MY LIFE
IN A FLASH

To RAM (OCA)

Best wishes

This book is especially dedicated to my mother, Surjit,
who died at the early age of 42 and to my late father,
Gurmej, who was such an inspiration to all of us.

MY LIFE
IN A FLASH

THE BIOGRAPHY OF
KASH 'THE FLASH' GILL

Kash Gill & Shirley Thompson

BREWIN BOOKS

First published by
Brewin Books Ltd, 56 Alcester Road,
Studley, Warwickshire B80 7LG in 2012
www.brewinbooks.com

ISBN: 978-1-85858-499-7

A Cataloguing in Publication Record
for this title is available from the British Library.

Front cover shot courtesy of Gurmej Badesha.
Photograph taken at Marco Pierre White's Restaurant
at The Cube, The Indigo Hotel, Birmingham City Centre.

Typeset in New Baskerville
Printed in Great Britain by
Hobbs the Printers Ltd.

CONTENTS

ACKNOWLEDGEMENTS

The authors are indebted to the following people, companies and organisations for their valuable contributions, various favours and support, which have been of great assistance in the publication of this book. Our diverse range of contributors:

The Gill Family: Julie, Elliesha, Kallan and Mitch; Resham and Mandy; Gamma and Lisa; Cougar and Daljit; Gurdip and Jan; Binda Dhillon and Satnam Singh.

World-famous Musicians/Entrepreneurs: 'Apache Indian', aka Steve Kapur, whose life and career closely parallels Kash's; UB40 musicians Brian Travers and Tony Mullings.

Sports Commentators/Broadcasters/other Media Personnel: Tom Ross, Head of Sport at BRMB provides not only the *Foreword* for the book, but many other perceptive observations about Kash; Phil Upton, BBC radio and television presenter, plus charity fund-raiser and Host & MC of VIP/Corporate Events; broadcasters Sonia Deol and Nikki Bedi; Adil Ray, Comedy writer, Actor and Broadcaster; Andy Walker, PR and Social Media Manager for Birmingham City Football club; Peter Wilson, Home Affairs Correspondent for *Midlands Today*; Satnam Rana, also of BBC *Midlands Today*. Tommy Nagra – Executive Producer, Religion & Ethics Department, BBC Manchester. Poppy Brady, freelance writer.

Footballers: Cyrille Regis; David Dunn; Dave Barnett; Kenny Cunningham.

Boxers: Joe Egan: boxer, entrepreneur and actor; Wayne Elcock: British Lonsdale Belt; English and WBU and WBF World Middleweight titles; Frankie Gavin: titles include Junior Olympic Gold Medal, 2007 first World Amateur Gold Medal Champion, Intercontinental Title London 2011, et cetera.

Coaches/Trainers: Howard Brown, Kash's trainer for many years; John Holcroft: community activist, gym owner and mentor for disadvantaged people; Norman Nelson, Anthony Whitehouse, Emma Fitch & Jay Sokhi.

Events Helper: Craig Saunders.

Thai Boxers: brothers and world-renowned experts Master A and Master Toddy.

Martial Arts Expert/magazine proprietor: Bob Sykes.

Bodybuilding: Dorian Yates, Bodybuilding Champion and 6 Times winner of Mr. Olympia – 1992-1997.

Kickboxers: a) Former opponents, Alex Tui; Tim Izli. b) Students: 'Balogun'; Stuart Nicholls, business manager, First Dan in kickboxing and student of Kash's for ten years.

Birmingham Businessman & magazine proprietor – entrepreneur: Paul Clifton.

Handsworth School Staff, Holyhead Road: Leslie Edlington and Ross Trafford.

'Safeguarding' and childcare consultant/referee/kickboxing coach: Hudson Richards.

Police/Handsworth Connection: Patrick Wing, former Chief Superintendent and OCU Commander, West Midlands Police; former Police Superintendent of Handsworth, David Webb; Handsworth 'Beat Bobby', Tim Green: 1974-1999; 'Mr Handsworth', Hector Pinkney MBE, Steve Dourass.

Photographer: Gurmej Badesha.

Newspapers: The Solihull Times (David Irwin).
The Harp: Siobhan Mohan, Editor; Vince Thompson, photographer.
The Birmingham Mail.

Restaurant: Marco Pierre White's Restaurant, The Indigo Hotel, The Cube, Birmingham, for permission to take our cover photograph from their roof.

Publishers: Alan and Alistair Brewin of Brewin Books Ltd. Amberley Publishing and authors, Eric Armstrong and Vernon Frost, for granting us permission to use two Handsworth photographs from their book, *Handsworth and Perry Barr Through Time*, pub. 2010.

Bookshops: Waterstones, Solihull Branch; W.H. Smith's Union Street, Birmingham Branch.

Additional Support: The Lord Mayor of Solihull, Councillor Ken Hawkins and the Lady Mayoress Mrs Janet Hawkins. The Lord Mayor and Lady Mayoress of Birmingham, Councillor John Lines and Mrs Kathleen Lines.

Libraries: Handsworth Library.

SPONSORS

I hadn't realised, when we began this book, how difficult it would be to get financial backing. Even some of the big names in Birmingham business declined to help. We are therefore *doubly* grateful to the following individuals and companies for their financial support:

Steve and Roy Bass; Care Helpline; Charles & Co, Solicitors; Connected Cars; Surjit Dhillon; Victoria Ewins; Cougar Gill; Harma Consultants; KBC Self-Drive Van Hire; Jaz McGill; David Nicholas; PT Communications Ltd; SBS Carpentry Ltd; Charles Simmonds, Immigration Solicitors; Jimmy Spices; Inderjit Takha; Thai Edge Restaurant; The Tower Ballroom; Peter Virdee.

FOREWORD

I first had the pleasure of meeting Kash at a WKA bill I was invited to by WKA president Paul Ingram.

I was immediately hooked not only by the sport but this tall rangy Brummie who didn't look like he could fight his way out of the metaphorical bag.

However when the bell went he was awesome. He had that world class ability that Champions need – controlled aggression with loads of technical ability. That wasn't the complete package; he also had the quickest hands I have seen and a classy style with the ability to showboat when he wanted.

Not long afterwards I was asked to host a series of kickboxing shows for SKY TV. It was here I got the opportunity to get to know Kash very well. His polite and respectful way of speaking to people told you he came from a good and caring family.

He gave me the chance to play first on BRMB radio a song specially written by Apache Indian for him to be played when he entered the ring in his first World Title fight. That went on to be a massive chart hit for Apache.

One of the things that stood out for me was how proud Kash was of Birmingham and Handsworth the area he grew up in, like me he came from the inner city and was proud to say so.

He is known worldwide as Kash the Flash but anyone who knows him will tell you that the "flash" part was only in the ring, outside of the ring Kash was anything but flash. He is a likeable, personable, man who is a perfect role model for any youngster.

He is known throughout the world due to him winning an unprecedented 4 world kickboxing titles but he is also liked all over the world by everyone who comes into contact with him because of his warm and enduring personality.

He has put so much back into the sport and the city since his retirement, by way of coaching and working with schools.

In these days of giving out honours and awards for nothing other than being a celebrity, Kash Gill has done more than enough inside and outside of the ring to deserve one.

Tom Ross, Midlands Sports Journalist of the Year 2012.

Photograph by kind permission of Jas Sansi.

"Who dares wins"
Motto of the British Special Air Service Regiment,
from 1942

In all walks of life we need something special – so glad
I've got my right hand... never leave home without it!

Becoming world champion was one of the greatest moments
in my life, but having three healthy kids, Ellie, Kallan and
Mitch – nothing can beat that – believe me.

Every time I stepped into that ring I always had fear –
which brought the best out in me. I was hurt many a time, but
never showed it. I even broke my jaw once and still won.

But heartbreak is the worst feeling of all.

Round 1

FLASH BACK (1966-1975)

The parish of Handsworth, situated just two miles from Birmingham City Centre, is set in the centre of the diamond-shaped Birmingham Plateau, surrounded by the rivers Trent, Severn and Avon and cut into by the Tame. This location, together with the fact that it was a forest area, shaped Handsworth's early history, more than any other single factor.

The name of the settlement originates from its Saxon owner, Hondes and 'weorthing', meaning estate or farm.

By 1086 there were two mills – Hamstead and Forge Mills, although only the Hamstead Mill was mentioned in the Domesday Survey. The graves of Watt, Murdoch and Bolton, the founders of the Industrial Revolution, can be found in St. Mary's Church. The ancient parish of Handsworth was in Staffordshire until 1911, when it became a suburb of Birmingham.

Just nineteen years later, in 1930, a baby boy, Gurmej Singh Gill, was born in the village of Powarda, in the Punjab, near Jalandhar. Little did his parents realise that their son was to become a wrestling champion... a village hero, or that their grandson would become world famous!

Twenty-year-old Gurmej Singh flew to England, in 1950, choosing Handsworth as his home, in the first wave of Asian-Indian immigrants to settle in the UK. That same year, India and Pakistan signed the Delhi Pact, each committing itself to upholding the rights of its minority populations.

As Gurmej began to put down roots in this Birmingham suburb, the Korean War was well under way.

Gurmej's fifth child, Kashmir Singh Gill, was destined to become the Four Times World Kickboxing Champion. Kash has four brothers and one sister: Resham; Binda; Gamma – Gurnam; Cougar – Herminder; Gurd – Gurdip.

Kash is the main narrator, throughout most of the book, aided by the recollections and observations of our contributors, which are shown within speech marks. Most text outside of the speech marks is Kash, telling the story, apart from Resham becoming the narrator for part of this opening 'Round'. The three other exceptions to the normal format are Rounds 4, 18 and 20, where it's more appropriate for Shirley Thompson to become the Narrator for a while.

Shirley is the 'scene-setter' at the beginning of each Round. Our contributors hail from all walks of life.

So please show your appreciation ladies and gentlemen, as Kash Gill steps into the ring, to begin his fascinating story... seconds out – Round One!

I was born in Dudley Road Hospital, now called City Hospital, on 2nd July 1966 – the famous year of the World Cup. At just under ten pounds I was a heavy baby: the nurses called me 'Tiger'. My dad said I was always a good baby – whatever that means! He called me Tiger too.

Throughout my early years I was known by everyone as 'Narni', which means 'youngster'. It wasn't until I began kickboxing at the age of fourteen, that my trainer, Howard Brown, gave me the name 'Kash', a shortened version of my actual name, 'Kashmir'.

As a young kid of two or three I was always on the move; never slept on time. By three or four years of age, I was kicking a ball and doing other active sports. Maybe that's why I'm into active sports now? Because I was forever playing football, tennis and cricket... full of energy!

My oldest brother, Resham, knows far more about our early family history than we younger brothers, so he's going to take over for a page or two, beginning with my parents' earlier life, before they came to the UK:

"Gurmej was visiting our mother's village," Resham begins, "when a wrestler came from one of the other villages and defeated everybody in the village. So they sent a messenger to grandmother's village, to get my dad back. He told me that it was a very pressured situation, because the whole reputation of the village hung on him. But he managed to defeat this guy and restore their reputation. He was only about sixteen when that happened.

"In 1990 I went to India with my wife and we visited relatives in the village. The house that my father had built was where the family were staying, but it was quite basic accommodation," Resham continues. "The home was surrounded by beautiful farmland, and fields of sweet-corn. My father later bought six-and-a-half acres of land, as well as his father's land. They were also growing wheat and their own vegetables.

"It's a lovely, rural setting. They have an irrigation system for the water, which they divert onto the farm. We come from a long line of farmers, on both sides of the family. My mother, Surjit, came from a village called Dhother, which is also her maiden name.

"I met my mom's two sisters – a very warm reception; delighted to see me; met my cousins – never seen them before. They were recounting stories about the old times; telling how the family had prospered more recently, in comparison with older times.

"My uncle told me that in 1947, when India became independent, one of Gurmej's uncles sheltered him because there was a lot of conflict on the borders and people were killed. They hid the women away; otherwise the Pakistani Muslims would have raped them. The men stayed behind, defending their village; despite being just a teenager, my father helped too.

"My father came over here from the Punjab, because his elder brother didn't want to come. My parents had already married, when they were teenagers, but they were separated for about five years, while my father established himself in England. When Surjit eventually came over on a ship it took her two weeks to get here. She landed at Tilbury Docks, near Gravesend.

"My father shared houses in Coventry and Birmingham, before he actually bought his first house and it was his Coventry landlady who noticed that he was physically well built, like a perfectly-formed doll, so she nicknamed him 'Dolly'. They called him that when he worked at the foundry too," explains Resham. "One of his other nicknames was 'Gedgie'.

"According to our youngest brother, Gurdip," Resham recalls, "the father of one of his work colleagues asked which village we were from, because that's how people of that generation identified who you were. It turned out that he knew Gurmej. Gurdip had gone there to do a home visit and ended up chatting about our dad. The old Sikh thing about getting bottles of whisky came into play – and this was eleven o'clock in the morning!

"He told Gurdip about how when they worked at the foundries they used to have this old 'dolly truck'. We didn't know this story. This guy's father said that they had a competition to find the strongest worker, so they each tried to lift this dolly truck and push it along a thirty-metre stretch. Apparently, my dad picked it up, took it thirty metres and brought it back! Slapped it down, dusted off his hands and said: 'That was easy!' Everyone's jaw just dropped – they couldn't believe it! The fact that his nickname was already 'Dolly', the type of truck that he'd moved, was sheer coincidence.

"Once he'd left rented accommodation," Resham recalls, "the sequence of houses was firstly, a terraced house in Wake Green Road, Moseley right by Sorrento Hospital, where I was born, in January 1957. It was still rented accommodation, but we didn't stay there much longer than a year.

"The reason we moved from Moseley was that when I was a baby the ceiling collapsed! My mother said: 'We're not staying here any longer. If my child had been in the cot he'd have been dead!' That was what prompted us to move to Waterloo Road, Smethwick.

"I was still the only child at that stage. Then in 1960, when my sister Binda was born, we moved to Handsworth. Gurmej bought 5, Waverhill Road, for two or three hundred pounds. He was one of the first Asians in the Birmingham area, to buy his own house. Over to you Narni!"

Thanks Resham. 5 Waverhill Road is in the middle of Handsworth, right off the Soho Road. It was a great area, I love Handsworth – I've got lots of great memories of it.

I was quite a happy little kid, but it was a big household, so no one got any particular attention from mom and dad: we got our independence early on. That's one of the things that happen in a big family. I realise that now, with three kids of my own, it must have been hard to give six kids much attention, even though there was an age gap.

Although I was very active, if I fell over on my hands and knees I'd just get up and keep going. Not many children do that... I was a tough kid!

There were about 120 houses in Waverhill Road and it ran downhill: I remember go-karting down the hill. It sloped all the way down. We lived there until I was eleven. I have lots of childhood memories there.

Our house was next to the church. I remember climbing on the flat roof, which was covered in barbed wire, to stop people getting onto the church roof next door. I cut my chest. My dad said: "How did you do that?" He gave me such a hiding! I didn't go to hospital and I've still got a heavy scar on my chest. It was an Evangelical church – it's still there. But they pulled a lot of the houses down.

We went to Sunday School because we got a little bit of religious education there. I enjoyed Bible Stories and took part in all the activities, although I don't follow the church now. They brought us into the activities slowly. I still see some of the church people now, like Mr. and Mrs. Brown. They say: "We remember you as a naughty kid." They tell me that to this day!

There were black and Asian families living in Waverhill Road; predominantly Asians. It seemed like everyone mixed together; it was pretty close.

As you've heard, my father was a hero, back in the Punjab, a far cry from being a trouble-maker. But in 1964 he was sent to Stafford Prison for a short period of time. That happened before I was born, but he told the stories. Mom had to cope on her own, with three young children. Cougar was born in July 1964, so it was a really difficult time for our mom.

As my father was a champion wrestler back in India, sport was already in our family. They didn't go by the weight back then. He used to tell me that he was 'King of the Village' and had a lot of respect from all the Indians over there.

As you went in at the front of our Waverhill Road house there was a little gate, with a step up to it – dad had quite a bit of trouble with that – when he'd had a drink or two! There was another step up to the front door. It was a terraced house, with four bedrooms; it wasn't the biggest of houses. There'd be three kids in one bedroom; two in a bed. My kids have got their own bedrooms now. They don't realise how lucky they are. As it was only a four-bedroom house, mom and dad were in one bedroom; my sister and a brother in another; the rest of the brothers in another and lodgers in the fourth one.

The garden was very small in the front, with no grass at all. In the back it was quite long and narrow, where we use to mess about playing cricket and all that. As you opened the front door there was a little hallway; on the left-hand side was a Front Room, which was kept for special guests; then there was a back room, with a fire in it.

It's strange – I can remember that house really well. There was a telephone in the Front Room, which was kept for guests. That dates back to the Edwardian times in England, where the front room or parlour was often curtained off and only used on special occasions. All of the best furniture was in there. I remember the Headmaster came round once, to talk about us being naughty kids at school, so he was shown into there.

Our kitchen was very basic: it was at the back of the house and just an average size. There was a coal-filled cellar: when it rained or flooded it got mucky. We played hide-and-seek in the cellar, as kids, although it was hard to get down there.

We had West Indian lodgers in our house. They had two kids – a boy and a girl. Their parents were very strict: they used to hit them with a belt, you know, proper punishment; you wouldn't be allowed to do it today. But our dad was the same. He hit me with a hockey stick when I was about seven, for staying up after a certain time. I got it straight across the arm!

We lost touch with the lodgers; at one stage the mother had a nervous breakdown. She was shouting and jumping around – I'd hate my kids to experience anything like that. I also remember the mother's funeral, which was in the Jamaican tradition: more like a celebration – singing and dancing. But as a young kid I didn't understand why they were doing it that way.

When we played hide-and-seek I'd put my head under the quilt, but I always got caught, because I had a fear of going underneath it, although I grew out of it. I was frightened of the cellar too, because it was dark. Going under the quilt was a similar experience to being down in the cellar – no light.

My childhood days were the best days of my life. I was telling my son about my book on the way to school this morning. I said: "I'd love to go back to your age. You don't want to be a man – you get bills and everything!" I remember those days well, like joining school when I was four. On my first day I was really upset and didn't want to go, but I soon settled down and enjoyed my school life.

At home I played with all the kids, but I always wanted to be head of the games – and in charge. Some of the kids didn't like it. I wasn't a bully, but sometimes you do it without realising. I used to be a bit of a scrapper as well. I'd get in fights with other young kids, for the sheer enjoyment of fighting! The kids down the road were West Indian; we'd fight them with bricks and stones.

I don't really have any best friends, even to this day. I just have general friends. I've always been a bit of a loner. I mix in, but then I keep to myself too. It's hard to explain really, but I was never in a group, always on my own. I seem to have been pre-programmed like that.

So how about my four brothers and one sister? You've already heard from Resham, the oldest, who was born in 1957. I'll bring each of them in, in turn, so that they can give you their version of events.

As the older brother, Resham was always out and about with his friends; he was never around with us very much. But my father held him responsible for the rest of us, because he was the oldest. We three younger brothers are taller than the earlier children: Gurdip is 6 foot 7; Cougar and myself are 6 foot 3.

Resham was the most academic of all of us. He went to Hamstead Hall, the old William Murdoch secondary school and became well qualified. We children went to two different branches of the same junior school, Saint Michael's, depending upon our age.

"As far as the lodger's breakdown is concerned," recalls Resham, "several women living in the same road and mostly related, had various things like that. The woman at Number 2 had breast cancer. They were all women who'd been taken out of their normal environment; they didn't have a full grasp of the language, and were living in another culture, so that's probably why the stresses and strains took their toll.

"With regard to my father going to Stafford Prison, one of his friends had got into difficulty, on a Saturday, with another group of individuals: it was two groups of Indians. We have a term called 'Rajinama', which is peace brokering. Gurmej had been to work. He didn't even get time to eat, because four of his friends came up and said: 'We need you to broker a peace deal.' In the meantime certain people told the pub landlord: 'These men are attacking us. We need to defend ourselves.' My father's group were made out to be the bad guys. This was all happening at the *Roebuck*, in Hockley," Resham explains.

"So effectively, they were ambushed; my father was stabbed and he incurred head injuries. There were just five men in my dad's group, who were confronted by up to seventy people in the pub, although not all of them got involved in the violence. The people in the pub were tooled up, but my father's group hadn't gone with any weapons, they were just going to broker this peace, but they were attacked.

"Not only did he take a walloping, but he was perceived to be the guilty party, because these people had rigged things up, to make him look like the aggressor. The pub landlord testified against him in court. Basically the story against him was completely twisted. Not being an educated man, he couldn't articulate what had happened. So although it was a case of injustice, had the judge been impartial, he would have perceived that the facts were stacked against them. But that didn't happen so Gurmej ended up doing a term in prison.

"I went to visit him on a couple of occasions, with my mother. On the second occasion, his friends took me on the train. Dad instructed them to make sure that I was looked after, so we travelled First Class," concludes Resham.

My youngest brother, Gurdip, elaborates: "If you look at the era, you'll find that they didn't have proper interpreters to sort things out; there were no tape recorded interviews with the police; it was just a report from a police officer. Dad was stabbed during that incident: he had a scar, just under his stomach. Because he was quite muscular in that area of his body, he was able to carry it; that's what saved his life: you could actually see where the knife had penetrated and twisted."

"When I was a little one I used to have a little top-knot on my head – and I'd run to my dad in the prison," remembers Cougar. "My uncle Gurdial drove us there, to visit him. This falling out continued for years and Gurmej never ever made up with his rival, who got him convicted.

"His son played for the same football team as me, the *Wondervaults*. He and I were mates; he'd come to the pub with me and my dad would buy him a drink. But Gurmej never talked to my friend's dad; the feud lived on for ever. He was very political," Cougar continues. "I think that's what the fight was about; they were going around, trying to recruit people, to help the elections."

In fact, dad actually served a few months; he was released early because of his good behaviour. Resham remembers a funny story about when our mother confused me with Cougar.

"Because they were so identical from behind, there was only a two-year age gap between them, she fed the one child, got distracted, then came back and fed the same one twice! So the other one had to starve – I think it must have been Kash who got fed twice!

"Another amusing story was that she bought a brand new wardrobe and then asked Cougar and Kash to break down the old one," continues Resham. "They were very young kids but they were so proud; they broke the wardrobe completely to smithereens, called their mother in and said: 'Look mom, we've done it!' 'Oh no – you've broken the wrong one!'"

The second to be born in the family was my sister, Binda:

"I was born in 1960," she explains. "I'm six years older than Kash. When we were little, before my mom died, we played in the streets and went to Handsworth Park a lot. The boys were always there: they played football, cricket, and hockey. The doors were never locked. The front door was always open, where we lived."

The downside of that, Binda, is that I remember our gas meter being robbed. We were in different parts of the house or garden when it was happening, so it didn't register immediately.

"But it was nothing like it is now. It was a lot safer," recalls Binda. "When people came over from India, we kept a few families with us at Waverhill Road, including my mom's brother. Dad supported them and found them work. If anyone needed money, he would give it them. He was very kind-hearted.

"When Gurmej arrived in the UK there weren't many jobs around," Binda continues. "He worked really long hours. But we get our sense of humour off Dad. That's what gets you through really. There were six children, but we were always having a laugh and a joke. My dad's approach to life was very positive and we inherited that from him. He'd say: 'If you earn an honest living, it's the best way. I never want you picking up anybody else's money – even a penny.' So that stuck with us really. We've never been in trouble for anything like that."

According to Binda, "The Asian way is work, work, work – and Kash has worked really hard to get where he is. Even before the time when my dad went to prison, he said that if immigrants went into a pub, they wouldn't be accepted. When he first moved into Handsworth it was predominantly white. But my dad stuck up for his rights and for other people; that's how he got into trouble sometimes – defending other people.

"He was so well liked," she continues, "that when he went into a pub, there'd be three pints waiting for him, because he would sort problems out for people, even if he had to go without something himself. We were brought up so differently. Now children don't want to share rooms, but we didn't have any choice. My older brother, Resham, slept in the attic, once we got rid of the lodgers.

"There was a kitchen at the back, at Waverhill Road," she continues. "We had a bathroom outside in those days. It had a bath and a toilet, but it was dark and dingy. It was just for our family. I got used to it, although I couldn't do it now. But we were brought up that way; we knew no better. There was a door, but no heating. The toilet was separate. The floor was hard – like dark stone."

Binda's description of our dark and dingy bathroom sounds quite comical. There was an upstairs room above the bathroom. We drilled a hole in the floor, me and Cougar. When Resham was having a bath, we'd pour cold water onto him, through this hole. We were quite cruel brothers really!

"When mom passed away, it was just us living in the house – no lodgers," continues Binda. "I agree with what you say Kash, about loving our childhood. We were really close. You said you enjoyed having scraps with the other kids – well I think even I did! Do you remember coming home from school to Waverhill Road and telling me that a black boy had taken money off you? I went straight to the school and sorted him out!"

Gamma, you were the third child to be born; that was in 1961.

"Yes Kash, a lot of the other residents in Waverhill Road were from our home village, back in India. Next door was our dad's brother's house, and then across the road was our dad's cousin's house. Next door to that were his two brothers, who were both from our village as well. Four houses out of six were relatives. There were two others as well, which belonged to friends.

"Like Kash, I played with the West Indian kids too," Gamma remembers. "There were never any problems. A lot of the time was spent playing football, in Waverhill Road. We'd go Handsworth Park with other people who lived in the same road, but also with cousins, who lived a bit further away. We played a lot by the White House, a historical house in Handsworth Park. It's still there now."

That's right Gamma. We played on a patch of grass near to the White House. But the house was locked, so we never went in.

"Nowadays parents often have to tell their children to stay in, but it was a much more trusting environment when we were growing up," Gamma continues. "If the Newsagents were closed, you just took a paper from outside and put the money through the letterbox!"

Child number 4 is 'Cougar'. He says that he could see that grit and determination in me, even as a young boy.

"Yes, you were a little sod when you were young," Cougar comments, "but I think you were just mischievous! You were climbing on this roof, in the back garden, and a wall fell on you! But you just walked away from it – it didn't hurt you at all! You just picked yourself up and I thought: 'yeh!!'

"We'd come down in the morning and stand in front of the fire – about four of us – and we'd end up fighting. That fight would escalate as you headed out of the door and you'd get a milk bottle thrown at you; you had to duck. Thank God none of us got hurt!

"But they were just 'growing up' fights. I remember waiting for some kid outside the house, and a tough black kid got on top of me. I ran off, but my dad said: 'What are you doing?' So you learn to fend for yourself – like a 'Rites of Passage' thing. We never held a grudge; the next day you'd have forgotten about it," Cougar remembers.

Do you remember how I was afraid of the dark?

"Yes, the cellar was darker than anything, but we had coal deliveries. The trucks used to come out. Binda was hit by a car as she ran into the road – and broke her leg."

Cougar and I are very similar. We'd go out in the morning and come back at night – all day in the park. When you think about so many of the kids now, stuck in front of their computers, ours was a much healthier lifestyle, wasn't it? Those things weren't available for us, as kids.

I was the next to be born, in 1966, followed by my youngest brother, Gurdip, in June 1969.

"I understand that there were thirteen blokes living in the house in Moseley at one time, when my dad first moved there," Gurdip explains. "Then gradually they brought their wives over. So we were all born and bred in Birmingham. The lodgers moved in because they couldn't get a house anywhere else. It was very much about sticking together. They would pool a pot of money together; houses would then be allocated to various people, but everyone would continue to contribute. So they'd be in lodgings to start with, but then gradually acquire their own houses."

Our father, Gurmej, put in more than most, to this pool.

"When dad first arrived," Gurdip continues, "he ended up in Newcastle, but workers in that area were born into the dock work, all working for the same company. So from there, dad made a quick move to Birmingham. The immigrants were given all the menial jobs, which the indigenous population didn't want. You'd sometimes have twenty people living in one house, but they all worked shifts; so one would be going out, as another came in. Then all the relatives came over," Gurdip explains.

"After my dad worked a double-shift, he'd go around door to door, selling silk goods. He couldn't speak the language, but half the time he thought they just bought something, to get rid of him! He wanted to make sure that he had a place, before mom arrived in the country. In the five-year gap before she came over, he made sure that he had a property and that he'd established himself. Surjit was fourteen and Gurmej was sixteen, when they married; there was two years between them.

"When Kash was about nine he was summoned to the headmaster's office at St. Michael's," Gurdip recalls, "because I was getting bullied by another boy, who shall be nameless. Kash threatened the boy with a small pocket-knife. Mr. Hincks, the headmaster, really told us off, because knives were more unusual at the time. We had the slipper too: he was banging it on the table! But Kash did it to protect me.

"We moved from Waverhill Road in '79, to Grove Lane, the year before I started Senior School," Gurdip continues. "There was a great sense of community in Waverhill Road, we all knew each other. It was fun-and-games growing up. Although we were mostly out of doors, we weren't too far from the house," he concludes, "so somebody always knew where we were."

Resham invited his friends round sometimes and I'd really taunt them. I'd jump up, and stand on the church roof next door – and spit on them. Or they'd be standing on the doorstep and I'd be abusing them, which is a really bad thing for a kid to do. I'd get elastic bands and shoot them at people too!

If any one of our siblings came under attack we'd all join forces to protect him or her. Another childhood memory from Waverhill Road was that when the electrician came round, me and Cougar threw fireworks through the letterbox at him. We'd come flying down the stairs and he'd come looking for us. It's lucky we didn't have a carpet in the hall otherwise the whole thing could have set alight! When a firework landed on the slates, it made the bang even louder! If my kids did that now, I'd be so mortified, but you don't think of the dangers. Those are the kind of memories that have been coming back to my family and myself.

Round 2

MOM AND MY ROUGH TOUGH DAD

Kash's mother, Surjit Kaur Dhother, was five foot seven inches tall and dark-skinned, compared with Gurmej who was light-skinned: people sometimes mistook him for a Greek. He was about 5ft 10 and a half; in his day he was quite stocky, but put on weight when he got older.

Resham, remembers their mother, Surjit, trying diligently to teach himself and his sister, Binda, her two oldest children, to count in Punjabi, despite her limited education. She spoke broken English. It wasn't the done thing to educate the girls, although her brother and father were highly educated.

Surjit wasn't inclined to sit around, chatting with the other wives. She always kept herself busy and was deeply religious. One of the central philosophies of her faith was that the only worthwhile human being is one who cares for others.

Resham, recalls: "She was a God-fearing woman. Her father was the equivalent of a village priest and used to conduct the ceremonies. As a child she took me to various 'Satsung', all over the country. They didn't have formal temples; they used church halls. They would have their congregation there. They served samosas at these meetings, so they were my inducement for going along!

Surjit meditated regularly, but I remember when a young milkman, juggling some milk bottles, cut his wrist. She went over and treated his wound; stemmed the flow of the bleeding and encouraged him to go and get treatment," Resham explains. "She said: 'It was just like one of you children getting injured.' "

Binda recalls: "My mother's family were vegetarian. The religion that they followed was Radha Soami." Kash believes that actor, Martin Shaw, followed the same religion too, because he attended one of the London festivals that the family went to. The TV series, 'The Professionals', was very popular at that time.

Both Binda and Cougar's wife, Daljit have books about Surjit's religion. Daljit has one entitled 'Sant Mat – the Science of the Soul'.

13

Although my dad's name was Gurmej, I used to call him 'Gummidge', as in Wurzel Gummidge, after I'd seen the film. It was easier to pronounce!

Gurmej sometimes brought home a group of friends at short notice and expected Surjit to provide them with food, a normal lifestyle for Indian women. There were several families in the road who were particularly friendly with each other, so the women of the houses took it in turns to cater for their guests. Surjit seemed adept at coping with such situations.

Gamma confirms: "Mom would make a base for a curry, make two curries and then cook chapattis on the third hob, so she was very adaptable. She also made homemade Indian sweets, which would be too time-consuming now, but at that time it was seen as normal."

If kids stole from our house, mom would chase them down the street. But if she was so good at coping, why did she have a nervous breakdown?

According to Resham: "It may have been linked to a sterilisation operation that mom had, to stop her having children. But if you transfer someone from their normal environment, to a new one... also don't forget that this was the era where there were no dishwashers, no washing machines; six children. It wasn't a major breakdown; it was fairly common amongst the women."

"It happened the year before she died," explains Binda, "but it was gradual. I went to India with her, when I was eleven. She was protective of all of us, but then she suddenly became suspicious, that something was going to happen. I'd go to the shops with her when I was little, but as we got older, we went shopping for her."

As a kid you don't really understand what's happening. She was acting out of character – it was really frightening! It wasn't long afterwards that they took her to hospital. Mom had previously been on medication so she'd been better then. About a week later I went to see her in All Saints Hospital, part of Dudley Road Hospital, near to Waverhill Road.

My mom said: "Come on, come on!" beckoning for me to come over. But I didn't go to her because I was afraid.

According to Gamma, "Like most of the families we knew, the husband was working because there was plenty of work, so we'd spend a lot of time with our mother, and were just waiting for our father to come home. We'd be on the bed, chatting to him.

"At that age your parents protected you from financial problems," Gamma continues. "We didn't have many luxuries compared with children of today. They might have four or five pairs of shoes each, we had one pair; you'd get a new pair when the others wore out. So we weren't wealthy but we didn't expect more than that."

I remember trying to follow Gamma, up the main Soho Road, but he suddenly ran across to the other side. I followed – and got run over! I was tossed in the air. Mom came up to me, kissed me and said that I'd be alright... that's one of my fondest memories of her. The shopkeepers found it really amusing that although they were trying to help me, to make sure that I wasn't injured or in shock, all I was concerned about was finding my shoe. I said: "If I don't find my shoe my dad's going to kill me!"

My brother, Cougar, remembers one of the shopkeepers tying a handkerchief around my left eye and knee. There were a lot of people on the streets, in those days, who knew each other. The older kids protected us.

Cougar confirms: "When we were quite young, the community was totally different from today. We could play out on the street. There was a heavy gate, where we played football. We didn't have any play stations or other electronic gadgets like nowadays. Our toy was a football. Kash was fortunate, because when my dad brought friends home, being a former wrestler, he'd get us brothers wrestling and doing press-ups, from a young age."

Cougar and me would be fighting on the floor. Sometimes it was for real, because I hated losing. Sometimes it would be with Gurdip; other times it would be Cougar versus Gamma. The winner got 50p. It was a bit of entertainment but it was also our dad's way of making us more aggressive. It wasn't a bad thing, against each other; it gave us that sense of competition.

Cougar's wife, Daljit, comments: "When I initially met Gurmej I was scared of him, because he was a huge man, with a huge presence! He was about 5 foot 10, but bulky – broad. His face looked very stern, but actually he wasn't really, he was a 'Gentle Giant'. But he commanded such respect, off people in the community. He had a definite presence about him. When we first got married, I found it hard, coming to a home with five men."

Resham remembers two family stories about Teddy Boys. One was when the foundry workers were getting mugged for their wages on Fridays, so dad confronted these thugs, over Smethwick Bridge. They had chains and were taking money out of the workers' wage packets. Gurmej took them all on and put a stop to that.

There was also another incident on the Soho Road. Our father and a group of friends were there, when some Teddy Boys confronted them. A sensible police officer said, "Look, instead of having mob violence here, why don't you each pick your strongest character and the two of them can fight it out." So they picked my father. He picked this other guy up and threw him into the road!

At the same time, my dad was being hit on the head by a woman who was calling him a thug! But to show British values the father of the guy whom he beat came over, shook his hand and said: "My son's never lost a fight. I shake your hand, because you've won the fight, so good luck to you," and that was the end of the matter. All of those guys lived in Handsworth, but that just shows how values have changed. At that time, when you knocked somebody down, that was it. Gurmej only had to look at us with disapproval and that would be enough, because we all respected him.

Gurdip and Binda visited the Punjab with our mother. "I was only three," explains Gurdip, "but I remember part of the rebuilding work at a holy place; everyone took part."

"When Gurdip and I first went to India, I was eleven years old," elaborates Binda. "That was 1972, three years before mom passed away. I had a good opportunity of spending three months there; meeting my mom's parents; her older brother and two sisters. I also met my dad's father and his brother.

"Our grandfather was a farmer; my mother's family were the same, although her parents were very religious. My mom's father did the religious ceremonies in his village; mom was about thirteen when she was initiated. Her family had a little house, in the village and some farmland. Her brothers worked very hard on the land. The oldest brother has passed away now, but her two sisters are still alive: one lives here and one lives in India.

"Mom's village was lovely. I went out all the time, on my bike; that's where I learned to ride it. It was a very rural village; nice weather. They grew fresh vegetables. Everybody knew each other."

Gurdip returned to India years later, in 1996, visiting the same village, with his sister-in-law's husband. They met all the relatives, including mom's sisters. The village has changed considerably. The structures of the houses remain the same, because it's so warm, but nowadays they have cookers and chairs and tables; literally a full kitchen. He and Binda returned again in 2003, when dad passed away... more about that in Round 16. Gurdip also returned in 2005, for a family wedding. Our dad's philosophy wasn't a particularly religious one; it was just about being a worthwhile human being.

According to Gurdip, "He always said: 'Never 'do the dirty' on anyone; have a good heart – and always help people if you can.'

"When I go to a wedding it's always: 'Whose son are you?' When I mention Gurmej, the usual response is that he helped certain people when they first came over, to get a job," continues Gurdip. "Because of his own hardworking reputation, employers would take his recommendation when considering others for jobs. At that point reputation meant a lot."

When we were younger my dad would finish work then go to the pub, a regular routine for foundry workers. Then he would come home at closing time which was 10.30pm. That's when he would eat! I still eat late now. It's a difficult habit to break. But as I got into my earlier training I had to eat earlier, not with the family, because of my training routine.

Gamma comments: "That was the lifestyle for other Punjabi families in the area too. Obviously I eat early now, but at that time it was a normal routine for us."

Dad went to the *Frighted Horse* when we lived in Waverhill and the *Woodbine* after we moved to Grove Lane. As young kids, we'd run up there at half ten, closing time. You were guaranteed a fight every Friday or Saturday night – and we didn't have to pay for it... it was free! He was a bit of a warrior and if there were two gangs, he'd act as arbitrator. They had a lot of respect for him.

Gurdip explains: "Some people get really drunk, but our dad never did: he was merry and sometimes he got emotional, reflecting on the past. After Kash's fights he'd have a celebration at the *Woodbine* in Grove Lane – it's closed down now. Everyone used to pass through – dad was so proud of Kash."

Gurmej would ring the landlord before they arrived, so that he could get the first three or four pints of Mild ready for them. I would fight my dad's corner because he was straight. I'm like him – we stick to our principles.

"He always used to say: 'Don't let anybody bully you'," explains Gurdip. "That was his philosophy. When I was fourteen I was walking home down

Albert Road, from Hamstead Hall Secondary School with two friends. There were four West Indian lads in their late teens, early twenties, who went round mugging young kids. They approached us, to take money off us. I said to my mates, 'Do that and they'll mug you every time. Give them nothing!' I got punched in the face by one of them, but I had a raw temper and I gave the one as good as I got.

"The other two lads were frozen to the spot. My dad had always taught us not to give anything up, so I chased them up the road, throwing milk bottles at them – I never lost my bottle!"

Cougar recalls: "There was a two-year age gap between Kash and me. Dad was always tired when he came home and he'd had a few beers. When he'd had a hard day, me and Kash would rub his feet with oil. Then we'd walk on his back, to try and get the cramp out and rub his back for him."

"With Kash, dad really encouraged his kickboxing, because he knew that sport was the best thing for us; it was therapeutic," explains Cougar. "He was very streetwise and he passed that down to his children. A lot of it was trying to justify situations; that's why I looked out for Kash, from an early age. From the age of thirteen I went to parties with my dad. At one party they said: 'Is that your son over there? He's just on his second pint of beer!' But he always let me have a pint with him.

"My dad's attitude was 'Why be bullied? Stand up for yourself.' He'd never instigate something," continues Cougar, "but if he or someone he knew was being intimidated, he'd sometimes get involved. But he was never the perpetrator."

My dad would come home on a Friday night with fish and chips for us, little things like that, so that was exciting. He had to work all hours to keep the family – and having a mortgage and all that – not easy. He always said to me "I don't want any of my kids to work in this environment."

He'd say "Never take anybody else's money, you earn your own living and live an honest life." All of us have adopted that way of life. He was always very careful with money: the Indian mentality was to save, save, save and very rarely spend.

When I was a little boy of eight, in 1974, there was a fireman's strike in Handsworth. I remember sitting in a tent with some of the firemen. Me and my brothers used to bring the firemen curries. We got to know them quite well. That shows you how much freedom we had as young kids.

Cougar, me and our friend 'Cookie' would walk over to the fire station and camp out with the firemen in their tent! It just shows how society has deteriorated; it wouldn't be safe for kids to wander about like that now. As a parent I look back on that and think: 'Bloody hell – there's a lot of leeway there!'

One of the firemen was Dave Warrington. He was the main guy. I was in Solihull about two years ago and I ran into Dave; he was shopping with his wife… he's retired now. It's amazing that he remembered me. It was part of a national strike for more pay and shifts, so the authorities brought in 'Green Goddesses': fire engines, manned by police and other people. But I had no idea that a family tragedy was just *months* away from us.

"Our mum passed away when we were all quite young," recalls Binda. "Kash had just turned nine, on July 2nd, his birthday. Mum passed away on July 30th 1975… she was only forty-two. I was fifteen; Cougar was eleven; Resham was eighteen; Gurdip was the youngest – he was six. It was a Wednesday when she died, I remember it well.

"The weekend before, on the Saturday and Sunday, she said that she had a pain in her heart: she pointed to the place where it was. She sat in the garden, saying that she didn't feel well, so we rang her brother, my uncle.

"Cougar walked her around the garden, hoping that would ease the pain. Being a child, he didn't realise the implications. Then my other brother, Gamma, said that he wanted a pair of trousers. It was a Saturday and he'd been to the market."

"Someone at a nearby factory was selling trousers with a side pocket and a lot of children were buying them," Gamma interjects. "Binda was there on the bed with her and I remember mom saying: 'Give him the money to buy them.' But we never realised how ill she was."

"On Sunday she got worse," continues Binda. "The doctor came. Then when my uncle Gurdial came on Monday she went in to hospital that same day. My uncle got quite angry with the doctor, because she said that she felt cold – it was her circulation. Uncle Gurdial has always been there for the family, in all kinds of situations.

"They called an ambulance that evening," Binda continues. "My aunt and uncle were there. The last thing that my mother said to me before she went to the hospital was, 'I want you to be sensible and always look after your brothers.' She knew she wasn't going to come back, I reckon.

"She went in on the Monday, to City Road Hospital. On Wednesday morning she passed away. It was heartbreaking! My dad's niece stayed with us for three months, she lives in Chippenham," Binda explains. "So that was a big help."

"She literally took care of the house, before Binda could," Gurdip explains "Her name is Gian… Gianur. To this day, I've got so much respect for her. She was going through her own turmoil, but she put that to one side. Our aunt, Gurdev Kaur, was a big help too. They came over a lot: they were a big support – and their children."

"I can remember when my mom died," recalls Cougar. "I was just turned eleven. Just before she went to hospital, dad said, 'Come and have some fish and chips.' Even though he worked long days, he'd leave his friends in the pub to come and have a Coke, spend ten minutes or so with me.

"I didn't understand how serious it was," Cougar elaborates. "At that time we had a front wall, which had been smashed. We were having it repaired and I remember telling her that the wall would be finished by the time she came home, so she'd be able to see it finished."

Gurdip remembers Gurmej saying: "Give your mom a kiss… she'll be home soon." "The day we got the news, we still went on the church trip," he continues. "Once you get the news everyone comes to the house to pay their respects. It's really difficult; you don't have time, in the immediate family, to grieve together. A sense of duty takes over, but I still remember the funeral.

"It was a hot Wednesday when she passed away," Gurdip continues. "I remember the front room window at Waverhill Road being open and everyone filing past the coffin. Resham and Binda were standing there. I went in and I stroked my mom's face; it's still a picture in my mind: she looked more asleep than anything. Then I remember the journey to the crematorium in the funeral car. There were three cars; I was in one with Kash and my dad. But the way people deal with bereavement now is probably completely different, because I don't think we knew how to."

"I stayed on another year at school," Binda interjects. "I was doing my CSEs. But it was a struggle. I left at sixteen. Dad asked me if I wanted to stay on, but it was too much. My English teacher, Mrs. Cooper said: 'Your grades have dropped. I didn't realise your mom had passed away. We could have given you extra help.' Because when I went back to school I told hardly anyone, except a few of my friends."

The night our mother died, Resham decided he should get married. "I was never asked again whether I *wanted* to get married. I was going to have an arranged marriage that didn't go well, because I had a letter from the girl saying that she didn't want to marry me and we had phone calls to the effect as well," explains Resham. "But I never actually shared that with my father."

Resham subsequently moved into a flat in Handsworth Wood, but after a while Gurmej realised that he might not see him any more, so Resham started coming back to the house and my dad got on better with him.

"Dad would have liked me to have had an arranged marriage, because what the older one does, the younger siblings will often do too," Resham recalls. "But it was only years later that I explained to him the circumstances. He was very understanding and said, 'If only you had told me what the reason was I would have sided with you.'"

Binda remembers dad telling her once about a guy who came to him. His son wanted to marry a girl who wasn't their caste. Gurmej advised his friend, 'Well either you lose your son, if you don't agree with it, or you marry them and keep your son.'

Resham later married Mandy, an English girl; he started that trend, I was the second one and then it was Gamma, although he's living with his girlfriend, Lisa. She and Gamma lived with my dad for five years, from 1998 to 2003, and dad was fine with it.

Binda and Cougar eventually had *arranged* marriages, but luckily they loved their chosen partners, so it wasn't a problem. Gurdip had a traditional Indian wedding. He married an Asian girl, Jan. They have two sons, Raajan and Jashaan. Mandy and Resham also have two sons – Emile and André. Binda and her husband, Satnam Singh, have two daughters, Mandip and Amandip. Cougar and his wife, Daljit, have three children: a daughter, Jeevan and two sons, Kietan and Gian.

After our mother's death some of dad's workmates suggested, as each of us approached the school-leaving age, that we might want to work at the foundry.

"But dad didn't want us to have to do that hard toil, which he had to do," Gurdip confirms. "I went to the Smethwick foundry once with Kash. It was only then that I realised the kind of environment he had to work in. At the end of the week our dad used to bring his clothes home. You'd have to wash them about three or four times and even then they weren't clean!

"On the first day back at St Michael's in Piers Road, after the summer holidays, when our mother had died, Kash held my hand while we asked the school secretary, Mrs. Joyce about a form for free meals," Gurdip continues. "We must have said something like: 'Our mom has just died.' Mrs. Joyce looked at us and burst into tears. Me and Kash looked at each other and just giggled: 'what's she crying for?!'

"Kash and I would walk home together after school. I hated Art, so I'd ask Kash to do some of my drawings for me. He wasn't very good at it either, but he'd help me do my homework.

"We had so much fun and enjoyment as kids. At Christmas we played *Charades*, but I remember realising at the age of seven that Santa didn't exist! The first Christmas after Mom passed away Resham and some of the other older ones tried to make it a bit special for me," Gurdip recalls. "I remember having a present, Christmas morning. The following Christmas, I put my stocking up again!"

We weren't particularly religious, but we believed in Christmas as a happy time. We had party food, but no Christmas tree. My kids have all of that because they were brought up differently. Although Gurdip was only six when our mother died, he remembers that she stood no nonsense!

"She had a great relationship with her brother, Gurdial Singh," Gurdip continues. "I went on bus journeys with my mom. Because I was the youngest she took me everywhere. After she passed away and we went to Senior School, our Uncle Gurdial made sure that everything was done properly. He'd go with us to Parents' Evenings, because our dad was busy at work.

"Gurdial has a Bachelor's Degree. He lives in Cranbrook Road, Handsworth. He and my mother were very close. The family nickname for Gurdial is 'BT', Bachelor of Teaching, because he's well educated. He took a keen interest in our welfare," concludes Gurdip.

We knew that a lot of people were against my dad. Because he was a powerful man he was quite open to being attacked, so either Cougar or myself would go with him, like bodyguards

Cougar recalls: "Surjit was a very *loved* woman. She was kind and warm and lots of women would confide in her, because they knew that she wouldn't take it anywhere else."

I remember looking out of the window, when she was going to the hospital. We were quite excited because the ambulance was at the front of the house. Being a young kid of only nine I said: "Mom's going in the ambulance – mom's going in the ambulance!" She had heart failure. Cougar mentioned the new wall built outside, which we were going to show her when she came back... but she never made it back.

I wasn't a huggie huggie mommy's boy or anything like that. I'd go out shopping with her sometimes. She would try to speak English in bits and dabs. Being so young when she passed away, my childhood memories of her are quite vague, but luckily my brothers and sister have been able to supply much more detail about her, for these early chapters.

Losing your mom at that age doesn't help you. As a young kid you think people are going to live forever – you just don't realise...

Round 3

THREE LITTLE BOYS

Three young boys grew up in Handsworth within close proximity of each other. Not only were they destined to become good friends, but also celebrities in their own right, in adult life.

Kash's birthday is 2nd July 1966; Apache Indian and David 'Kwame' Barnett, were born within just a month of each other, in 1967: Dave on 16 April 1967 and Apache Indian, aka Steve Kapur, just twenty-five days later, on 11 May.

Dave, Kash and Steve explore the cultural and social inspiration in their Handsworth childhood, including sports events and music carnivals in Handsworth Park, a regular haunt for many residents.

The three boys could play football safely on the streets, enjoying greater freedom than children nowadays. Steve lived at the opposite end of Handsworth, in Holly Road, the closest of the three boys to Handsworth Park and Lozells. Like Dave and Kash, he spent his formative years in this racially mixed area, with large Black and Asian communities, the home of Reggae bands such as 'Steel Pulse'.

Future football personality David 'Kwame' Barnett spent his childhood in Greenhill Road, at the Rookery Road end of Handsworth, bordering Lozells.

Although we lived in the same district, Dave Barnett and I didn't really know each other as schoolboys. We met in the early 90s. Having both been brought up in Handsworth meant that we could kind of relate to each other, straight away.

There was an article in a paper, some time ago now, saying that Dave had taken up kickboxing, because it helped him with his football. So I contacted him, and then took him over to Aston Gym; a friend of mine, Paul Sutton, is the owner. I introduced Paul to him, and then coached Dave at Paul's gym. He's a talented footballer.

According to his friend, Cyrille Regis, Dave came into football a little later than usual. He's been around a lot of clubs, had a good stint at West Bromwich

Albion and worked under Barry Fry at Birmingham. Birmingham City won the *Auto Windscreen Trophy* at a national competition played at Wembley, to a crowd of 100,000. Dave played in central defence and was part of the winning team.

He's had a good career at Birmingham City; he's a solid defender. I've got a lot of respect for him. He used to support me at my fights. He'd bring down Ricky Otto, Peter Shearer and other well known names from Birmingham City football team. I already knew Wayne, Ricky's brother, through karate.

Ricky was a talented footballer, but didn't quite make the grade, because of his lifestyle. Dave Barnett's lifestyle was religiously football, similar to my attitude to kickboxing. He was dedicated to keeping fit.

I've got a photograph of Dave holding my oldest son, Kallan, when he was a baby. Even though we don't see each other weekly, I can phone Dave up and he's there for me – and the other way around. If you need any advice, he's a good guy to speak to.

He played for a variety of clubs in the Football League, including Dunfermline Athletic in the Scottish Premier League, Port Vale FC in the Championship, and also for Birmingham City. He made more than 200 league appearances in total.

Dave's father, like mine, was an immigrant to the UK. He was from Jamaica and he became involved with Law; he had an entrepreneur's mind. His mother was a dedicated nurse for many years. She retired in 2010, on the same day that Shirley interviewed her son. His half-brother spends most of his time in London, as an interior designer. Over to you, my friend!

"Like Kash, I was an active child and always into sports. As a toddler I used to kick a football and later played on the streets on Greenhill Road and the surrounding roads. Hilltop Farm, by the *Uplands* pub, in Handsworth was a popular playing area; it's up the other end of Handsworth from Waverhill Road, where Kash was living. I went to Wilkes Green Junior School and St George's Secondary School, just before the Newtown area. I left school at sixteen and played for Wolverhampton Wanderers from 1983-1985.

"Sport was my 'be-all-and-end-all' as a child. I played for the school, did Athletics and belonged to the Cricket Club. Both of my parents were very sport-orientated, so sport was very much in the genes," Dave continues.

"In total contrast to Kash's street, our road was about seventy per cent Irish. At the end of it was Saint Augustine's School and the church."

Several people have confirmed that there wasn't a significant racial problem in Handsworth, while they were growing up in the 1960s and 70s, but nowadays there's a much greater divide.

"Yes, there wasn't that much segregation; we'd just play and if you got on, you got on," confirms Dave. "But to be realistic, there *were* pockets of the Afro-Caribbean community who would keep themselves to themselves. It was the same with the Asian community, because, if you think about it, the Asian community came over here and set up businesses and gradually built up empires, so credit to them. That led to a certain amount of division, but at the same time there was unity too. People would be more comfortable with others of like mind-sets. But as children, we mixed together, regardless of colour.

"I had aspirations to join Wolverhampton Wanderers. I was training there and looking forward to a potential apprenticeship, but it never materialised. So I went to London, where I met Cyrille Regis's brother, David. I was about seventeen at the time and David Regis was on the course; we've been friends ever since. I had a flat in Golders Green. David lived with his parents. I'd go round there and he visited my flat.

"We trained very hard and I had a full-time job teaching sports at a Health Club. David and I had a crazy lifestyle at that point, in the middle of London. We were out till all hours, although we were still focused on trying to become professional footballers.

"In 1988 David Regis and myself played football in New Zealand, for about nine months. Culturally and socially it was good for us to get out of London for a while. A friend of the club manager where we trained invited us to come out and see what New Zealand was like. When I returned I signed to play professionally for Colchester United, from 1988-89. David signed for Barnet. So it worked out really well for us," Dave Barnett continues.

"As Kash explained, I met him in the early 90s. Although Birmingham's a large city it's also the type of place where people tend to know each other, so I'd already heard about him before we met. In that respect, it's been compared to a village. If you imagine Handsworth, you're playing against Broadway Holte, Aston Manor, in various sports, so, attending other functions, you meet a lot of the other children."

I ran evening classes at Holte School, Wheeler Street, Lozells, but there were a lot of shootings there around the year 2006, so I had to close the kickboxing class after a couple of years. It was impossible to carry on, with the gun dealers, crime et cetera.

I was twenty-four when Dave Barnett and I met as adults, although I almost certainly would have met him around the area, when we were children, without knowing his name.

"I think Empathy is the key," continues Dave. "There was a mutual respect between Kash and myself, because we both know what it took, first-and-foremost, to have a goal. Many young people have problems now, because they haven't got a specific goal and a vision for the future. Kash and myself each had a vision: Kash wanted to be Number One in kickboxing and I wanted to make the grade in professional football.

"It depends upon your background really," continues Dave. "In Handsworth, growing up, we were fighting every single day. So we were able to do Kung Fu, kickboxing, whatever. It was a natural transition, because you had to defend yourself."

That's absolutely right. Kickboxing's quite a new sport compared to Kung Fu. Howard Brown went to America in 1977-78, when Dave and I were just ten or eleven and was one of the first guys to bring kickboxing to the UK.

When I turned fourteen, in 1980, I started kickboxing at the *Handsworth Leisure Centre*.

I was one of the first kids within the area to start kickboxing as a sport, but Howard started it off, was into it for a couple of years and then took me on board. People used to ask me in those days: "What's kickboxing?" But it really came on in the 1990s. Nowadays Sky coverage and the film industry have made it more popular.

In those earlier days that Dave's talking about a lot of black and Asian kids did Kung Fu, because they were into the Bruce Lee films, so Kung Fu was the main thing. You'd get a few doing Karate, then kickboxing came along after. Even now, just thirty of forty years on, kickboxing is a relatively new sport.

"If there were any disagreements, you just had a 'straightener': we just straightened it out with bare knuckles. It was between you and the person and the best one won. It's totally different now on the streets, because someone can just knife you or shoot you!" Dave concludes.

Dave's early memories have jogged my memory, about being in fourth year at Secondary School. I was about fifteen and already into kickboxing.

In the class it was early in the morning. I was trying to hide someone's glove in the top roof, because I was the class joker. I was lifting this heavy tile up and it slipped out of my hand, went over the heads of three kids sitting there, hit the table really loud and smashed into pieces! But if it had hit that kid on the head, David Simpson, it would have killed him... Oh my life!

If the tile had fallen on him it could have changed my life completely. That really does stand out in my mind. I told the teacher that I was trying to release something, but he knew that I'd been fooling around. But thank God no one got hurt! That's the first time I've mentioned that to anyone... it's quite frightening, isn't it?

If I went out into Birmingham City Centre I wore shoes with a good grip on the soles, in case I got into a fight! Normally I wore trainers but if I was going out to a club or something I made sure I had the right footwear. When we were training in our gym classes we had predominantly bare feet, so I'm very conscious of my footwear, which is a strange thing to dwell on. I'm kind of thinking about fighting, which makes me sound a bit crazy!

In Junior School, at St Michaels', I must have been nine or ten, when we had PE lessons I'd say to the other kids: "Do you want to punch me in the stomach?!" Everyone was fascinated by me taking any number of punches. Nine or ten kids would line up and take a shot at my stomach. I'd laugh and say: "That didn't hurt!"

But one big kid, Calvin, who was really tough, hit me once – and I'll tell you what – he nearly brought tears to my eyes! He hit me in the stomach, but I didn't show that he'd hurt me, although I wanted to cry really. Doing that was like a gimmick. The teacher was in the hall, getting the equipment ready.

As a young kid I was always climbing really high into trees and across roofs. I climbed up on the back of our house roof and the bricks were really loose. They suddenly collapsed and about fifteen bricks, hit me on the head, one after the other! I just stood up, dusted myself off and carried on, but I was more scared of my dad finding out than I was about being injured!

My brother Cougar describes me as a natural leader; because of the sporty side, I was quite athletic, at a young age. A lot of the kids didn't mind that; if you could lead you'd do it, wouldn't you – without thinking about it? If anyone wanted to challenge me – then they would.

I used to climb up on the church roof and annoy Resham! Gurdip remembers how there'd be a service going on, and there was a skylight in the church roof. Cougar and I would be peering down and knocking on the skylight, just to be disruptive! Gurdip never did that, because he was the youngest, but he'd tell on us! The church was only open so many days of the week, so we'd use the entrance area, an exposed foyer, to play football and cricket.

We'd also use the factory gate. If you went down Waverhill Road, about 100 yards down, on the left-hand side, there was an alleyway to the back of the houses and a steelworks factory. Gurdip had a paper round when he was eight. We used that alleyway as a cut-through into Holliday Road, on the other side and as a back way for walking to school.

We also used that area to play in and practise our football. There was a big wall; we used to practise 'headers'. It was more about having competition with the other kids – how high you could kick the ball in the air and things like that. Every now and then you'd have a 'dust-up' with a kid from another road.

Resham did Kung Fu with Gamma. Resham came home the one night when I was a little kid; they'd been learning knife defence. He gave me the kitchen knife and said: "Come on then – try and stab me!" So I went straight for him and stabbed him on the upper side of the wrist. Thank God it wasn't the underside; otherwise he might have bled to death! Resham gave me a real hiding for that! I was scared because I was only ten or eleven. They took him to hospital and stitched him up. He's got the scar from that, so we still have a laugh about it. When I teach my classes, we use plastic knives, which is much more sensible.

Resham sometimes invited his friends round, when we lived at Waverhill Road. He studied in his attic bedroom. Our electricity power was in the corridor. Being naughty kids we'd turn the power off! He was so annoyed: he'd come all the way down from the attic and chase us! He was a bit of a swot. We kept doing it, again and again!

I saw the demonstrations in Handsworth Park and followed Muhammad Ali's boxing matches. My sister woke me up once when I was about nine or ten years old: she pulled me by the hair. I got up and I started shadow boxing, which is really strange, because I wasn't into boxing at that time. That's probably why I'm where I am today, because it was almost instinctive with me!

As they grew up, Gamma and Resham had their own friends and went out to pubs and nightclubs in Birmingham City Centre. I took the other path, avoiding nightclubs and drinking. I always had a bag on my shoulder on a Saturday evening, going to my sport.

I enjoyed sport at school. I wasn't any good at Maths, but I was pretty good at English. I got good marks for my stories, because I've got a vivid imagination. I was good at essays: I could write page after page. My woodwork exam was terrible: I remember putting the object I'd made into the box and it all crumbled to pieces!

Around the age of eight I desperately wanted some child-sized red boxing gloves. They were in a toyshop window, on the Soho Road, which is famous for lots of shops. I cried every day for those gloves, but never got them. That's why I treat my kids so well, when they ask me for things.

Handsworth Park was around ten minutes from where we lived. We'd run there and run back. My brothers and sister would often end up there too. We'd sometimes go to the Hockley Adventure Playground, at the far end of Soho Hill, for a change. Hockley borders Handsworth.

I was proud of Handsworth. It was such a mix of people and such a busy place. I quite like busy places. My childhood memories are really good. Obviously it's a high crime area, but when you're born in it, you don't see it. I felt pretty safe living there.

When I visited South Africa, in 1997, it was known to have a high crime rate, but being born into that kind of environment, it was just a 'breeze in the park'!

St Michael's Infant School, in Thornhill Road was the first primary school that Steve Kapur, went to. The Head teacher, Mr. Selwood, was a good head teacher. Although we went to different branches of the same junior school, Steve was doing his thing and I was doing mine, so we didn't actually meet at that time.

Steve was always into his music. I began to know more about him at senior school; he was DJing and things like that. He used to say: "Kash, you're always running!"

He made a special track for me, after I came back from Australia, *Chok There*. He changed the lyrics from one of his songs, so that the words were about me. That was in 1991, when I was twenty-four, just as he made it big in the Asian Charts: he went to Number One. Apache's a year younger than me. One of his early musical influences was a Jamaican nanny, who lived next door to him, in Holly Road.

"Yes. Jamine – I'm not even sure if she's still there," recalls Steve. "Her son was actually the park keeper. They were an established family that everyone knew. She carried on looking after children for years. I went back to see her, as an artist, when I was twenty-odd. She was what we would nowadays call a Child Minder.

"There weren't many nurseries in those days. I remember it vaguely, because I was between the ages of five and upwards. It was sounds and languages and culture; smells. We were exposed to all of that.

"There were two things in particular that drew me towards Jamaican Reggae music, even from an early age: the first was the bass... the *depth* of the music, plus what it was talking about. It was very 'conscious'; listening to all the Bob Marley music and stuff: it was about love and about what was going on. He was singing about things that were really important," Steve remembers.

"Just as Kash attended martial arts demonstrations in Handsworth Park, I'd attend the music carnivals – although people sometimes don't understand why I did that. My parents were from the Punjab, like Kash's parents. As much as you look up to them and you're learning from them, they almost had to learn from you. They hadn't been in this country; they hadn't been to the schools. That's why you sometimes get problems within Asian families. Some parents don't *want* to listen to the kids, so the kids end up having this double kind of life: thinking, 'well hold on. I went to school and it's a different religion.' Sometimes it might conflict with what your parents have told you.

"You go to a British school and they take you into church. Your parents can either sympathise or listen, but they can't relate directly to what you're saying, because they've never been to either," Steve explains.

I agree with what Apache's saying there; it was a similar situation for me. If you compare it with the way that the kids are integrated now at school, I'd have been embarrassed to tell other kids that we ate chapattis and curries, because young Asian kids were in a minority when I was at school.

It was an education at school, with all the different races. But our parents were very Indian. We were a typical working class family, quite streetwise, but there were some things that you'd have to explain to dad. Things that were happening at school were a totally different experience for Gurmej. It's quite hard to explain really. It was a different world.

At school we'd be learning about the Christian Faith, but we weren't that religious at home, whereas Apache's family were more so. But we always believed in 'A God' and went to church next door, so I was brought up learning about Jesus and the disciples and so on.

Our father brought us up as Sikh children. In India the Sikhs are considered to be a superior race and tend to get all the best jobs. But when you're in England we're all the same, even though the parents still believe that you're more superior than others.

There is still conflict between the older parents with the caste system, which is very strange because the system doesn't apply in England nowadays, although it might, when I was younger, if it was an Asian employing you! My dad's first generation, we're second generation and now with the younger ones, the third generation, that's fading away.

"My parents were receptive to what I was telling them," continues Steve. "I was lucky, because I noticed that a lot of my Asian friends were having problems; they had to hide things from their parents – they weren't really listening. That's when you'd have people leaving home or going out with boyfriends and girlfriends. All of this clashed with arranged marriages… and all that stuff was going on.

"My parents were also quite receptive to different cultures; for them to even drop me off at the next door neighbour makes a statement in itself. They would have black friends and white friends, like we would, in school and in the park… it's different cultures, religions and communities, all around you, so it's always about that balance.

"I went to St Michael's Primary School: the Soho Road-Thornhill Road junction one, rather than the Piers Road one. Although I remember Kash from school, I would remember him more from the community, from Handsworth Park.

"To me he seemed like a quiet boy. He was really into his sport and his running and his training, from an early age: first or second year secondary school.

"You wouldn't really see Kash hanging around with a lot of people; he was always training; he'd be running up the road. Come rain, sleet or snow, if you looked out of your window, there was Kash doing his training… he wasn't stopping to talk to anyone! I'd never see him out smoking or drinking. The discipline that he had, at such an early age – wow! And the support that he had from his family, including his brothers; he seemed to have a really good network there.

"A lot of discipline, but very quiet; still to this day he'd rather keep himself to himself. He is very independent: he doesn't open up too much. I've actually got closer to him over the last four or five years, doing things together; school events. We're both established names in music and sport. We should do more stuff together.

"I probably first met Kash in and around Handsworth Park, playing football. I enjoyed sports at school and was all set to be a Sports or English teacher. Then I became interested in Reggae music and started buying records as a hobby. There was a shop in Grove Lane, which I used to pass. I started buying some records from there."

I remember that store Steve. It was right near the chip shop; it was there for years and years. But now it's been converted into an Off-Licence; my friend runs it. It was the in-place for people to go; mainly Jamaican people went there, for the Reggae music.

"Right... and it was the *only* shop that sold Reggae. But again, there were all black people outside, with dreadlocks and everything. I used to wonder – can I even go in there? But eventually I started buying one record, two records. The whole culture around sound systems, in Handsworth, Birmingham, was that you'd start buying speakers and start a discotheque, so that was my little hobby," continues Steve.

"I remember even taking my wardrobe outside in the garden. I painted it black and cut three holes in it. I was crazy with the sport. I wasn't into drugs, and I was into music, but it was very black-orientated, so people like my parents were saying: 'Wait a minute – hold on!'

"I actually grew my dreadlocks when I was young, about eighteen. People were going: 'Oh, he's trying to be black,' or 'He's going against his culture.' I've got dreadlocks and I'm into this Reggae music. I've got a lot of black friends, and it sometimes seems to people that I'm disrespecting my culture – and you get hassle... from your own communities.

"But the thing is that no matter what I did it couldn't be more natural: it was just a reflection of my own community area. There's nothing political about it. Although I became a singer-songwriter and I write poetry and all sorts of stuff, it wasn't obvious when I was younger that I was going to be a musician. Anyone who knew me at school would have thought that my interests were sport, sport, and sport! I went to Birchfield Harriers; I was an athlete there. I did Long Jump, Triple Jump and Fifteen hundred metres.

"I remember going up and down the country, just as if you were touring with music, but everything was sport. I'd go to school at eight o'clock in the morning, to do an hour's training, before school started. A lot of it was Athletics but I was also captain of the school football team. So I had all of these achievements and I was Head Prefect at Handsworth Boys' School too. There were over six hundred boys at the school; they were mainly West Indian and Asian... just six white boys!

"It's closed down since. In the end it turned into more like a little Borstal. It was on Church Lane. Our school was at the back; the one in front was Handsworth Girls. Having single sex school at that age isn't such a good idea. In terms of respect for the opposite sex and being able to work with them in the classroom I think it's a very good thing to have an integrated system, although there are arguments for and against.

"I did three A Levels, but I didn't enjoy school at that stage, as they didn't do sport. I tried a little bit of College, between sixteen and eighteen. Then I started getting more into the music. I would take my sound system and I started DJing in some of the smaller clubs – some of the Reggae places around Handsworth and other areas of Birmingham. I bought myself a little Luton van and carried my sound system around in it. I became known as 'Steve the Van Man' and ended up taking all the sound systems to their venues. But that gave me a lot of experience in setting up various systems. I was twenty-two or twenty-three at the time, but this was my new hobby now, taken to another level.

"Eventually I thought: 'You know what? I used to love writing at school, but I couldn't even *think* of singing,' so I started writing a few poems and a few bits and pieces. But I made it about all my experiences of life: things that I heard at home, like arranged marriage, but in a Reggae way, with Indian sounds added to it. I mixed sounds from the country too, from pop songs. I wanted to go into a studio, to record a song, just to say that I've got this song and this is mine.

"In Christmas of 1989 I went to the studio, to make a record. Then I brought it home and played it to my friends. They said: 'Well, is that really you? I'd love to have a copy of that record.' To cut a long story short, I ended up making five hundred records, because it worked out cheaper. I'd given out ten records and everyone liked them, so I offered the other ninety to record shops, on 'sale or return'.

"I switched off from it then. I thought: 'Well I'm not even listening to the radio; not even going back to the shops. But in those few weeks, apparently, everybody was playing this record, called *Movie Over India*, because every time we went home, there was a 'Bollywood' movie on from India.

"I made it using the subject matter from home, with all the little sounds and words that I'd heard; names of film stars and all that, do it in a Reggae way; let's use some patois language that I've heard, which I look on as a language from Jamaica. It's also easier to learn language if you sing it; so I'm learning these languages and my own language, because I would insert bits of my own Punjabi language too: bits and pieces from home.

"I went back to this record shop, three weeks later, and they said: 'Oh, are you that little kid that came with the record? Bring us all the records you've got!' And you know what? The song became Number One in all the Reggae charts across Birmingham. And everyone's like: 'Wow, is this two guys on this record?' But to me it was just like making sense of everything around me.

"Although my real name is Steve Kapur I called myself Apache Indian because my favourite singer from Jamaica was called 'The Wild Apache Supercat'. Again, there was no idea of trying to be an artist, but when I went to fill in this form for my record they asked if I had a singer name. I said: 'No,' but as I liked Apache so much and I'm Indian I chose the name 'Apache Indian'. As my sound system was called 'Sunset', they said: 'Right, your record label can be *Sunset Records*.'

"But in 1989, *Movie Over India* got to Number One in all the Asian and Indian charts too and that hadn't been done before. People said that it was bringing together communities. That got picked up by a Reggae label in London, so it eventually reached Number One in the country, in early 1990. I got signed to that Reggae label and they said can we have two more songs? *Boomshackalack* was the record that made me really famous... that was later on," Steve concludes.

Thanks Dave and Steve – more from those two in later 'Rounds'!

Round 4

INNER CITY YOUTH

When the Handsworth Riots of 1981 were taking place, Kash was just a teenager, reacting to the situation that suddenly flared up within his home area. Much has been written, over the years, about the causes and outcome of what became a series of riots.

In this 'Round' and Round Five we're looking mainly at two riots: 1981, 1985 and then, briefly, four later ones in 1991, 2005, 2009 and 2011.

Kash relives this dramatic episode in his life, aided by eye-witness accounts from a cross-section of people. These two Rounds combine the memories of former Police Superintendent David Webb, Kash, beat bobby Tim 'Gringo' Green, Kash's brothers and sister; Steve Dourass, Howard Brown, Adil Ray, Hudson Richards, Norman Nelson, John Holcroft, Apache Indian, Wayne Elcock and Brian Travers; also, media personnel Tom Ross, Phil Upton and Peter Wilson.

Our intention is to shed light on what it actually felt like for Kash, his fellow residents and contemporaries, to be at the epicentre of the riots. The substantial amount of information gathered would make a fascinating book in its own right. For the purposes of this biography, however, we have been obliged to condense the material.

As David Webb recalls, "In 1981 the riots started elsewhere in the country. They were down in Brixton, London; Moss Side in Manchester; they were in Liverpool; St Pauls in Bristol and so on. Riots were going on during the week. We in Handsworth, because of all the projects that we had, were OK; there was no one coming near us.

"But at that time in Handsworth there was a man named David Buchere, a young black guy who was often in trouble. He'd been arrested for possessing an offensive weapon. He was in custody and people were protesting down at my police station, Thornhill Road Police Station that week, about him being in custody. So that's the introductory background."

My relationship with David Webb grew after he'd retired. We'd get sports equipment from him, when he opened a sports outlet called *Aries*

International, just off the Holyhead Road, in Booth Street; my brothers Resham and Gamma also worked for him.

Extracts from a conversation between David and my co-writer, Shirley, provide a backdrop for subsequent memories from others in this Round. Over to you Shirley.

David Webb spent twenty-seven years in the police force and was Superintendent at Thornhill Road station in Handsworth, for seven years. He was born in Hertfordshire on 13 April 1935, ironically the same date as the Sikh Festival of Vaisakhi. From the age of nine years onwards he played a wide range of sports, joined the army in 1953, the Bedfordshire-Hertfordshire Regiment and boxed and swam for them.

After joining the police force in 1955 in Hertfordshire as a village constable, he served in various departments until 1966, rising rapidly to the rank of sergeant. He was later promoted to Inspector, in the West Midlands Police, when it was formed, in 1966, and was based in Walsall. Rapid promotion continued, through the ranks, until his transfer to Handsworth in 1975. According to his book, *Policing the Rainbow*, he originally hadn't a clue where Handsworth was.

"It was a big surprise to me when I heard that I was going there. It's twelve miles from Walsall, but it was another territory, Birmingham City, and a different lifestyle. In those days there were lots of abandoned houses in Handsworth called 'Squats'. They were occupied by young West Indians who had problems at home; young girls mixing in with young Rastas and so on; all sorts of *Blues Parties*, as they called them, going on at night; drugs parties. That caused the neighbours to become very angry and the police kept having to sort these situations out. It was very difficult. There were a lot of burglaries too; crime was rife in the area. There was constant thuggery and anti-social behaviour.

"The Battle of Winson Green, on the 17 May 1976, occurred when Thomas Relf was imprisoned there. He was a man who refused to sell his house to non-white people, so he was imprisoned in Winson Green prison. As a result of that, they held demonstrations outside Winson Green prison. The National Front and all sorts of other people gathered up there. They started throwing bricks and other missiles, at the police."

So although the *Brown Report* had recommended the value of preventative strategies, the *Cranfield Institute Study of 1977* made the point that that would mean increasing police numbers, with the emphasis on foot patrols?

"That's right," David Webb explains. "Rather than Reactive Policing, we were trying to adopt a village style of policing in the area, which meant that we totally communicated with the community, so that they knew us and we knew them – a proactive approach. I've said it a thousand times: teachers, social workers and police officers did not *live* in Handsworth; they did their job and then went away. They had no actual social contact, unlike the County System, where you lived in a police house; your children went to the local schools; you used the local shopping precincts. You were part of that community and had a vested interest in it. Unfortunately, in the inner city areas that wasn't the case.

"In India the policing was done in a certain way, so they never thought that police officers would be able to sit down with them, talk with them, go out and have a meal with them; go to the churches and the schools and inter-react," David continues. "So we had to overturn that and let them know that the police would act and respond to the community.

"We tried to get various organisations to sit down together, so they could see what each of the groups was doing. We had projects with the probation service and social services: we went on camps; we had our own youth club and called it the *Lozells Project*. We went out on trips, all to show that the police understood the community problems and that we sympathised with them.

"I was Superintendent of Handsworth from 1975-1981. It took two or three years to implement my changes and make a positive impact on the community. Newspaper articles show that between 1976-1978 inclusive we were getting huge global press coverage. I still have a letter of congratulations from Lord Scarman's secretary, written in August 1981," David explains.

"When we had the 1981 Riots happening all over the country we got off lightly and Scarman came to Handsworth. He based his *Scarman Report* on what he found in Handsworth: the community working together; people talking together; because we knew all the community leaders and they knew us. When the *Handsworth Festival* began in 1980, it involved all the various communities in Handsworth joining together. From 1984-1994, it became the *Handsworth Carnival*.

"October 1977 marked the beginning of the *Lozells Project*. Its aims were to reduce crime and vandalism, forge closer links with the community and encourage local people to help to resolve the problem. However, in 1985 it was the Lozells area where more extensive riots flared up!

"In 1981 I retired, because my tactics and my policies weren't being followed and there was a move back towards a more reactive type of policing again, because it was cheaper and required less police effort. Getting out of a car and going down like a fire brigade situation requires far less effort than going into youth clubs and schools; working very long hours: they *thought* that was non-productive.

"The opposite has since proved to be the case because now all of the police forces are going back to my style of policing from the 1970s and early 80s, because it *is* productive.

"I said in my book, *Policing the Rainbow*, that Community policing is much harder than the other style of policing – it wasn't glamorous like *Starsky and Hutch*. Also, that 'Stop and Search' was too expensive a method and inflamed the black youth.

"During the day when the 1981 riot started we were patrolling the streets of Handsworth, following rumours that the National Front were going to march along the Soho Road. So we tried to keep it cool; there were very few policemen about: me, in plain clothes, trying to reassure people.

"Unfortunately, the shopkeepers were a bit wary, because of what had happened around the country, so they started boarding their shops up," David recalls. "In the evening, all of a sudden a crowd of people, who were involved in the David Buchere situation, were standing opposite the *Frighted Horse* pub. They started chucking bricks at me. Apparently, on *CD Radio*, it came out that a riot was going on in Handsworth. So people started to come into Handsworth, to take part in the riot."

Most of the people who were arrested were outsiders… they weren't from Handsworth. People started running up the Soho Road, knocking windows in and so on. Back to you Kash.

Thanks Shirley. Cougar and me used to watch from the rooftops, during the 1981 riots. Afterwards, metal shutters were introduced for shops and are now in common use. A common misapprehension at the time was that West Indians were attacking Asian shops, because they resented the Asians' success.

"No, that wasn't the case," David continues, "the people who were arrested there were all sorts: Indians, Irish, White – not one particular group. In one TV programme that went out later, in 1985, some of the West Indians are saying: 'We were paid by some of the Asian shopkeepers to come and smash their shops up, so they could claim on the insurance!' That's some of the allegations that were made – totally false. But that's how the Riots started in 1981.

"That was the shortest of the riots. We had the main part of the riots under control within forty-five minutes and the situation was all over within two days. We had the community coming out on the streets – young blacks and young Asians: protesting, saying that we should support the police. 'We don't want riots in Handsworth,' et cetera. That's why Lord Scarman was so impressed when he came here, because people were protesting that they had a good community. It spread down into Lozells later, which grew into people making petrol bombs.

"1985 was a different ball game. I'd retired in 1981, although everyone kept coming to me in '85 as if I was still the Police Chief. I was still chairman of the *Handsworth Community Relations Panel*."

The Chief Superintendent for the area, as the rank had now become, decided that as there was a lot of drug-taking going on, one or two places would be raided and that sparked more problems. It centered on the *Acapulco Café*, in Lozells.

"I'm not criticising the police, I don't do that because all of my children are police officers," David continues. "At that particular time the *Community Relations Panel* said that it wasn't the same situation as it was in my day. Unfortunately they did not have the communication, respect and trust that we used to have.

"Chief Superintendent David Love was in charge at that time. It's OK to mention his name because it was in all of the papers at the time. I'm not disagreeing with his policy. If he wanted to say that there were drugs then that's his decision. There *were* drugs when I was in Handsworth.

"I used to go to the landlord of whatever pub they were being pushed and give them a warning. So he'd be telling all of the people in the pub: 'Look, there won't be a pub here tomorrow if the Superintendent closes it down!' Usually they would move to another place; that's still happening this very week: there's more cannabis being sold and grown in the West Midlands than there probably is in Afghanistan!"

David's resignation, at the age of forty-five, was in October 1981. A longstanding Conservative, he subsequently stood twice as a Liberal-SDP Alliance Candidate. According to my brother, Resham, David did much more for Handsworth than would normally be expected of a Police Superintendent. He received honours outside of the police force, from the Rotary and the Academy in India, in recognition.

The situation's certainly come a long way since my father, Gurmej, arrived here from the Punjab, when he was very much a minority, there were no temples or mosques and he had few belongings.

"They are now solicitors, barristers; their children have been educated," David continues. "All their children and grandchildren are westernised now and much more like our own anglicised society… if you can get people so that they're not frightened of each other. There's not enough publicity about the good things that are happening. Hopefully Kash's biography will help with that process."

So what was it like for the 'Bobby on the Beat'? Over to Tim Green, or 'Gringo', as most people call him:

"I grew up in Harborne, attended King Edward's Grammar School, Five Ways; joined the Birmingham City Police Cadets at sixteen, then the regular West Midlands Police Force in May 1974. After serving thirty-nine years altogether I retired on 31st March 2011."

Gringo was in the Major Investigation Team from 1997 to 1999; 1990–2004, Steelhouse Lane Robbery Intelligence; 2004-2007, joined the Major Investigation Unit again."

When our family first met him Gringo was a Beat Officer in Handsworth. His 12-year period in the Force, from 1973-1985, is particularly relevant to my book. I understand that it was a total culture shock when you first began working in Handsworth Gringo?

"Yes, but when I started on beat patrol in Handsworth, in 1973, at the end of my six-week introductory period I said: 'I want to come back to Handsworth, because it's an *amazing*, colourful neighbourhood.'

"The West Indians had come over and established themselves and the Asians… mainly Indians; there were a few Pakistanis there at the time. I just found the whole vibrancy of the place was wonderful and I always wanted to go back!

"Following my training, at Ryton, I was posted to Thornhill Road Police Station in Handsworth and that was it… I had the most incredible time there. I've lived in Handsworth for thirteen years now, that's how much I love it."

I first met Gringo when I was fourteen. While patrolling he was called out to investigate an incident at Grove Lane; he 'hit-it-off' with our family straight away.

"Yes we accepted each other very quickly. You were very confident and forthright Kash, you knew what you wanted. Gamma was much quieter. You asked a lot of questions about the Force and I honestly believed, at one stage that was the way you were going. You were very respectful. I always thought that you were the oldest; I didn't realize, at that stage, that there were older brothers.

"I remember Gamma and Gurdip vividly too. Probably the most important thing was that I trusted them, straight away. I understand that their mother was a very religious person and would put everyone else before herself. So they got that grounding from her. Their mom would be very proud of all of them, wouldn't she? They *have* fulfilled her desires."

All my brothers and sisters have said how lucky we were to have Gurmej, keeping us on track; some of our friends weren't so fortunate and got into bad company. The same thing has been said by some of the other contributors to our book… that their parents were strong enough to prevent them from getting caught up in the gang culture.

"I came from a predominantly white area, and to suddenly be thrown into these new cultures; I was just fascinated by it all," Gringo continues. "The police were very thin on the ground in the early 1970s and 80s, so many of the Handsworth families hadn't had much contact with us at all. We were quite aloof as well: running in and out of jobs so we weren't finding time to speak to people. Being a beat officer, which I was for two-and-a-half years, allowed me time to stop and speak to people.

"You aren't allowed to patrol on your own now, but at that time you'd patrol alone at night too, although it was probably just as violent then as it is now. You knew that when you sent for assistance only two or three policemen would come, as only a few were on duty; nowadays there are a lot more.

"But I've always been a talker. I learnt very quickly, especially with the Afro-Caribbean's, because as soon as a police officer spoke to them, their defence barriers went up. Some police officers would react to that, but if you talked, you might be able to calm the situation down. I am proud of the fact that over the thirty-nine years I've only been assaulted twice, even though I've been involved with the most serious of crimes and cases.

"Before *Handsworth Festival* started in 1980, there was a Summer Competition for schools in Handsworth Park, organised by myself and a colleague, Tony O'Loughlin," Gringo continues. "Twice a week, during the summer holidays, we had up to ten schools competing in a football competition, based on a League situation. It covered Lozells, Handsworth and part of Aston, so it was the Inner City Riot Zone, basically. The teachers, God-bless-them gave their time and brought the teams with them. We ran semi-finals and finals; a member of Birmingham City, Aston Villa or West Bromwich Albion teams used to come and present the trophy.

"I particularly remember Brian Little, who was absolutely fantastic," recalls Gringo. "He watched the whole event – what a role model: he was a lovely man! Mark Dennis of Birmingham City was brilliant too. Then we had Tony Godden, the West Bromwich goalkeeper. We're looking at a period from 1979-1986 and beyond.

"We started with junior football and then we moved on and involved seniors as well. We invited local clubs to put a team in, i.e. the FCF Club in Handsworth and Shere Punjab put a team in. Kash played in a few of the 5-A-Side competitions, which were played at Holyhead School. Gamma played in the 11-A-Sides, with the older kids, in Handsworth Park.

"When *Handsworth Festival* was running there were all these big names in the concerts, but our competition cost nothing. The Jewellery Quarter donated trophies – the Cup, which was played for every year. Unfortunately, when I left the Beat it stopped, which I always thought was a shame. People still talk about it today… Mr Webb will tell you the same. People still come up to me in Handsworth today and call me PC Green, and talk about the football competition. There was an edge to it, because the police put a team in and everybody wanted to beat the police! But it was always played in the right spirit."

When we grew up there Gringo, Handsworth people *did* help each other – and older boys would help the younger ones too.

"That's right Kash. I was there during both riots. In 1981 I remember taking cover behind a dustbin lid, having rocks thrown at me. But in both riots outsiders caused it, although inevitably some of the locals got involved. You'd just see a crowd running, but the entrepreneurs amongst them, people whom I won't name, but I know very well, used it as a cover to break into shops and steal and loot. Unfortunately, the reason that Handsworth was always at the epicentre of the riots, was that two people in the post office died in the fire; they were murdered. So it became not only a riot but a murder enquiry as well.

"At the *Villa Cross* pub, opposite the *Acapulco Café*, someone had the nerve to put up a sign saying 'Birmingham City Council Drug Centre'," Gringo continues. "That's all gone now. On the weekend before the riots, *Handsworth Festival* was held in Handsworth Park. However the very next evening, on the Monday, the Post Office was burnt down, although at that stage, it was still mainly locals involved.

"But on Day 2 of the '85 Riots, a Tuesday, I was in the CID and went down to investigate," Gringo recalls. "It started because a uniformed bobby on a bike put a Fixed Penalty ticket on a car that was parked right outside the *Villa Cross* – and it suddenly escalated. The owner got arrested because he came over and had a go at the police officer. He was taken in.

"There was a place called *The Night Spot* in Lozells. The boys ran down there and decided this is it – we're going to kick off! By that time outsiders had come down, looking for a fight. There were criminals amongst them.

"We got word from the Community: 'Look there are people coming into the area!' So all the shopkeepers shut up shop and we had a policeman on every corner all the way up the Soho Road; all the way down the Lozells Road.

"The people of Handsworth and Lozells did *not* want the Riots to happen. But there are some longstanding situations which can never be resolved," Gringo continues. "There were people using the situation to cover their criminal activities and that includes the drugs. As it turned out those people involved with drugs were very influential. One guy told me, when I asked if he was unemployed: 'No, I get up every morning and go out and sell drugs.' He was a proper Rastafarian, who believed that smoking sensibly and selling drugs wasn't a problem!"

Gringo describes my dad, Gurmej, as 'very direct and friendly'.

"Yes, although I was unaware that his wife had died, but all credit to the man, for bringing the family up as he has done. He would sometimes help me trace people. I used to hold what I called an 'Open Evening' at the *Woodbine* public house, which Mr. Gill used to drink in. Most of the time you'd be knocking doors, knowing full well that people wouldn't be there, but you knew that in the evening they'd socialise. People would come into the *Woodbine* and I'd deal with the paperwork, which could be summonses, production enquiries – anything like that.

"If for example, someone had been stopped in Kent or Somerset, a Production Enquiry would come through; as long as their documents were OK, that's all I had to do. I'd mention names to Gurmej and the next time I came in, 'Mr Singh' would be waiting there, to speak to me. It was just two little rooms; a little 'walk-through'; a little Smoke Room on the side, a bar and that was it – tiny – but a big part of the community. In 1964, way back, before I met him, Gurmej had been in prison, so he'd had experience of both sides. So for him to be like he was with me – all credit to him.

"If you look at gang members now, the majority of them do not want to be involved, but what else can they do? But that wasn't as prevalent in the late 1970s-80s; gangs have grown more powerful since then. I'm a great believer – and I've told Kash this a hundred times – that if you look at America and then eight years later look at us, we're doing what they were doing. America had a lot of trouble with gangs, and then all of a sudden, that's come on our doorstep.

"Tony O'Loughlin, who I mentioned earlier, was very instrumental in setting up *Little League* in this area. Steve Cluney was a policeman who was well involved with that too.

"In October 2006, the *Birmingham Mail* produced a *Remember When* issue, which included *Handsworth through Time*. There's a photo of me in there as 'Gringo'.

"When I was on the beat I had quite long hair – I don't know how I got away with it... and a drop-down moustache that I was famous for. I played in a Charity Football Game at Tally Ho – Handsworth CID versus the 'Aston Villa All-Stars', on the rugby pitch. Charlie Aitken shot the ball and I dived to the right and saved it. Tony Butler was doing a charity commentary for the match. He said: 'A great shot from Charlie Aitken. Well saved by the Mexican goalkeeper!' So the name 'Gringo' stuck from that day onwards. A lot of people don't know me as Tim; they know me as Gringo!

"I was always taught to be 'firm, fair and friendly'. You've got guidelines to work within, but as Scarman says, 'There's a shade of grey.' People who work in a world that is simply black or white can't be effective. All Common

Law is based upon what a reasonable person can expect. The majority of police want to do the job that they joined to do."

Thanks Gringo.

In 1981 I remember going up the Soho Road and everyone was looting the shops. I picked up a pair of tracksuits, but I was only a kid. I ran as fast as I could, but in the end I just threw them away, with fear. I picked up a bottle of wine as well, but I don't even drink! You just copy what everyone else is doing. There were the marches with the BNP going on for a lot of the time. Within the community it was blacks against the Asians, which I don't agree with. They needed to unite against the white people who were trying to send them back to their own country. The same thing applies today.

In 1975 and 77, there were BNP marches. I remember going up there and just trying to copy them, as a young kid, throwing stones at the police with the riot shields. It was against the BNP, but obviously the police were on the Front Line, protecting them. As an eight or nine-year-old my heart was really pounding, but it was the excitement. But if my kids ever did that now, I'd be distraught!

We were just brought up with the idea that the BNP wanted to send Asians and Blacks back to their own country: they were the enemy. Obviously we were born in the UK, but they wanted to send us back to India. They didn't like the colour of our skin. This was around the time that the National Front was staging marches in Handsworth.

The Anti Nazi League was against them and they gave us lots of stickers and leaflets. One of the Asian Labour councillors in Handsworth supported the League, because they were seen as being on our side. We got involved with them for the excitement: we didn't actually know anything about politics! I was about ten or eleven years old. That's the time I told you about – when I threw a brick at the police!

The more recent problems in Handsworth, in 2009, were probably because the blacks are much more segregated from the Asians now; when we were growing up we were more integrated. But you're finding that the young kids now are all sticking to their own roots. A lot of the fighting between gangs is drug-related: they want to run their own drug empires separately, the blacks and the Asians. It's only a small percentage, but it's taken out of context.

It's become much worse. People want to sell drugs, rather than work 9-5, because there's more money in drugs, so they're willing to take the risk.

As you know, I've kept away from drugs, always been clean living to this day. Because you are brought up in the area, you don't recognise deprivation yourself. I'm sure we had it in our house: passing down your clothes and so on, but you don't see it as anything unusual. Our road wasn't that bad actually. We didn't see any really bad poverty. Our family were a lively bunch and unlikely to get ourselves into that kind of situation.

During the first Handsworth Riot on the 10 July 1981, the police were under heavy bombardment from people. They had their riot shields. As a fifteen-year-old young kid it was frightening. My birthday was only eight days before – what a birthday present!

It was frightening to see people throwing petrol bombs at the police. I was on my own. My brothers were somewhere around, but we were all spread out. I kept my distance. It was kind of like a football match. The police would run, then the rioters would run – all at the same time. At first the crowd would be quite brave, but then everyone runs, in different directions.

Although our father said, "Don't go near the riots. It's dangerous," we tried to get a better view. We knew all the side streets in Handsworth, so we'd just find a roof and watch from there. Even from a distance, if you're high enough, you can still see quite far away. Sometimes I'd climb to the top of a lamppost. I was a bit of a clown when I was a kid – and very good at climbing.

Then you run away, hoping that they don't catch you, because you're just watching really. But you can so easily become a part of it, as with the tracksuit trousers and bottle of wine. I threw the tracksuits away – but I kept the wine! The Badial Supermarket, on the Soho Road, was the one I looted the wine from and possibly the trousers.

I saw a lot of police getting hit and shop windows getting smashed, because they never had shutters in those days. Now you go on the Soho Road and every shop's got shutters.

As David and Gringo have told you the second and larger riot began in September 1985 and lasted two whole days. Hundreds of people attacked property, looting and smashing, even setting off firebombs. In its aftermath, two people were left dead – both of them burnt to death – in the local post office.

Two unaccounted for, 35 injured. 1500 police officers were drafted into the area. Around 45 shops were looted and burnt; the damage ran into hundreds of thousands of pounds. The riots were to spark a series of similar riots across the country, notably the Broadwater Farm Riot in London, which also resulted in fatality, a murdered policeman, Keith Blakelock. Film-maker and artist Poca Caesar extensively photographed the second Handsworth riots; it was also witnessed by Bronx graffiti artist, Briman Goldie, who documented the devastation in a *Channel 4* Documentary – so there's actually a video there.

Lozells, where the second riot took place, was a different sort of place. It already had a reputation. I always kept away from Lozells. We stayed on the Soho Road. Most of the shops that were smashed were owned by Asians. People said that they only smashed Asian shops but there were only Asian shops around! There were one or two West Indians shops, but they were predominantly Asian. I used to run around there occasionally – lucky that I wasn't running there that night!

Although there was a lot of crime in Lozells, Handsworth was the one with the reputation. The second riots, unsurprisingly, spread into Handsworth. I remember reading all of the newspapers at the time, to see if we recognised anybody in the pictures; watching TV and stuff. I was four years older by then: competing and training at that stage, so I kept away from all the violence and had something more important to channel my energy into.

That's an important message to the kids out there: find something else and keep yourself out of crime. My sister, Binda, remembers the 1985 riot, which lasted two days; it happened just before she moved to Germany.

"I didn't really go out; it was a scary time. My brothers were quite protective of me anyway. They were more involved in the situation; the younger ones were watching it going on."

Binda attended Handsworth New Road Girls' School. When Gamma went to Hamstead Hall Secondary School, which all of my brothers did, the number of ethnic minorities was very small.

"It was a predominantly white area," Gamma recalls, "but I never had any racial difficulties. I spent a lot of time playing football in Handsworth Park, during my school lunch-break and got into Kung Fu when I was thirteen. It was an early ambition of mine, to make a career in martial arts, like Kash. I was doing quite well in the third year at Hamstead Hall so I was put in the O level classes, but I didn't like the school environment. Eventually I did a Marketing course, followed by the Civil Service."

Generally speaking all of my family felt safe living in Handsworth, apart from the riots.

"In this day and age," continues Gamma, "you get a lot of people worrying about sending their children out. When we were growing up there would only be the odd person who was trouble. Everyone knew each other in Handsworth; mixing together was no problem. We had people from different communities coming to our house.

"I was about nineteen when the 1981 riots happened. There were rumours that something was going to happen. As it had happened in Brixton and Toxteth, it was likely to happen in Handsworth, because conditions for us were as bad as they were for them," Gamma continues. "There was high unemployment, including me and my friends. Our football team was probably what kept us sane. We were Albion fans. I was the captain and manager of our team.

"I was in the wrong place at the wrong time. We were driving around in our football tournament van, when the police pulled us over, at two or three in the morning. When the riots happened although we got caught up in it, none of us were interested in looting the shops. Kash was younger of course and just got caught up in the excitement of the moment. I'm sure lots of kids would react like that, when they're younger."

Round 5

THE HANDSWORTH EXPERIENCE

Steve Dourass, a former Area Fundraising Manager for Macmillan Cancer Support, was working for the 'Post & Mail' when the first riots began:

"I remember the Handsworth riots very well. I was a Birmingham Post Sales Representative at that time in 1981. The weather was humid and sticky and it felt really uncomfortable. My Circulation Manager told me that things were happening in Handsworth, and that we were producing a 'riot' special edition of the Birmingham Post. My role was to get extra copies out to the newsagents across the region and to ensure that 'handwritten' posters were displayed. It was a dreadful time for the community."

Our youngest brother, Gurdip was a twelve-year-old Scout when those 1981 *Riot Special* editions came out.

"Resham was running a Scout Troupe, on Saint Michael's Hill. The Scout Hut was in the church there," recalls Gurdip. "We normally finished at nine o'clock on a Friday night, but each of the Scout Leaders took the youngsters home early, instructing us all to stay indoors.

"Somebody we knew had been to a 'Stag' do," Gurdip continues. "He walked down Handsworth High Street, drunk, and didn't realise until the next morning that there'd been a riot! But because I was the youngest I was always protected, to an extent, from things like that.

"There was a bike shop in Grove Lane," he explains. "During the 1985 riots it was a bit like the *Keystone Cops* or *Police Academy* films, because young Afro-Caribbean lads were riding off on bikes. If one was a bit too small, they'd throw that back into the shop and pick a larger one! We guarded our own house. Binda didn't come out at all – but we were ready!

"Although the 1985 Riots actually started in Lozells, it spread all the way down, because in a riot, people go for the commercial areas, to see what they can get. If you asked people who took part in those riots what it was actually about, I don't think they could give you an answer. It was just a 'free-for-all'! Because of my age, it was more a case of guarding the house, with a hockey stick in my hand!

"A hundred yards up from Grove Lane is Branksome Avenue, which branches off Grove Lane," Gurdip recalls. "About ten West Indians pulled this van into the middle of the road and were about to set it on fire, but there was a bus coming! So they moved the van out of the way, let the bus pass, then turned the van on its side and set it alight. There may have been some kind of principles involved in that! Those 1985 riots were more difficult. There were Copycat Riots too: people tried to out-do each other.

"When we were growing up there were fair fist fights, no other weapons. If you have a fight like that now, the crowds get their mobile phones out, sending pictures to everyone!

"But I was always OK in Handsworth, because people knew that I had four older brothers, so I never really got any hassle, although I did get into some 'dust-ups' that I didn't tell the family about, because whoever I'd had the fight with would get another smack off Cougar or Kash, even if I'd won the battle.

"Racial awareness is probably more prevalent now than it was then: we were kids and it didn't matter what the colour of your skin was," Gurdip continues. "When I was around thirteen Kash would be running to the bus-stop and I'd be there with a milk bottle – throwing it at him. That helped him later, with all his ducking and diving!"

Resham explains: "The National Front was causing provocation by coming into an area that was densely populated by migrants. They knew exactly what they were doing. There were youngsters within the community who wanted to be assertive and say: 'Look you're not coming into our patch, causing trouble,' so they put up a counter demonstration of strength – a bit like the Anti-Nazi League do now.

"You can ignore these people, but it's a tried-and-tested technique that they use: go in, provoke a response; create tensions. They return to their own areas, having distributed propaganda, leaving the community to pick up the pieces.

"When you combine this kind of community tension with people who have lost hope of employment, particularly young men between the ages of

16-30," continues Resham, "there's an easy temptation to get involved in loitering. Also, it's a good excuse to have a knock at somebody. It's usually the police who get in the middle of these things, so they vent their frustration and anger on the police.

"In a democratic society it's important to protect people's right to free speech. Whether they agree with it or not, the police have to protect whichever force comes in to demonstrate, so they had a duty to protect the National Front. That was seen by some individuals as defending aggressors. Many of those police officers would have been sympathetic to the local community, but they're paid to do a job.

"There was greater preparation for the second riot; people had learned from 1981 how to make firebombs, so the damage was more devastating and it lasted much longer too. In the early 1980s Handsworth was described as the 'Angry Suburb'. David Webb was known for being at the forefront of policing and was certainly respected by the community," remembers Resham.

Tom Ross recalls a television car being burnt out on the Soho Road during the 1985 riots: "It was a dangerous time for the BRMB radio news reporters who had to cover the disturbances. I kept as far away from it as I could!"

My former coach, Howard Brown, was born in Handsworth, in 1957, a child of First Generation Jamaican Immigrant parents. There were seven boys in the family and one girl. Four of the brothers are fighters. Howard and his younger brother were boxers and kickboxers, plus a cousin and a nephew.

Howard attended Handsworth Grammar School, from 1969-1976. There are probably more Asians there than whites nowadays, but in Howard's day it was the total opposite, as he explains.

"It was a great school, but I got into loads of fights, mainly because of cultural conflicts, between me and some of the wealthier lads, but we all became good friends. I can't complain, although earlier on I didn't do my homework and I'd get in trouble regularly. I didn't take it seriously until I started to take GCE O Levels.

"But I got a good job, with Lloyds Bank, for seven years… they wanted me to play for the football team! I had all the other qualifications as well and finished off in Smallbrook Queensway branch at Gloucester House, for a couple of years. In between all of that, I was kickboxing," Howard concludes.

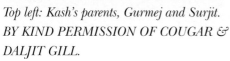

Top left: Kash's parents, Gurmej and Surjit. BY KIND PERMISSION OF COUGAR & DALJIT GILL.

Top right: Cougar, with Kash (seated on his mother's lap). Photograph taken on 7 April 1968, when Kash was 1 year and 9 months old. BY KIND PERMISSION OF COUGAR & DALJIT GILL.

Bottom left: From left to right: Gurdip and Kash, the two youngest sons, c. 1977. Kash aged 10 and Gurdip aged 7. Their mother Surjit had died just a short while before, when Gurdip was 6 and Kash was 9. BY KIND PERMISSION OF COUGAR & DALJIT GILL.

Bottom right: Waverhill Road, Handsworth. From left to right: Gurdip, cousin Judy, Kash and Popsi, Judy's brother. BY KIND PERMISSION OF COUGAR & DALJIT GILL.

Handsworth Park features prominently in this book. The Gill children spent many happy hours playing there and Kash used it as a regular running route. BY KIND PERMISSION OF ERIC ARMSTRONG, VERNON FROST AND AMBERLEY PUBLISHING.

A modern day view of Grove Lane. The Gill family moved there from Waverhill Road. BY KIND PERMISSION OF ERIC ARMSTRONG, VERNON FROST AND AMBERLEY PUBLISHING.

Kash always knew that he'd climb to the top of the tree! Taken in the back garden of the family's Grove Lane house. Handsworth Grammar School is in the background. BY KIND PERMISSION OF COUGAR & DALJIT GILL

Above: Tim Green, aka 'Gringo'.

Left: Former Handsworth Police Superintendant David Webb, in conversation with a young Handsworth demonstrator. BY KIND PERMISSION OF DAVID WEBB.

Kash and Dad at Grove Lane. "This is how you make a fist son." Dad's are never wrong!

Kash takes part in the Sutton Coldfield Fun Run, 1988.

Above: Who looks the coolest in the 80s? Kash and Cougar outside their Grove Lane home. The Ford Cortina Mark 3 was Resham's first car. What a banger!

Left: Kash in action at the BAI Boxing Gym, John Bright Street, Birmingham.

Left: Dad and the lads. BY KIND PERMISSION OF COUGAR & DALJIT GILL.

Below: Close family, left to right: 'Gogi', now a doctor in the USA; Kash, Popsi and Gamma – on his back again! BY KIND PERMISSION OF COUGAR & DALJIT GILL.

Above: Kash's Living Room, decorated with trophies, for his proud father.

Left: Flash Promotions: the public weigh-in, outside Birmingham Council House, prior to one of Kash's events. Resham is doing the interview.

*Above: John Holcroft and his partner,
Pauline Wright (centre, front row) with
a group of supporters, outside the new
community hall, in Villa Road
Handsworth, January 2011. John has
worked tirelessly to help the
disadvantaged in the community. Kash
is waving from the back row.* BY KIND
PERMISSION OF POPPY BRADY.

*Right: Kash in the garden at Grove
Lane, with two championship belts and
no shoes!*

Adil Ray, TV and radio presenter, comedy writer and performer, was also a Handsworth Grammar School boy, from 1985 until 1992, starting there nine years after Howard had left.

"We were the first Asian family to live in Yardley, a suburb of Birmingham. It was difficult for the first couple of years. Having previously lived in a predominantly white area, my first experience of a multi-cultural area was going to school in Handsworth," Adil recollects. "It was rather like 'trial-by-fire', because my first experience of the new grammar school was the day after the Handsworth Riots! I remember walking up Grove Lane and there were boarded-up windows and glass.

"My dad, Abdul, a bus driver, came from Pakistan; my mom is from Kenya. Dad arrived in 1965; mom arrived in '67. My mother worked as an Interpreter-Manager, one of the first women to work in immigration. She became an unofficial advisor, like a Third Ear, if you like. There was lots of immigration at the time. This was from the 1970s until 2000: she retired twelve years ago.

"My mother had told me that they were sending me to the best school in Birmingham, so it was quite bizarre! From Day One it was a 'wake-up call'. But looking back, it geared us up to go: 'Right – OK. It's a tough world out there – anything can happen!'

"The pupils were mainly white pupils at Handsworth Grammar School and about 20% Asian and a handful of West Indians, nowadays it's mainly Asian. Almost within our first week we were becoming slightly more vigilant and a bit more streetwise. But to be fair, I don't think any of us quite understood why the riots had happened and what it was about.

"There were about a hundred in my year and about twenty Asians, but it felt like more, because we had a real presence. The Sikhs, Muslims and Hindus all bonded together, because we recognised the need to. I really enjoyed that part of school," Adil recalls.

"We didn't have any friends or relatives who lived in middle class areas like Harborne and Moseley. After school finished at 3.50pm the pupils who lived there just wanted to get on the bus and get off home! The rest of us just hung around and would take our time; probably drop into some of the shops there on the way home. But not buy anything! We'd go into newsagents and say we were 'just looking'.

"In Handsworth, around that time, the Asian retailers started to do well and what would originally have been a small shop suddenly would turn into a big supermarket, or a big clothes shop. Although I didn't really know any of these Asian families it kind of gave you a sense of – yes, we've done really well, haven't we? We felt a part of it and we fitted in, because suddenly the Asians began driving around in smart cars too, so we identified with their success – a good example of how the Asian work ethic had begun to bear fruit," Adil recalls.

"After my university work placement I returned to Birmingham for Work Experience, with an Asian Radio Station known as *Radio XL*," concludes Adil. "That's how Kash and I first met, when I interviewed him for the Station."

Hudson Richards' childhood experiences contrast sharply with the Birmingham situation.

"In Jamaica, where I lived between the ages of twelve and sixteen, people were carrying guns and machetes," he recalls. "We heard gunfire in the evenings and then we'd hear about people who had been killed the night before. Some of them had tyres put around them and set fire to. So when I came here and a guy came at me with a short knife, in Smethwick, after I was used to machetes, it was almost laughable!"

Norman Nelson has known me around twenty-three years and has been the DJ at all of my events. We first met when he was doing a Thai Boxing event in Handsworth Park. He grew up in Handsworth, off the Hamstead Road. Having been born in 1962, he remembers the Riots too.

"I danced for a living for a few years, like *Diversity*. Back then if you weren't from the street, people used to think: 'Oh look at those gymnasts!' We incorporated Mime too and performed abroad a lot.

"During the 1981 Riots my father wouldn't allow me out. We lived just below what was known at the *Beehive*. During the 1985 Riots I'd just returned from dancing abroad. I couldn't get near my house because they'd barricaded Hunters Road.

"There were police; crowds coming towards us. It was really harrowing, because we didn't know anything about it… just pandemonium all round. From where my agent dropped me at the flyover, to the corner of Hamstead Road, would normally take me about three minutes walking. I eventually got home and found out what had happened the next day. I actually know the person who started it, who shall be nameless! But it all started from there," Norman concludes.

Stuart Nicholls, a former kickboxing student of mine, remembers the 1985 Handsworth Riots: "My dad came home afterwards; he did a building job in Handsworth and someone had nicked all of the bricks... to throw at the police!"

Community activist John Holcroft has devoted much of his life to helping the disadvantaged. One of four children, he was born during the war, in 1944, up in Chorley, Lancashire. His widowed Irish mother struggled to keep the family together. After sailing around the world a few times with the Merchant Navy, John became a builder, travelling around the country, including the Birmingham area.

"In 1968 I started my own company, mostly in the West Midlands, but I got nicked and went to prison for five years. A lot of the prisoners were misfits, but I had this empathy with them and helped quite a few of them. I do believe in destiny and that God sends things along every now and then. I'd been an alcoholic, but when I went to prison I stopped the drinking. It was like a religious experience... I was forty years of age and what had I done?

"After prison I went to Handsworth, bought a big house up for sale for only £17,000 and turned it into an Old People's Home. As a builder I had some idea about how to sort it out. I bought another house on the Soho Road. My sons decided to develop it on their own. I was more interested in helping drug addicts and alcoholics.

"Jesus said: 'Whatsoever you do to the least of my people that you do unto me.' The Drug Addicts and the Alcoholics seemed to fall into that category. They can't con a conman can they? I've got a chequered past, as they say, so I had an empathy with them, which meant that I could help them.

"I used to write to Prime Ministers, to MPs, for financial help with what I was doing. But instead they put me on *World in Action* in 1992, which exposed villains: is this man, who has been to prison, a suitable person to look after vulnerable people?

"It took me five years to sue them for libel successfully. They came in secret and filmed under-cover, but they were trying to destroy me. Maybe I'd been arrogant with the Council? I'd ruffled a lot of feathers.

"Money doesn't turn me on at all. When I was doing that building up in Handsworth they were all black lads who were helping me. The big drugs guy in the area gave me a free hand to help these guys. They began to believe in me: 'Leave him alone. John's OK.'

"I had people living there who were in rehab, but they've never been to prison again since they met me. There were all sorts of things there to keep them involved, including a gym. Their ages ranged from 8-60. Then we got another building, but the actual Centre is all under the one roof.

"It took twelve years to get the Centre under way, using money I got from suing *Granada* – and it's still going strong. I just oversee it nowadays. Our policy is to get the Asians mixing with the blacks. We've got all different nationalities here.

"Kash seemed to have similar ideas when he came along to *St Theresa's Gym*. I didn't charge him any money, because otherwise he'd have to charge the kids. I liked what he was doing, because he *was* working with all nations, teaching them properly – overcoming problems. There were gangs of Asians, Blacks and Whites. Kash has a lovely personality and lots of 'bottle'. He was at the gym for about four years.

"They decided to pump money into the area in 1987, following the 1985 riots," John continues, "but it wasn't being spent properly. A lot of it was going back to Jamaica, rather than to local people, who needed the money. They did up the front and backs of the Soho Road shops, but it still didn't help young people who wanted the experience of a job. There was no clear sense of direction. They *thought* the government were going to keep giving them money, on a regular basis! But that stopped about eleven years ago, around 2001.

"However, the West Indians' attitude totally changed. They said: 'Look what we've done and look what the Asians have done'. They took a real good look at themselves.

"But they're struggling again now, because some of them haven't learnt how to run a business, so they now look at the Asians, Kurdish and the Iraqis, some of whom make better businessmen than them – they're doing very well. At first it was just shops then some of them started up in things like the building trade.

"So the social situation in Handsworth is changing yet again. It *was* becoming friendlier, where Asians and Blacks were coming together a little bit, just around the start of the New Millennium. Then the Gulf War started and we had a lot of Iraqis, Kurdistan and Iranians coming here. I offered to help them, because they were walking around the area in their white clothes and people were saying: 'Oh look, here's the next bunch coming to get the Social Security!'

"There was going to be trouble, so I started a Centre up there for them. It was Number 10 – where the Gym was: somewhere where they could feel safe; there was no smoking, drugs or alcohol, because we'd be closed down straight away. There are all sorts of people running it voluntarily now... good people. When new people come to the Day Centre they often need food as a starting point. We've also got a Hostel down on the Soho Road, which sleeps twenty-four. We help people mainly from the Winson Green area," John concludes.

Freelance journalist Poppy Brady's article about the brand new Centre, was featured in *The Voice* 27 January 2011. It was illustrated by her photo of John and his partner Pauline Wright, outside the new community hall in Villa Road, with other supporters, including myself.

Poppy writes:

'Here's living proof that the Big Society is alive and well in one of Birmingham's most deprived inner-city areas after movers and shakers in the community organised themselves to open their own base.

A disused building in Villa Road, Handsworth, has been transformed into a community hall complete with kitchen, offices – it even boasts a hair salon and homeopathy centre.

John Holcroft, the founder of the Handsworth-based charity Law, Leisure and Learning, has launched a new community hall which proudly carries a striking mission statement in bold red letters: Empowerment of the People.

It's a pilot scheme set up by the charity which is assessing the need for such a centre in Handsworth – and so far it's been overwhelmed with requests from people to use it and hire it out.

An irrepressible community activist, John defied months of kidney dialysis sessions to get the project off the ground.

"There is definitely a great need for something like this in the area and I just hope the Government's plans to empower local communities in the Big Society will in turn empower groups like ours under the office of Civil Society.

"We've been inundated for requests to book out the community hall which holds about 200 people for birthday parties and christenings. It's shown us there's a great need for something like this, possibly something bigger."

Law, Leisure and Learning, LLL, was set up in 1997 by John,' Poppy's article concludes, 'to provide some of the unmet legal, leisure and educational needs of the Handsworth community.'

Steve Kapur remembers: "With the Handsworth Riots it was never a Black versus Asian thing, as I remember it. Black people were always linked to drugs and crime and they didn't have the big businesses, but I don't think that it was racially motivated. I was there during the 1985 Riot. I remember cars burning and everyone trying to get out of the way; people looting down Lozells, because I just lived around the corner from there. It was horrible to see! I wasn't caught up in it in any way but it went on for several days – very frightening."

Footballer Dave Barnett, who we first met in Round 3, was living in the Soho Road and Murdoch Road area in 1981:

"When parts of Lozells burnt down we were around that vicinity," Dave comments. "There was looting going on; there was chaos; the police were around; there was a lot of anger, but we were streetwise, even though we were right in the middle of it. It was not something that you could shut the door and be oblivious to. You get involved… it's your community. But I was more of a bystander."

BBC Radio Presenter Phil Upton explains how we both have certain experiences in common, although he grew up on the South side of the city:

"Kash and I are both from a generation where we suffered quite a bit of racial abuse at school; we had quite a bit of verbal," observes Phil. "We were in a minority, growing up as kids, in this city. I grew up in Northfield. It was made very clear to me at school that I was in a minority, with my father having come from Pakistan and my mother from Ireland. Kash fought his way out of it too, in the respect that he became a kickboxer, in order to get himself out of the khazis, quite frankly."

Boxer Wayne Elcock is also of mixed-race parentage, like Phil. He has featured on a range of television news items, over recent years, in connection with his fitness and role model activities with West Midland youths.

"I was born in 1974," Wayne begins, "and spent most of my early life in Shard End, which is right next to Castle Bromwich, in Birmingham; my family all still live there today.

"There weren't many black or mixed kids around there, when I was a kid, I could count them on one hand! It was a predominantly white area so there was a lot of racism going on. Because there were so few mixed race kids we stuck together, protecting each other. I could look after myself, so I was never bullied. It was more a case of them name-calling and then sprinting away.

"I got into a helluva lot of fights, on behalf of coloured or mixed-race lads who were weaker than me. My dad's from Barbados and my mom's from England. My dad came over here in the 1950s, just a few years after yours Kash. Like Gurmej, he's a disciplined person. If it wasn't for my dad then God knows where I'd have been today!

"The parents of many of the people I grew up with were in prison, or were single parent families; it was that sort of area. We grew up in a road called *The Shardway*, blocks of flats, which have since been demolished.

"I remember being four or five years old and you'd wake up every morning to find that someone had stolen a car from outside the flats; there was a passageway below the flats and you'd hear people coming back from the pub. They were forever fighting; people got stabbed and God-knows-what else!

"So you had to be very 'switched-on' and like Howard Brown I was forever getting into fights! Don't get me wrong: I was never a bully myself. I didn't care about how old the kid was. I'd go in there and try to sort it out, like my dad and yours Kash – I really do think these things pass on. You'd see a lot of domestic violence in that area, because there was a lot of tension... and single parents. I'd try to sort that out too.

"My mom, Sheila, was white and English, so she had it ten times worse than me. Some of the names she was called down our way were unreal! Mixed race families are a lot more common today, but at that time it was far more unusual. You were stuck in the middle. Mixed race are some of the toughest kids about, because you had to be!"

Peter Wilson, Home Affairs Correspondent for *Midlands Today* covered the Lozells Riots, as they became known, in October 2005:

"The police got some 650 officers into a very small area of Birmingham, to keep the peace," explains Peter. "Racial tensions were very high. The difference was that this wasn't about the police; it was about the racial tensions between that community and the Asian community. There was a rumour that a young black girl had been raped in an Asian shop... which was also being pumped out to Pirate Radio stations. It wasn't true. It was one of those urban rumours that became the accepted truth. There was legitimate economic tension plus tension between Asian and Black drug gangs, which were operating within that area."

Musician Brian Travers of *UB40* is proud to have lived in the Balsall Heath district of Birmingham, for many years:

"It's like Handsworth, but the other side of town. They weren't the suburbs – they were the most active and poorest parts of the city, which brings us round to what we're going to talk about.

"I was born in 1959 – I was fifty-three years old in February, so I remember the first wave of people arriving from the West Indies, from Pakistan and from India. Of course immigrant people only get to settle in the most poorest of places. The only way that they could make it through was to help each other. Moseley was a bit more middle class, but Balsall Heath, in particular became very run-down and dirty, a kind of bed-sitter land, with houses split up for four families to live in.

"When the Asian people arrived we started seeing little food shops opening, so that they could eat their own food," remembers Brian. "It's taken this last thirty-five to forty years to turn Balsall Heath around: it's not a filthy little neighbourhood any more, although it might still be tough, but that's only an outsider's perception."

Shirley interviewed Patrick Wing, former Chief Superintendent and OCU Commander, with the West Midlands Police, for another biography. Patrick has helped the community to turn the Balsall Heath situation around, so there are members of the police force who *do* care.

"Good, we've had a few people doing that," continues Brian. "It's always been a very active community, because people are socially-minded, they do look after their families, their children and their elderly parents – and thank God for that! That spread over into our neighbourhood and *our* lives. Asian people would look out for us, as children too. They'd say: 'Try this food – I bet you never had anything like that!'

"As a result, Balsall Heath came back alive: there were cinemas and restaurants. Birmingham's definitely a Balti centre. They enhanced Birmingham most definitely, with their music and their culture.

"The institutionalised racism which exists within white society has always been a bone of contention with me," Brian continues. "I'm from an Irish family, so as a child, when the bombs went off in Birmingham, I can remember bricks being thrown through the window, by white people who'd never read a book in their lives. Therefore every Irish person was in the IRA... and responsible for what had happened. That was white-on-white racism, so imagine what white-on-black-Asian racism was like.

"The influence of Asian immigration into this country has changed it for the better, there's no question about it. As children, because of the Asian-West Indian influence, we were into Reggae music. Apache Indian is a good example of that: Steve, with a wonderful Asian music heritage, being influenced by West Indian music. There's a good reason for this: West Indian people didn't have anything to watch on television, or listen to on the radio. So music, anything to do with home, was very important; they'd gather around music and gather around records. In a multi-racial society, in neighbourhoods like Balsall Heath and Handsworth, the effect was profound, on all of this.

"Reggae was a way of commenting on the social conditions around them and their concerns about that. It speaks for itself really. So that kind of explains why *UB40* do what we do, because it was the music that we listened to.

"And I'm glad, because we grew up to be non-racist, non-judgemental about other people. Our band is a broad mixture of different races. We've got Arab, West Indian, Irish, English, and Scots. It's great. *UB40* are a microcosm of Balsall Heath or Birmingham or modern-day Great Britain, a multi-racial outfit, no more or less, we're just musicians.

"The important thing about this is that back in the early 1980s people were so poor. We had a Tory government. Even the privileged classes were struggling, but they were making it. Working class people were just handing their houses back – they couldn't pay for them. Timing-wise, that fits in with the first wave of riots in Handsworth and across the country, in 1981. They were taking place in Balsall Heath the day before and the day after the Handsworth Riots, but they just stopped reporting them, because they joined in with others – we're all in this together.

"Martin Tindal and the National Front were extremely Right Wing: they were marching on the streets in jackboots! It was the British Movement and the British National Front at that time; the BNP came later.

"So just those facts alone were enough... late 70s – early 80s, when Kash was a developing young lad. The poorest in this city were the Black and the Asian people – they certainly weren't being given jobs. They had to start restaurants or shops; market stalls. They're a very tenacious people; they know how to survive, but they were given a hard lesson. They were brought to this country with the promise of a better life, after the Second World War, but they were treated terribly!

"There was nothing in the establishment that catered for the ethnic minorities, so they had to provide it for themselves. West Indian music and Asian culture and food became really strong. The only way that they could survive was through themselves: giving their own people what they wanted – and what they missed from home. We all caught on eventually, I'm glad to say. We're still catching on now," Brian concludes.

Cougar recalls: "I was coming back from a football match, on Grove Lane, and Gamma was coming back towards the house. I could see two guys bullying him. The next thing, there were about six police cars and a van. Me and Gamma got taken into Thornhill Road. I was in a cell for about six hours. The other lads made up a story, saying that a gang of Asians had jumped on them, but the police let us go, with a caution. It's one of those things, isn't it? It just happens.

"With the Handsworth Riots we just followed what the crowds were doing. If you got too close into it, on the Soho Road, you were in trouble. People were driving into shops and raiding them, but I never got caught up in anything like that. When the police discovered what was going on, they set up road blocks, which put a stop to that. But there were people carrying things out on their shoulders!"

Daljit, Cougar's wife, grew up in Derby. "It was quite a quiet place: a town that then became a city. We hadn't been married very long; it was just totally alien to anything that I'd known. All the lights went out, so I hunted for candles. That was around 1991. There was a woman named Edie, who lived a few streets away from Grove Lane.

"When the lights went out, Kash's dad was asleep upstairs, but apart from him, I was alone in the house, because Cougar went off, to make sure that Edie was OK. It felt like he had gone for ever, because the next thing I knew there was screaming and shouting; people were running down the street. I knocked on dad's door and said: 'I'm really scared!' But then Cougar came back.

"People were running down the road with televisions, knocking your door and saying, 'Can you just put this in your house for me?' If there was banging I just went upstairs," Daljit continues. "But it was really frightening!"

"We had to arm ourselves with baseball bats," Cougar recalls, "to protect our property I bought a machete. I've never had to use it, but if they came in, they could kill your family. You have to think like the criminal.

"More recently, Apache had a birthday party at his wine bar, opposite the Law Courts," continues Cougar. "Kash got there later, but I'd driven into town earlier, with the children. It was really strange – why are there so many police here? On the outskirts of town I stopped a policeman, for directions."

Daljit adds, "The policeman said 'You'll be fine here, but don't go into the middle of town, because some rioting has been going on,' but it is frightening. I remember ringing Kash to warn him about what had happened. We decided to leave the party early."

"When you're in these kinds of situations," Cougar observes, "you have to stand up and fight for yourself. But I'm quite tough, having grown up in that kind of area and so is Binda. It *is* a bit of a culture shock. A Rastafarian came in to our kitchen at Grove Lane, but Binda, brandishing a rolling pin, marched him straight out of the back door!"

We began this final section of the chapter on Thursday 11 August, but, by an *incredible* irony, the riots that we had been describing flared up again with a vengeance. Furthermore, the situation was far worse than those of the past. Looting began in London on Sunday evening, 7th August 2011 then rapidly spread to most suburban areas north south east and west of the city, including Ealing, Tottenham, Croydon and Hackney.

Copycat riots subsequently spread to Birmingham City Centre on Monday night, 8 August 2011. Front page headlines in the *Birmingham Mail* the morning after read: '87 arrests as looters rampage in city centre'. This happened as gangs rioted for the third night in London, amid calls for the army to be sent in to restore order. On Wednesday 10 August five hundred police officers were drafted in to patrol the West Midlands hotspots. The trouble spread to West Bromwich and Wolverhampton.

According to a police statement, "There is shock and anger about what happened and many of the people involved were astonishingly young."

As before, Handsworth was badly affected and looting was widespread. On Dudley Road, in nearby Winson Green on a Tuesday evening three young Asians, from respectable families, were mown down and killed by a car, whilst trying to protect businesses in the area. Tariq Jahan appeared on television, holding up a photo of his son, Haroon Jahan, who had been killed alongside two brothers. Kash later attended his funeral, out of respect.

One of the fundamental differences between these 2011 riots and some of the previous ones is that this time trouble broke out in several different areas of England, within a short space of time, so police were dispatched to a wide range of trouble spots. Many were drafted in from other UK forces.

It would appear that, rather than having a genuine grievance, as with some of the riots of the 1980s, these new attacks were by looters, many of them in their teens or even younger, simply intent on material gain. 21st century technology enabled them to broadcast pictures of themselves on the Internet and chat on social networking sites, glorifying their exploits!

It's too early to say how the situation will be resolved in the long-term. Parliament was recalled and a televised debate within the House raised many issues. By the following day, Friday 12 August, one week after the first riots, over 1700 arrests had been made across England. Arrests and court appearances continued well beyond Christmas 2011.

Under-age looters received a maximum 6 months punishment, plus fines and could not be named in the Press. Some adults received custodial sentences, depending upon the severity of the crime.

The courts were open all night, on several evenings, to deal with sentencing. Police raided the homes of individuals who had been caught looting on CCTV and confiscated goods. *Radio WM* asked Kash, amongst others, to comment on the lootings.

FIRST STEPS TO THE TOP

"Kash was a trailblazer, because there were no professional Asian kickboxers in the UK, prior to him. Because of the Asian culture, the fight game was not for them. Their parents, quite rightly, would push them towards academic subjects."

Howard Brown

From the age of sixteen Binda was like a mother figure to us, after our mother died. She cooked the meals and looked after us, which was a lot of pressure for a young girl, so all credit to her. The Asian girls usually have an arranged marriage but she didn't marry until she was twenty-five, which is very rare for an Asian girl.

When she cooked for the family I was dieting, so I could never eat the curries and the chapattis. I would eat healthy foods like chicken and salad. I'd get separate food and eat out.

I sometimes fell out with Binda over petty things. If I fell out with someone it might last three or four months. I was probably the most stubborn person in the family. On the other hand, if that stubbornness is channelled into determination, it can be a very useful asset, particularly for a sportsman.

I fell out with Gurdip too when I was about sixteen or seventeen: I didn't talk to him for three years. Once, we had a fight in the kitchen and he stabbed me in the hand. I ended up in hospital but I just said I'd cut it on the fence. Gurdip is a very respectable family man, but as a youngster he was sometimes quite rebellious. We were inner city kids in Handsworth, fighting in the house. I think that's what made me so tough.

My brother Cougar and me would have an occasional fight, because we were closer in age. I had some fights with Gamma too. He's the only one who made me cry, because he'd put my arm up my back. That's why I started to do kickboxing. He did Kung Fu, but whatever Gamma tells me, I do the opposite, so I went into kickboxing!

Another incident that made me determined to be able to defend myself took place near Hamstead Hall Secondary School, involving kids in Cougar's year. There's a place called Hilltop Farm, which is a cut-through for the school. When we were walking through, the kids in the older year chased me and my friend. I was scared because they were a group of six or seven. They dragged me into this pool of water, which was like a stream. I got drenched. So after that I decided to do something, so that I could look after myself. That was definitely a turning point. I was just coming up to the age of fourteen.

Another memory from Hamstead Hall School was what was supposed to be woodwork lessons on a Friday afternoon. There was Amos, a good Jamaican-Indian friend of mine; his proper name was Michael and little 'Suki', Surinder, too: he was only short. At lunchtime we'd see who could do the splits the furthest! We'd have competitions like that.

Woodwork was one of my weakest subjects… it was a disaster! So that was my exercise period really. Amos was into the martial arts films: he was quite flexible. Again, we'd have challenges: who could do the most sit-ups and so on. I was easily led and more interested in doing the exercises than the lesson.

Another pupil at Hamstead Hall, who had no aptitude whatsoever for practical subjects, was Tommy Nagra. He was two years younger than me. Being academically inclined, Tommy gained seven GCSEs and eventually a degree in Media Studies-Communications at Sheffield University.

Like myself, by fourteen years of age Tommy knew precisely which field he wanted to work in… in his case journalism. He has done exceptionally well, becoming an award winning programme maker and creative leader, and, since 2008, has been Head of Television at the BBC's Religion & Ethics Department, based in Media City UK, Salford. His parents were *also* from the Punjab. The family lived in Elmhurst Road, Handsworth.

Tommy appears again, in our final chapter, at a venue where *neither* of us could have envisaged ourselves, during those early Handsworth days!

After leaving the Sixth Form at Hamstead Hall Secondary School, I went to Handsworth Community College, with a few friends of mine, who were also from Hamstead Hall.

At lunchtime we'd go up to the top floor of the college, where no one else was around. We'd say: "Let's have a round," which, in those days, didn't mean going for a drink, it meant having a fight! We'd hit each other really hard.

Handsworth College is on the Soho Road, opposite the top of Waverhill Road, on the left as you're coming out of Town.

There were three of us: Cookie, who was a tough kid. I was into kickboxing by then so I was in good condition, about sixteen or seventeen. There were a couple of others too, including Suki again.

According to Dorian Yates, "There's always been a link between bodybuilding and martial arts. My gym, just off New Street, in Birmingham City Centre, was half bodybuilding and half martial arts, many years ago. I've had that gym since 1987, but there's been a gym there in some form or other since the mid-60s. Kash will know Master Yau who used to run the Kung Fu Centre nearby, before it became bodybuilding. Ask him if he ever trained there. It was in Old Temple Street."

Gamma and Resham were the first in our family to train at Master Yau's gym and Howard Brown used the facilities too. It's the same building as Dorian's gym. Master Yau is Chinese. He's well respected in the community and had a really popular gym. He was really 'kicking' down there – a good word! In the 1980s Gamma said I should come down to the gym and do Kung Fu, but I wanted to do kickboxing. So I won that argument because, in my opinion, we'd beat Kung Fu any day of the week!

Master Yau took me to one of the tournaments in Austria in 1984, although on that occasion he managed it badly. One of the fighters was overweight, but I'd made the allocated weight, so it was unfair to move me into a different category.

Master Yau is still Birmingham-based, but obviously a lot older; he's produced a lot of world champions. He had the old team like Neville Wray, Clive Parkinson, and Humphrey Broomes. He brought all of those top names into the UK.

According to *UB40's* Tony Mullings, "Kash was well known, even back then. He would have been the only Asian fighter. There were a lot of kids of West Indian origin involved in it, because they were into combat sports. The Asians had this image of being too soft, physically, to take those kinds of sports on. Kash was the only one, at that time to do any kind of formal training in the martial arts. I do believe it was because he had a similar kind of upbringing to me... you had to learn to fight to protect yourself."

Former Police Superintendent David Webb, from the Handsworth Rounds, has known me ever since my teenage years.

"Kash was always very respectful and we could have a laugh and a joke," David recalls. "When we first met he wasn't a brilliant boxer – it wasn't quite his style. But when he got into kickboxing he was a different fighter altogether."

I also met magazine entrepreneur Paul Clifton around this time. Paul's first premises were in Birchfield Road. Would you run through the sequence of events for me please Paul?

"I remember Kash as a fourteen-year-old student, when he first started. But he actually joined the *Karate Association* because it was two things in one: karate and then the kickboxing kicked in, if you pardon the pun, so it then became the *English Contact Karate Association and the English Kickboxing Association* – they were one and the same, so Kash signed up to ECKA then."

It was Howard Brown who actually signed me on, at *Handsworth Leisure Centre*. I'd previously seen him giving a demonstration at Handsworth Festival. After that a friend of mine called Steven saw Howard's advertising poster in the *Leisure Centre* window, about the fact that he was starting a new class there, which worked for me. Steven went along too, to try it out.

"We set up in John Bright Street, a four-storey building that was also the home of Birmingham boxer Pat Cowdell. We'd had a fire at the Birchfield Road premises, so we re-located to the *BAI* – the *Birmingham Athletic Institute* in John Bright Street and we stayed there for three or four years. Kash trained there with his coach, Howard Brown. That was primarily in the early mornings, in the Boxing Gym, which was on the ground floor. Our offices were on the first floor and part of the second. The *British Kung Fu Association* was based there too," Paul explains.

This was the same gym where Paddy Lynch ran his classes. On the ground floor was the boxing, amateur and pro, where Azuma Nelson and Tim Wetherspoon were guest boxers from Africa and the USA respectively. That gym was used for matches, by top international names. As kids we'd come down and peek through the door. Azuma Nelson was very fast and powerful. He fought against Pat Cowdell.

I started on the ground floor, then moved up to the top floor, for kickboxing. The middle floor was for Kung Fu; the ground floor was Pat Cowdell's boxing gym, that is, the one he trained from. It was called *Birmingham City Boxing Gym*.

"Kash would be at least fifteen at that stage," Paul Clifton continues. "By that time he was building up to a fight career without really knowing that he was, because Howard was turning him into a full contact fighter. Howard himself was a great fighter – an undefeated Amateur Kickboxing Champion, who worked really hard to be as good as he was; he took training very seriously, as he did coaching.

"Howard knocked his opponents out by kicks to the legs! He fought Rod Kei from Mexico, at the *Aston Villa Leisure Centre*. Rod had to be helped out of the ring: he couldn't walk for three of four days!

"Then Kash fought Alex Tui; he really gave him a beating. Everyone enjoyed these fights – the aficionados and the fighters. That time was, I suppose like in the Fewtrell's day and the boxing area, where everyone had a punch up on the night, then went down to the local restaurant, had a good time out and spoke about it for a few weeks later," Paul recalls.

"It's interesting that in kickboxing, although weight is important, the opponents can be a range of heights, Alex Tui and Kash, for example. It was mainly about the weights, but having said that, finding opponents, in the early days, was quite difficult, so there was lots of room for manoeuvre. Kash was one of the first professional attitude fighters," remembers Paul.

When I left school I did a year's business course, which gave me a lot of useful tips. I went straight into kickboxing from school – that's all I've ever wanted to do. My brothers have regular jobs, mostly in various branches of Local Government, but I've never had any other occupation.

"It's interesting to consider the psyche of a good fighter," Paul continues, "because the best fighters seem to be those who can keep their cool, in the face of adversity. Any fighter, just as any golfer or football player, has to be technically gifted. He also has to be fully conversant in every aspect and avenue of concern for him and his industry. So, if you've been in a fight there's first confusion; then there's anger, frustration and adrenalin. Fighters tend to approach that differently: they tend to come in from the point that 'This guy's a threat to me, so what weapons does he have? Will he go for a right-hand lead, for a kick?' He knows all of this beforehand if he's a professional and he's done his homework.

"I would describe Kash as a Cerebral Warrior. That's the ability to disassociate himself from the situation in hand; even for a split second; to be able to analyse the game in hand. If you're in the ring and somebody's throwing ten to fifteen punches a second at you, literally," explains Paul, "then normally confusion would reign in most people's minds, under such circumstances. To be able to analyse that in a calm and controlled fashion is where the cerebral warriorship comes in – in the sense that you have to analyse it: break it down, countermand it – and then deliver those counter actions.

"Mike Haig had started a magazine," Paul recalls, "and he was having it produced by a company called *New Enterprise Publications*. We met up, because I was given the job of producing this new magazine, *Combat*. It was part of my apprenticeship, to get my graphic arts licence. Eddie Shah launched the *Today* newspaper and the unions fell apart, just before my apprenticeship came through, so now graphic artists could do anything that they wanted to do. So I left *New Enterprise* and formed a new company and Mike and I went into partnership. We moved to Birchfield Road and the rest is history. They were great days, in the late 1970s-early 80s.

"In 1987, we launched *Traditional Karate*," recalls Paul. "After that I launched *Taekwondo* and *Korean Martial Arts*, in 1996. Then in July 2004 I bought *Fighters* magazine (and gave it to my daughter, Paige, for her 16th birthday) which we re-launched in 2005, as a magazine for the full contact arts (MMA, Thai Boxing, Kickboxing etc...)."

The environment that I grew up in nurtured those survival instincts that Paul defines as 'cerebral warriorship'. However, the downside of that is reflected in Howard Brown's point, that when I first started fighting I wasn't good at controlling my aggression. They had to hold me back for my first few fights, because if somebody hurt me physically, I'd retaliate almost instinctively, like a kid on the streets.

Howard left his bank job, to become a professional instructor. In 1975, he'd been watching *World of Sport*, with Dickie Davies.

"I joined the local karate club," Howard remembers, "and also started to amateur box for the *Golden Gloves*, the same club that my brothers boxed for. It's now called *Small Heath Amateur Boxing Club*. The karate club, in Hockley, was called the *Hachi-Shim-kai*.

"At the same time I started my career in kickboxing – in Full Contact Karate mainly, although I did do some Thai Boxing as well, the ultimate form of kickboxing: I was to go down that path years later, with my main coach, Master Toddy, who you'll meet in Round Eight," Howard continues.

"What I liked about Thai Boxing is that you had to be *very* fit. The result was ultimate, unless you reached a point that *can* be dodgy, but usually the winner is clear cut. If you knock the other guy out then you've won – simple; whereas in traditional karate, if you knock the other guy out, then you get disqualified! That didn't really suit me, because I wanted to show my fitness and toughness. When I was getting warm my opponent was blowing and the contest was usually over!

"I started travelling abroad in 1978, to compete in amateur tournaments," Howard continues. "I fought my first Thai Boxing Match in Amsterdam in 1978; met a lot of friends there; did a lot of training, and then got into a new aspect of Martial Arts, which I hadn't seen, because of my karate background. Thai Boxing is absolutely huge over in Holland."

At one time Howard, I was better known in Holland than I was over here!

"Yes you were, because in Holland you were on television all the time; there were posters of you and myself. When we landed at the airport, the posters were on display at the airport and all around the streets. It was just so professional. Boxing over there is not as big as it is in England, but kickboxing was as big or bigger. They had brilliant fighters who we remain friends with, to this day. So that formed a large part of our formative years.

"Going back to 1980, when fourteen-year-old Kash sauntered into my gym, we already had quite a few outstanding lads join, of various ages. Our teaching system wasn't as formalised as it became later. A lot of what we did was 'hit-and-miss', in terms of structuring classes. We just did a warm-up, which was the way that I was taught karate; we ran through some basics; we paired them up for some technical work and at the end of class we did sparring. They were training for only three months and then they were sparring – which is totally wrong. We were just doing 'put them in their place' sparring, if you like; with the gloves on, it was kickboxing sparring.

"Most people wouldn't come at us hard, because we were too good. We were the instructors and they respected us. But Kash would! So we'd hit him a little bit, then we'd hit him a little bit harder, because we thought that would put him in his place. But the next week, he'd do exactly the same thing again! Godfrey Butler ran the club with me: he was very tough and taught me a lot about boxing.

"We realised that Kash was promising, although he was only fourteen. We weren't trying to knock him out, but we'd hit him hard. With the grit that he showed we realised that he was going to be quite special. But not only that, he was technically excellent. He picked up techniques, straight away.

"But the thing is with Kash, his father used to be a wrestler, so he was proud of Kash taking up the fight game. That worked in our favour, so I wasn't battling against parents. His father was very supportive – a terrific man! So Kash turned up to everything; he had the money for his equipment, or whatever was needed. Other Asians just couldn't believe it!

"I had other Asians say to me: 'You've got an Indian guy, but I bet he's not very good, is he?' I said: 'You've got to be kidding!' But that was a natural assumption, back then. It wasn't until a few years after Kash had been fighting that we started to get some Asian lads entering the fight game," recalls Howard.

During those teenage years Howard, I'd go out running, then come straight back and put on a kickboxing video.

"Right at the beginning, with the *raw* talent, you became technically proficient much quicker that I ever did," Howard continues. "You were just gifted – and obviously, very focused and determined. Normally, you can't see that in someone, especially when they're fourteen; you'd be thinking that maybe this time next year you'd have found girls – and that would be it; but you were *completely* the opposite.

"It wasn't long before Kash was as dedicated as we were. We couldn't let him kickbox in the ring, because he was too young. But as soon as he was seventeen we put him into his first fight – straight away! All of this training was taking place at *Handsworth Leisure Centre*.

"We *did* move from there eventually, because I opened a full time gym, in Broad Street, Birmingham, in the 1980s; we'd train there, during the day – professionally. Kash was there every day. We never had any problems with his fitness and technique. We thought: 'This kid's going all the way.' To succeed in the fight game you need fitness, dedication and you need to be naturally tough. Now you can have a great heart for the sport but if you physically can't take the punishment then you're not going to make it at the highest level – it's as simple as that – it's genetic!

"But we knew that Kash had everything. So we lined up his first fight. In the fight game you need to learn to be patient. Kash has got patience, but when he *first* started, if someone hit him hard, early in the first round, he'd try and knock them out – straight away. You can't do that, because if they're good fighters, they'll knock you out, because that's what they want. You have to step back.

"With Kash it was anger: 'How *dare* you do that to me?!' We used to be pulling our hair out – I had hair then! I'd be thinking: 'Kash – what are you doing?!' He'd come back to the corner, after the first round and we'd say: 'Look, will you *listen* to us? Just relax. You can get him back later – we'll plan it.' This went on for a couple of years. He always had that little weakness, but it became ironed out. Everyone was talking about him, within a year. He was obviously a talent," concludes Howard.

This is the first time I've told anyone this, but in the changing rooms, before a fight, when we were putting on gloves, I'd think: 'Don't pull them too tight – just in case I have to pull them off quickly!' I wonder if that goes back to my street mentality… fighting with bare knuckles? Or perhaps I felt vulnerable, having my hands so encased in gloves? Maybe it's a 'control' thing… that I needed to be able to be free to instantly react? Whatever the reason, that 'hang-up' plagued me for quite a few years!

When there was a drain in the road, I'd always avoid the drain. I would never land on it. I had this fear that if I stepped on it that would bring me bad luck. Even to this day I'm still running and still avoiding the drains! I won't go in-between two sign-posts. I have to go round them, which is a strange thing. And sometimes I'll run on the same pathway of slabs that I always did. It's like a good luck thing isn't it – almost superstition?

Regarding my early training for the first two years, between fourteen and sixteen, I was doing the sport as a hobby, just going in and enjoying my bouts, but by 1982, when I was sixteen I realized that I loved the sport. So it began to change as I left school and I could spend more time in the gym. I began helping Howard with coaching around that time too, like an apprenticeship really.

I remained single-minded. While many of the other young people around me were going to city centre nightclubs on the weekend and enjoying themselves, I would stoically continue with my training, as Gamma confirms:

"We had our own separate sets of friends. I used to go to the clubs most nights: places like *Romeo & Juliet's* and other Broad Street clubs. But Kash never went out very much. He seemed like a bit of an 'odd-ball', but as it turned out that was OK, because he was focused on his sport.

"I was into martial arts, Kung Fu in particular, from the age of about thirteen and then Resham came along and joined the club too," remembers Gamma. "Then I got into football and we formed a club called *Funspot*

Acorn. Funspot was a gambling arcade on the Soho Road – they were sponsors and bought us the kit. We played in the West Bromwich League, so it was more in the Black Country. We started a team for people of about my age, mainly unemployed. We used to go round the pubs, *The Frighted Horse* and everywhere else. Although there was not a lot of hope for some of the team members work-wise, it kept us focused on positive things.

"When Kash opened a club in Handsworth" Gamma continues, "there was a massive queue. I started training with him there, from my late twenties onwards… and I've trained with him ever since… for about sixteen years now, for Fitness and Health. I've never been interested in going in the ring – you've got to be brave to do that!" Gamma concludes.

Cougar comments: "Kash got a lot of respect and confidence from doing his kickboxing. Once he started the kickboxing with Howard Brown, he did fantastically well. From where he was, to what he is now, everything that he's achieved, he's deserved.

"Once Binda went to Germany, I was the main person running the house," Cougar continues. "Kash was the fighter so I never burdened him with chores, but Gamma and Gurdip had to do their bit."

Gurdip remembers: "When Kash saw that demonstration by Howard Brown in Handsworth Park, there wasn't a lot of interest, at the time. Then the Sports Club moved to Bromsgrove and Kash asked dad if he could catch a bus to the City Centre; from there he caught a train to Bromsgrove. He did that for a couple of years, taking his kit with him. But it would be a more difficult decision now, as to whether to let your child travel that distance."

I always said that I didn't want any of my family watching me fight, until I fought for the World Title. Back in 1986, when I won the British Title, Gamma turned up, so I was a bit nervous, although there weren't many Asian contact fighters on the scene at that time and I was winning.

I remember going to a couple of shows and receiving racists taunts, but I didn't mind – it just made me fight better. Nobody liked it when I beat these other kids, but that's how I made a name for myself. I wanted to have all the Razzmatazz – put my name in my hair and wore flash dressing gowns. I had all the glitz. That's how I became 'Kash the Flash' and spread the name all around the UK; all around the world.

But my inspiration came from Howard Brown, my coach. Even though he wasn't with me 24/7, he was the undefeated Featherweight World

Champion, and defended his title many times. I've won it a different way. Howard was a Handsworth lad too, as you'll know from Round Five, although he'd moved out of the area by the time I was coming on.

I had no guidelines, other than watching other people, so a lot of it was down to myself, how to be coached and so on. Although my dad had been a wrestler you couldn't compare the two sports. He'd say to me 'Why are you dieting – why are you not eating?' because his way was to build up his strength and his weight. He was probably a Middle Heavyweight, about 5ft 10-and-a-half. I'm just a touch under 6 foot 3.

I kept myself on a diet because I wanted to be Number One in my sport. The most important thing for me was to be training. I'm a determined person. If you want to be the best in the world, there's only one way to do it. I wanted to be remembered for doing something special. I had that goal to become a World Champion – and I followed that goal. And I did alright.

I used to work at several gyms; this particular one was in Broad Street. I'd get there and open up this cold gym, with damp on the floor. Normally that was around ten o'clock in the morning. I'd probably had a late night, training. But it was horrible, especially at night. There were rats running around!

The last couple of fights I was in I lost, because there weren't enough people available to spar with. Sometimes when we had no ring in a hall, we had to set up chairs to create a ring in the middle. We'd leave them upright. It was quite dangerous, but it was nothing like the real ring; sometimes we'd put rope around.

I was a Thai Kickboxing fan. All day long I'd watch Tommy Hearns, Muhammad Ali, but I'd also watch tapes from Thailand: Master Toddy gave me the tapes, from all the top Thai boxers and I'd watch them week in, week out. In Thailand Thai Boxing had been around for hundreds of years, but Master Toddy and Master A brought it to the UK, in 1975 and 1986 respectively.

By the 1980s kickboxing and Thai Boxing had become very popular. I was a big name in the UK, so around 1987 I was invited to Holland. They were very good at leg-kicking out there. I was lucky to fight a few times, at that stage. It got my name around Europe, because it was televised in Holland, by Canal Plus TV.

It seemed a lot bigger in Holland and in Europe than it was in the UK, so obviously we drew in bigger crowds: five thousand people in Amsterdam.

ALIVE AND KICKING!

Kash went through a really traumatic period in the early stages of his career, when he was with Howard. He was losing month after month: five defeats in a row. Although it nearly broke his heart, he remained determined to succeed, no matter what happened. Some were hometown decisions, but he took them on the chin. One such example was a London fight. Although Kash seemed to dominate the match, they gave the decision to his opponent.

It happens in all sports and it happens all around the world, in the fight game. People get ripped off, but they also know in their hearts who the winners are.

Another good example of this losing streak happened in 1986, when Howard and I travelled up to Bolton. At that stage I was down to about 73kg.

Howard elaborates: "We'd received a 'late notice' call from Master Sken, who comes from Thailand. He's a training partner of our coach, Master Toddy; the two of them arrived from Thailand in 1975. They then separated: Master Sken ran classes in Stockport; Master Toddy ran classes which we trained at, in Manchester. I used to take Kash with me, so he's as much Master Toddy's student as mine.

"Anyway, Master Sken phoned me and said that he had a problem with one of his top fighters. Humphrey Harrison, a brilliant fighter, had his opponent pull out from the fight. He phoned me up on the eve of this competition, asking if Kash could take the fight. Humphrey was a couple of pounds lighter than Kash. Anyway, I agreed to do it.

"We got to Bolton and they wanted us to weigh in. Kash was about two or three kilograms heavier. We thought that because it was short notice there'd be no problem, but Humphrey insisted that we lose the weight," remembers Howard.

"Our problem was that we were so over-confident. When Kash was younger he fought a heavyweight and knocked the guy out. It was very unprofessional, but I even had World Title defences where the opponent was overweight; I fought Rob Kei and Paul Lenihan: both of them were three pounds over. Technically, they were supposed to lose that weight, otherwise they couldn't compete for the World Title defence title. But I said, 'Forget it – just give me a good fight,' because I was that confident. I was a co-promoter, as well as a fighter. It wasn't advisable to do that, and technically illegal, but we did it all the time, it was just the way we were.

"So when we arrived in Bolton and Humphrey said lose the weight, we thought he was joking! As Kash was such a high class fighter we thought that we were going to come in and teach him some manners! Master Sken said he wouldn't take the fight unless Kash lost the weight. I asked Kash what he wanted to do and he said: 'I'm going to lose the weight,' because that's his nature.

"Skipping in the changing room for 45 minutes (half an hour followed by a quarter of an hour), he still had one pound to lose," Howard recalls. "The show started at 7pm and we were now at around 6.30pm. In the event, they rescheduled the fight until at least 8.30pm.

"I thought to myself: 'I don't think we should even bother with this,' but Kash said no. Humphrey came in and I said: 'He's only got a pound to lose now. Let him rest and he'll fight you.' But Humphrey said: 'No – he's got to lose the other pound.' This was just Humphrey – no one else was bothered. He came in personally into the changing room, to check the scales.

"Kash was skipping with three tracksuit tops on – all sorts – just to lose this weight. And they moved the fights back, so that he could skip some more. When he made the weight exactly, Humphrey came in and said: 'Yes, that's OK.'

"I look back on it and I just shake my head – how I was so stupid! It wasn't Kash's fault, it was mine. I should have said: 'Kash put your clothes on. We're going back to Birmingham.' But we didn't want to let Master Sken down. We were so confident we thought: 'It doesn't matter. If we skip for a day we're going to thrash you anyway!'

"We were walking out towards the ring when Kash suddenly said to me: 'I've got no legs!' The place was absolutely packed, with two or three thousand people. We got into the ring; the fight started but Kash had nothing left. Humphrey hit with a low kick, straight away and floored him; then hit him with an overhand right. Kash got up but I just threw the towel in. In my entire career everything I've done in martial arts, in training, competing – everything – that's my biggest regret… that night.

"Humphrey was putting his hands up before the crowd – the big hero. We thrashed him… We beat the big noise from Birmingham easily! I'm thinking, 'if only the crowd knew what had *really* happened.' It was disgraceful.

"Afterwards there were write-ups in the Northern magazines, saying how Humphrey had destroyed 'Kash the Flash'. But we just had to put it down to experience – although I'm not sure that we wouldn't do the same thing again! But the fight game's changed now: we wouldn't let our students go through with that – there's just no way!

"He had a fight in Italy, against a Swedish fighter," Howard continues. "There weren't many Swedish fighters, but the ones that there were, were brilliant. There was a lad called Thomas Rasmussen. I think it was the second round. He hit Kash with a low kick to the thigh. Kash, like me, was an orthodox fighter, in other words, we're right-handed and we fought most of our fights with our left foot in front. I guess about sixty or seventy per cent of competitors do that. We train for both sides, so we're able to switch into what we call the 'Southpaw Stance', which is with your right foot in front.

"It's a good job that Kash was so technically gifted, because Rasmussen hit him with this kick and he said to me: 'Howard, my leg's gone!' It was a ten-rounder and he had to fight the remaining eight rounds from a Southpaw Stance, against a world class fighter – and Kash won.

"I was so proud of him, but the *damage* that was done to him during that fight; that's not the only time that happened. He's just been in so many wars, because Kash is a 'do or die' fighter: he knocks you out or you knock him out! Nine times out of ten he's knocking the other guy out. That's why it's so exciting, because it's 'edge-of-the-seat' thrills and he provided that, as soon as the bell went; which was a nightmare for me as a coach!

"We've had some ups and downs, because everything is experience. But the only regret that I have, with his career," concludes Howard, "was the mistake that I made with the Humphrey fight."

Paul Clifton comments: "Humphrey Harrison took Kash's energy, but that's the fight game, unfortunately, but there *was* a weight discrepancy before the fight. Howard was saying that they often turn a 'blind eye' to that – and it *was* short notice, but that's the difference between Amateur fights and Professional fights.

"The short notice aspect is the Amateur stakes again," Paul explains, "If you can't get somebody to fight, then you have to find somebody else.

Because there's a crowd and tickets have been sold, you have to put the fights on. It's not like the Pro fights where they sell the tickets in advance and go through an agency. There were no sponsors in those days."

Champion boxer Frankie Gavin and I talked about coping with that type of situation, getting through the difficult times. A few years ago, I ran into Frankie at the Virgin Gym. He asked me, as one fighter to another, "Kash, how do you keep your motivation?" He wasn't a professional then, but he turned the corner afterwards and had won seven out of seven as a professional, by Jan 2011. So now he can answer his own question:

"Being World Champion is what motivates me," Frankie explains. "Once you win it, it's keeping on form, which is hard. I had a very similar experience to Kash's. I was Great Britain's best hope of a boxing medal in the 2008 Summer Olympics, but was unable to make the weight and therefore unable to compete. I later beat the kid who won the Gold and was the first British boxer to be favoured, going into an Olympics."

That's right Frankie. I've had some fights where *Aston Villa Leisure Centre* has been packed out. When I've won everyone's there for half an hour afterwards, shaking your hand, touching you. When you lose, the arena just goes empty. You just wander around... what's going on? That's the difference: when you're successful people hang on to you; when you lose they don't want to know you – they disappear!

"Absolutely, when you're winning you get hangers-on, but when you're losing, some of them won't give you the time of day," agrees Frankie. "You say: 'What's the matter with you? Can't you even say hello?' And they'll probably say something – behind your back. So when you're winning it's fine. I've got a handful of mates who'll stick by me no matter what; if you're lucky, you've probably got two handfuls."

Hudson Richards has diversified a lot, career-wise, but now works as a 'safeguarding' and childcare consultant, which gives him more time with his family. He first saw Howard in action, in a hall in Harborne.

"What really caught me was Howard Brown's spirit: he had a really gentle heart. I'd been trained by totally different guys, who would walk around with bamboo canes. If you were standing incorrectly they'd hit you!

"I didn't know any better," Hudson continues, "but the discipline was really rigid; you daren't put a foot wrong. Howard has quite a colourful past including a spell in prison, but when it came down to his training he had a really gentle spirit about him. He was firm, but for me gentleness means 'power under control'. And to this day I teach that to my students. It's not about treating everyone the same; it's about recognising that people have differences and treating them accordingly.

"So I attended a couple of sessions and didn't look back. Through Howard I met Kash, in 1989, at the Harborne club, when he was helping Howard. Kash later opened up the Handsworth club, so I started going there. I also went to Halesowen. It would depend upon my shift times. I'd given up the other martial arts, to do kickboxing. I then took a break from kickboxing, but went back to it from 1991 onwards. By then I was a qualified social worker, so I had a bit more time to devote to it," Hudson concludes.

Coming from a big family we couldn't afford expensive holidays, so 1984 was my first chance to go on a plane. It was to Austria, but I ended up spending a week in hospital there. So what a debut that was – because I didn't make it back on the plane: I had to come back by train and then ferry… which I'd never experienced either! As I was quite a young kid it was quite frightening to do it on my own, but it was exciting too.

I started taking it more seriously when I had my first full contact fight in 1984, at which point I started watching more of the contact stuff. I also played those Thai Boxing videos, although I wasn't intending to take part in the sport – just exploring the possibility.

Once I had my first taste of the fight game in 1984 I became seriously interested in fighting. I went to watch Howard Brown, in some of his competitions, at the *Tower Ballroom* in Edgbaston, *Central Hall* and *Wembley* too… and I fell in love with the sport.

In 1986 I fought a Dutchman, Ricardo Noslin, in Newcastle, and thought I'd won. There were two other Dutchmen on the Bill, who also lost that night. I asked for a rematch in Holland, scheduled for two months later. We went over as planned, but he never showed up.

Seated in the audience, however, was 'Mr. Perfect', Ernesto Hoost, who later became a K1 Ultimate Champion, famous for his head kicks. It was suggested that Ernesto might replace Ricardo as my opponent that night, but as he had a match pending, he declined the offer… thank God!

During a radio interview Sonia Deol asked me, "What's the worst injury you've had, because you must have had quite a few?"

The worst injury a fighter can have is a broken heart! No, my worst injury was probably a broken jaw. That was during a fight at Wolverhampton. I was posing a little bit, because I was 'Kash the Flash': I was dropping my hands and jumping around the ring! My trainer was in from Thailand so I was trying to impress him too. Believe it or not, I won the fight!

I went home and was drinking a cup of tea when Gamma walked in. I showed him that all my lower teeth were loose. So we went down Dudley Road Hospital and I had my teeth x-rayed. I was so worried. When I came back the doctor said: "You've got a broken jaw." They operated on me. When I woke up the next morning I had lots of wires coming out of me: I was like that for six weeks. But I was just thankful that I wasn't going to lose my teeth. I had to follow a liquid diet for six weeks, which wasn't easy.

And the biggest thing for me, at this stage, was to regain my confidence...

Round 8

5-D TRAINING

The five D's in the title of this round are dedication, determination, dieting, desire and discipline. For the uninitiated, myself included, here are some basic differences between three of the martial arts most frequently referred to in Kash's book.

Martial Arts Categories
Full Contact: kicks above waist only to body and head.
Kick Boxing: kicks to inside and outside of opponent's inner and outer thighs, as well as body and head.
Thai Boxing: can use knee, elbow, clinch, or kick any target. Probably the toughest sport of the three, because your opponent has a wider range of options.

A typical day:

As a fighter, my days were much the same. I'd wake up between 8.30 and 9am, unless I was seriously dieting, in which case I'd wake up a bit earlier. Occasionally I'd have a breakfast cereal, but normally I'd just have a cup of tea, get cleaned up, put my kit on, then out to the gym. So I didn't have a lot of energy in my training sessions. I'd feel really groggy in the mornings because I'd been running the night before.

I always say to my students: "It's quality not quantity," because I used to train intensely for an hour-and-a-half. You'd be doing twenty minutes skipping, five three-minute rounds of shadow-sparring: using hands for the first two rounds, then hands and feet for the next three rounds: your footwork. When I first started I did fifteen rounds, every day! I'd constantly dance around – like Muhammad Ali, my boyhood hero.

In the early years of my career pad-work wasn't too important, but as I progressed two of my student friends, Levi Lovell and Rob James, who later became a policeman, would help me. I'd do 12 x 3-minute rounds on the pads. Sometimes Paul Sutton would let us use his backstreet Gym, *Electric Avenue*.

Levi became a good friend: we used to train together and fight as well. He and Rob became good pad-holders. When I tell my students that I did twelve rounds of pad-work every day, skipping, plus shadow-boxing and punch-bag work, they can't believe it. Every day I'd do double circuit training: 10 x 10s; a one-minute break and then do 10 x 10s again – a hundred exercises; press-ups, sit-ups and so on. You'd constantly think about your exercises. What made me a World Champion is that I'd do all of that at the end of my training, which was tailored towards being strong in the legs for my fights.

So after an hour-and-a-half in the gym I'd go home and have an afternoon nap for an hour. I'd actually go to bed. Then I'd sometimes do another half hour's skipping, or go to the *Stock's* gym in Birmingham, now called *Bannatyne's*, on the corner of Corporation Street, near Masshouse Lane.

So I'd go in there for a 35-minute workout on the treadmill. Again, it's quality not quantity. Fast one minute, slow the next: down from high speed. My training was divided into fast and slow. Some of the gym members would look around... who's on the treadmill?!! Then I'd go into the Sauna and the Steam Room, to relax muscles. I'd do that every day, in 10-15-minute bursts. That was part of losing the weight.

After going home, having a rest and something to eat, around 2.30 to 3pm, I'd then get ready for teaching, in Harborne, Halesowen, Sutton Coldfield or Birmingham. My classes were between 6-9pm or 7-9pm.

It was like a normal job. Sometimes you'd think: 'Oh I don't feel like it tonight,' but it's a constructive way of passing the time, other than training. It keeps your mind occupied when you're doing it, especially when you've got fights coming up. So the teaching really helped me relax and I enjoyed coaching the kids.

After I'd finished, tracksuit, trainers and I'd often run home. Or if I was at home I'd run five or six miles that evening. If I ran home from Sutton I'd need to collect my car, but I couldn't afford taxis then, so Cougar and Daljit would come over to Sutton Coldfield with me, to pick my car up. By the time I got back it might be midnight, so I'd be going to bed. Then I'd get up in the morning and start the same routine, all over again.

I'd have somewhere between eight to ten hours sleep, every night. If I'd been teaching in Harborne it would be a shorter run, so my day finished earlier and I'd be in bed by 11pm. The only thing I'd watch on TV sometimes, when I got in, would be boxing, because there was a lot on ITV and BBC.

The next day I might decide to do a shorter run: instead of ten miles I'd run three or five.

I'm quite superstitious on my runs. If I'm doing a 'five' I'd say: "I've got to do this particular training regime, because that's what I did last time." I'd train just as hard, for every fight.

The training I've just described began when I was eighteen, where I was running long distances and training really hard, all the way though to thirty-six years of age. So I maintained that vigorous regime for at least eighteen years. When training partners weren't available, for the gym, I had to work extra hard.

Let's imagine that I've got two training partners in the gym, Robert and Levi. I'd give the lads twenty minutes to half an hour to warm up. Normally we'd have three five-minute rounds, or just fifteen minutes straight. Once you've done that you'd have five seven-minute rounds of shadow sparring, which is imagining that you have someone in front of you, keeping your eyes focused; keeping your hands out; making sure that every shot counts. I tell my students now: "Any punch I throw, I never waste a shot."

After that, if Rob was there I'd do five three-minute rounds kicking with the pads, then the same, but with boxing. Then two further rounds where I'd mix it up, so that's a total of twelve rounds pad work, which is much harder than sparring.

All of this is continuous and a typical training session would last about an hour and fifty minutes. After the pad work I'd probably spar with Levi or one of the other lads. But sparring was often difficult for me, as I had no sparring partners at my more experienced level. When I trained with Howard or Godfrey 'Razor Edge' Brown, Howard's brother, that was fantastic, because they were more experienced than me.

The next time I went to the gym, if I had no partners I'd do extra time on the bag – ten three-minute rounds. These were all the methods I was using. Then I'd finish it with a circuit, at the end: for example, 10 exercises fast; ten press-ups et cetera. I'd do that day after day for eight weeks.

For someone who's never experienced that, it's difficult to imagine just how hard it is. Sometimes when I went into the gym I'd think: 'oh, not a circuit today!' But when I'd done it, it was an empowering achievement.

Being a superstitious person, if I missed my circuit I thought it was going to affect my performance. This was all at that peak of my career: I couldn't be doing this now, because you have to be really fit. So I was doing this from the 1980s through to 2002. With hindsight, my training was probably over-intensive; it was only around the year 2000 that we began to understand the human body in more detail; there wasn't the backing from Sports Science Departments that today's young sportsmen have.

I lost my last fight. Mitchell was born in 2001 and I had my last fight in 2002. I'd been out of the ring too long. I'd had no preparation sparring-wise. The weight limit was 71kg. The night before the fight I weighed 66kg, because no one was monitoring my training. I had a good feed, because I stayed at the Hilton Hotel at the NEC – the *Metropole*. I went up to 67kg which is still far too light: 5 kilos below.

That's why I'm fit now, because I'm feeling the benefit of all of those years of hard training and I'm still doing it to this day. Sometimes I'll think: 'I wonder if I can still run the same distance?' Occasionally I'll put my trainers on and do it... although at forty-six years old I'm not as quick. I never used to tell people my real age when I was forty; I'd say I was thirty-five or thirty-six.

The good thing about my early fight career was that I'd get fights all around the country... London, Brighton, Leicester, Nottingham. It was fantastic. Me and Howard got a lot closer too – travelling. He used to fight too. Obviously, you have your wins and your losses. At the time I was giving away weight, but Howard had every faith in me as a fighter.

When they get past forty 95% of people get bellies. I always advise them not to go drinking at the pub, but to keep their fitness. That's what I recommend to the pupils when I give school presentations, that they keep a healthy lifestyle.

I was starving my body when I was training. I'd have no breakfast and just Lucozade and peanuts for lunch; sometimes I'd have a white bread sandwich with ham salad. If I had chicken I'd take the skin off, because it was fried. That would be my evening meal. I would have a breast or a leg of chicken, for protein. I'd have very few fizzy drinks, because of the sugar.

I remember going to the weigh-in for a fight in Sicily. I went to the bathroom after I'd eaten and I felt quite sick, because you're trying to eat, to meet the required weight; but because you've not eaten for all those weeks your stomach can't take the extra food. At many fights I've felt really faint at the weigh-in. But I've always kept my power. Thank God I've got a good right hand – it's got me out of trouble many times!

I've always had strong determination, to keep going when I just don't feel like doing anything. But once you get there it's a fantastic feeling, once the adrenalin begins to flow. Having that bag on your shoulder, dieting and training: the three things go hand in hand.

My dad was the same wasn't he? Lots of stamina and working two shifts at a time, but with Asians it's money-orientated; it's the incentive to get the money and look after the family. He subbed his other family in India too; he was constantly sending money over there. Originally my father thought he'd only come over here for a short stint; that he'd need to go back one day. Most of the immigrants thought that way to begin with.

My father advised me to do a lot of fitness work, because he came up against a lot of racism, and it meant you could 'hold your own' if you were threatened. So it worked for me. It seems strange that I should feel like that, because Gurmej was really proud of me, but maybe the converse of that applies too – that when you're that close to someone you always want to please him? My older brother Resham sees it from a different perspective:

"There was a very strong bond between the two of them, but if Kash lost a fight, he would have felt it more from my dad's perspective, whereas my dad would have just been pleased that he wasn't injured," Resham explains.

"Every time that we went to a fight dad would be nervous. He'd have a couple of drinks before we got there. But every single time he looked at the opponent Dad said: 'He looks like a big, strong lad. Are you sure our Kash is going to be alright?' Dad was looking at Kash's opponents as people who could potentially cause him injury. It wasn't defeat," Resham comments, "because at that level, you can't win all your fights."

Howard told me: "If you lose, you need to lose with dignity. You need to learn how to do that, as much as enjoying your successes, because that's the mark of a true champion."

But I was developing and trying to do the low kicks and use knees and elbows. Howard took me to a certain level but then we'd travel to

Manchester once or twice a week, because he was fighting there, under Master Toddy, a specialist from Thailand.

Master Toddy and Master A are brothers. Master Toddy was one of the most respected coaches in the world. He's the one who brought Thai Boxing to the UK, first arriving here on 8 April 1975. Master Toddy recalls:

"Howard Brown, one of the world champions came to train from Birmingham to Manchester. Of course the first words out of his mouth were about one student of his who he swears to be very talented. I didn't take notice at first because at that time we already had 22 world champions and to bring in another one would be too much.

"Howard was very persistent in reminding me to please take a look at this fighter. Then one day this boy came to train. I saw the way he trained and the way he moved; at that instant I knew this boy named Kash would definitely be another champion.

"We started training and training, then came time for Kash's debut in the live show we did. It was there he met a Thai champion who went by the name 'Superman', one of the top fighters in Thailand. He stood toe to toe for 5 rounds and lost by a decision, against this Thai champion. I was so impressed. Since that day I trained him even more and spent a lot of time working with him.

"And so it happened, Kash invited me to go to his corner for a world title fight against Alex Tui. This guy was an unbeatable fighter, and very strong, like a bull. To me, Kash had very little experience in Muay Thai by comparison. I remember being in his corner and again this was another hard fight, proving to be the most difficult one he had to date.

"We were in his home town. He came to my corner once again and said 'I will win. *Teach* me.'

"I have never seen such a hard fight in my life. I told Kash, 'If you want to win you've got to step forward, stand toe to toe, and strong right hand!' As I watched the fight it was like he was facing a brick wall, but Kash has a big lion heart. He stepped forward and knocked the world champion out!

"You would not believe the reaction of all the English fans, I still remember it so vividly, at that moment everyone was so happy. It's as if you were rooting for your team at the world cup who, from being behind the entire game, make a comeback by scoring the winning goal at the last second! Everyone in the audience went wild.

"I don't even remember how I did it, but I managed to jump over the ring and I hugged Kash. I thought, 'Wow! This fighter has a great lion heart and he made it again!'

Kash never got an easy fight but he always managed to make it every time, like a true underdog.

"That day is still in my heart," recalls Master Toddy. "I remember walking out from his corner the proudest man and everyone was touching me just because Kash had won, but really it wasn't because of me Kash did it, it was because he has always had the heart of a lion."

Master Toddy's brother, Master A, gives his version of events:

"I came to England in 1986 to help my brother Master Toddy at his Muay Thai School, to coach and train all his champions. The first time I met Kash I said to my brother, 'Wow! He's so tall!' The first time I coached Kash on the pads I found it a bit difficult, with his height! But soon we started to understand each other on the pads and sparring (yes sparring me, 5ft 5 inches) but we managed and it was very enjoyable to train and spar with Kash. We worked together over the next few years, on all Kash's world title bouts, with great success, until Kash's retirement from the ring.

"Kash continues to be a celebrity in the martial arts world, now training his own champions. 'Kash the Flash' is his nickname, because he's flash when he fights in the ring: fast hands, fast kicks! Kash remains a great Champion who is well respected by the whole martial arts community.

"We continue to work in close contact. It's always a pleasure to travel to Birmingham to teach seminars for Flash's up-and-coming students. I look forward to many years of continuing to work together."

Master Toddy is much older than Howard: he's a senior; but he's now over in Thailand, coaching. I went to his Manchester gym once, when I felt really under the weather, but he said: "You're here to train – get on with it!" So I felt really out of order.

Howard was good at giving instructions, but Master Toddy was more of a Motivator: he really lifted you. "Fight like a Tiger!" was his famous saying. Ironically, 'Tiger' is what my family called me when I was a young baby.

I remember fighting a guy from Thailand and Master Toddy really got me off that chair! For my first World Title, back in 1991, I had Master Toddy, Master A and Howard Brown, all in my corner team… the best corner team that anyone could have.

Master Toddy has his own base in Las Vegas and has trained at least twenty-five World Champion Thai Kickboxers. Thai Boxing is when you use the knees and the elbows; Kickboxing is when you use your legs. There are three different disciplines: kicks below the waist; above the waist and then all three.

If I'd taken it a little more seriously I could have gone much further with Thai Boxing. I had the chance to do it for six months, which I didn't take – but maybe I would have done it now? Although I *am* a kickboxer, I get a buzz from doing Thai Boxing as well; using the knees and elbows is quite exciting too.

You would think that, once you mastered the technique, it would be easier to win with Thai, because you've more weapons at your disposal. But my knees were so sore, because you're kneeing the pads for about two hours! Just knee after knee after knee: they use the Thailand method. When I tell my students that I did that for two hours, they don't believe me! It's the same with the bags, but once you've mastered the technique, they're not so sore.

I am a perfectionist. I remember getting home and I'd had a really hard day at the gym, I was really under the weather. One of my family said: "Are you running tonight?" I felt I had to, although my body needed a rest. That night was the worst of my life: I ran really slowly, so I was very upset.

I could have said: "OK, I'll leave it and give my body a rest," but it was like: "Oh, you're getting lazy you are." I just felt compelled by my brothers and sisters, to go on. Maybe it was for a reason? I just felt compelled to go on – I don't know... but it's part of life.

I wasn't *just* doing it to please my family; being superstitious as well, if I missed a day, where I wasn't running, I'd do things like only running on the same path and the same slabs. So it was a bit of pressure from others, but from myself as well.

Nowadays training techniques are more sophisticated. I was probably dehydrated for a lot of my fights; very dizzy; a lot of the time I hardly ate anything. I wasn't drinking enough water. Since I've been a coach I make sure that my students drink enough water and eat the right food. But for me, it was a hard path and how I became so successful I still don't know to this day, because I *did* struggle with my weight.

Going back to one of my earlier fights around 1990, I had to really struggle, making 10 stone 12. I was fighting Ronnie Deleon at the NEC. I hadn't eaten much all day and was dehydrated too. I enjoyed eating the small Jammy Dodgers. So I went downstairs and just had one, and then went back upstairs to bed. But then I went back downstairs again and finished the pack of twelve... I just could not believe it! The next day I spent an hour-and-a-half running, just to work it off. I shouldn't have done that, because you need food and energy in your body, but it was a fixed idea that I had in my head. People used to ask: "How did you make 10 stone 12 at 6 foot 3?" I'd say: "It was bloody hard work!" Nowadays I'm a healthy 12 stone 4, but I still watch what I eat – I'm not really a kebab man!

There are other martial arts that we haven't yet mentioned. Hudson Richards, Tony Whitehouse, *UB40's* Tony Mullings and Bob Sykes will describe them to you.

"I've been involved in martial arts for quite a while. I did Wado-ryu and other martial arts but I didn't particularly like them. Litijitsu was OK, it's a form of karate and had aspects of Jujitsu too," Hudson explains. "So you could use all of your limbs, but in a very traditional guise, so for example, we all wore the angry white pyjamas!

"I advise my students that if something happens, at least tell your teacher, because they're in 'loco parentis'. That way, they can't say that they didn't know. But the second point is about gentleness – 'power under control': you don't have to knock somebody out, just because you can; thirdly, if you have no choice, you do what you have to do to survive, which can sometimes actually mean taking the beating.

"We had a Yellow Belt who was mugged. I was horrified, but really surprised to see him come in to the club. He was thirteen years old. His face was all bruised," Hudson recalls. "He said: 'They got my stuff, but they didn't get me.' I thought that he was going to be afraid to come out of his house. But he said that the training I'd done with him worked.

"Self defence is not about what you do to the other person," Hudson continues, "it's about what you do to *you*. Sometimes that might involve you taking them down. If they attack you and you're lashing out, you're not making a choice: they're making it for you. So you have to be able to choose your own reaction. The guys who are dream stealers don't have any dreams of their own; don't let them take you down with them, or affect your future prospects."

Tony Whitehouse has known me for about twenty years.

"I met Kash when I joined the first class that he started in Harborne," Tony remembers. "I'd seen him before that, but actually got to know him at that class, which myself and a few kickboxing friends decided to join as students, back in the late 1980s. I'd been doing traditional martial arts before that. I started off with Shotokan, and then, like Hudson, moved on to Wado-ryu: both disciplines are Japanese."

Tony Mullings is into a type of Kung Fu called Lau Gar. Kung Fu is Chinese and Karate is Japanese.

"Lau Gar is not the same as kickboxing," Tony explains, "and I wouldn't really know how to describe the difference. I'm not into the technical side of it: I did it more for self defence. I suppose Kash did kickboxing for the same reason too, being a minority. I was around sixteen when I started. It's a semi-contact sport – no elbows or knees; it's linked with meditation. We used to get picked on quite a lot, by dare I say it, a lot of white gangs. But it was mainly kids. Sometimes you'd get yourself into trouble, just by being in the wrong place at the wrong time.

"David Cole and Audley Bell were my best friends at the time. We all did Lau Gar together. David was a South Birmingham Lau Gar Champion... a *very* good fighter.

"We started doing it at the old church in Cotteridge, when I was sixteen," Tony continues, "then later moved to a Sparkhill Club. I practised the sport for seven years. We moved about a bit actually. One of my tutors worked in Birmingham's Fish Market. He trained us at a gym down by Temple Passage, where Dorian Yates' club is now."

Bob Sykes' biography, *The Journeyman*, was published in 2006. Bob was into karate for about six years, heard about kickboxing, in the late 1970s and always wanted to try it.

"I went along to a kickboxing gym in Barnsley, run by a chap called Arthur O'Loughlin," recalls Bob, who is just four years older than Kash. "I'd already got my Black Belt in karate. I got in the ring and this lad who'd only had six months of kickboxing just jabbed my head off and I thought: 'Well, I want some of this!' So I was in from there on, from 1982 to the present time.

"My brothers were cricketers and footballers and so was my dad, but I could never handle the cricket ball. I was totally uncoordinated but eventually got into sport through running; one of my brothers, Graham Sykes, still runs now, all over the world.

"But I got better and better. I was one of the *Longwood Harriers*, the local running club.

"I got into karate, at fifteen without my dad knowing, because I'd always wanted to do it. I used to see these films where a small guy could beat a big guy. It wasn't as popular then as it later became.

"After working in a mill for a few years, and a few months in the army, I realised that the only way that I was going to get anywhere in life was through Martial Arts, so I threw myself into it. No one did Martial Arts full time then. It was 1981, the Conservatives had just got in again and the factories were starting to shut down. Everywhere in the country industry was on the decline.

"A lot of mills became Martial Arts centres. If you looked at East London, Liverpool, Birmingham, the North-east of England, every main industry was declining and martial arts became more popular, because people who were out of a job were looking towards leisure activities.

"It's very much a working class affair, martial arts. Back then, in the era of kickboxing, which Kash and me were a part of, everybody was scrapping. You could have a scrap with somebody at your club and there would be no comeback, because people would have really tough fights and sometimes almost be killed. Nowadays if you did that you'd end up in prison, so everything was still relatively raw and fresh, like in *Boys from the Black Stuff*. That's the era that I came from and so did Kash.

"By 1985 when I met Kash, I was into Thai Boxing, but I wanted to be on a stage with everybody watching. I wanted to be performing," explains Bob. "That tension was more important to me than actually getting a throw."

Every time I approached a ring I was *really* nervous, until I actually got into the ring – and then I was fine. Was that the case with you Bob?

"No, nerves can be healthy for a fighter, but I was just *excited*. Obviously, there was that fear, but I was always excited to be there. People were watching me and shouting my name – and I didn't even know them!

"The first time that I saw Kash I was supposed to fight in this event, in Barnsley, in November 1985, but I was down with a cold, so I pulled out and went to watch. It was a really good show, promoted by Arthur O'Loughlin.

I'm watching Kash fight and he was from Birmingham, fighting a lad from Barnsley. It was one of the early bouts of the evening. We like a good fight. Then one of the Barnsley lads shouted out: 'Come on Kash Kebab!'

"It was very funny. This fuelled Kash. You saw his pride. He's a Sikh isn't he? They're a very proud, warrior race. This ignorant Barnsley, miners' strike voice, with a pint in his hand and a fag in his mouth fuelled Kash and I saw him just totally annihilate his opponent! I thought: 'this guy can scrap!' But I never thought that I'd be watching him in the future, at that stage.

"It was one of the best kickboxing events that I've ever seen," Bob continues. "There were some brilliant fighters. Kash was on the Undercard then, because he'd just started. But the show was really well promoted. Even to this day I don't think I've seen a better staged event.

"In Sheffield, in 1986, I actually had a fight with him. It was only the second time that I'd seen him, at the late George Wellington's kickboxing event. We both fought Top of the Bill. That first fight was a very close call, in my opinion. It was closer than the second time we met – put it that way! It was a good fight and went to three rounds. I enjoyed it, but it was Kash's game and being up against him was quite something. It was a perfect fight for me, because he stayed at a long distance and we didn't engage as much as we did the second time, so it worked out well for me.

"Kash won it on points, so fair play to him. It was totally enjoyable and we both came out of it unhurt. During the second fight that we had, in late September 1986, I challenged him a bit more. I was just happy to be Top of the Bill with Kash the Flash Gill. It was in Nottingham, at the *Victoria Leisure Centre*. It was a bad time for me at that point.

"Kash was all over me; he dropped me twice. He was bigger and heavier than me. I'm 5 foot 8, so he's considerably taller. But a thousand people came to see me and Kash fight. He was just brilliant!"

On pages 64-67 inclusive of *The Journeyman*, Bob and I demonstrate *Techniques of Kickboxing* in photographic form. Also, we are really grateful to Bob for giving us permission to reproduce edited extracts from his colourful account of our second fight, from pages 60-62 – *The Kickboxing Years*.

"There I was back in 1986, facing 'Kash the Flash' Gill, getting myself ready to start our seven round contest for the British PKA light middleweight crown. Kash, who was fresh back from his World Amateur Full Contact win in the sleepy Gallic town of St Nazaire and who had prior to that, beaten Taekwondo's Kenny Walton in the Combat Karate TV pilot, was in a serious mood. 'Pain for Bob Sykes' was his prediction. This I felt could have been due to our first meeting (in that same year) in Sheffield, during which I'd taken him to the full distance, where although Kash received a win to his credit, it hadn't necessarily been a clear-cut decision.

In any case, there I was, stood face to face with a fellow kickboxer, who was intent on doing me some serious damage. But I was more fascinated by the fact that over one thousand spectators had come to watch. Furthermore, I felt more than capable of beating this six foot three, kickboxing crazed southpaw.

Refereeing was none other than the Arthur of the Britons, aka Arthur O'Loughlin. Arthur was a good friend and certainly the best kickboxer ever to emerge from Yorkshire.

During the first round I fought out of my skin, throwing kick upon kick – jumping back kick, spinning kick, roundhouse. However, no matter how many kicks I threw, I still felt I was losing out to Kash's right jab (I can still to this day feel it bouncing off my forehead).

Round two continued at the same hectic pace with my sporadic kicking outbursts being met by the Flash's back leg round kick and flurries of overhand and hooking punches. Things were beginning to look grim and, as Bey Logan put it at the time, 'the writing was on the wall'.

During a crucial part of our contest my entire perception of time began to slow down, when I connected with a booming right cross to the top of Kash Gill's head. As the punch hit its mark, everything slid into a state of slow motion and what noise there was seemed irrelevant. What must have been only two or three seconds seemed somehow to stretch itself out into ten or twelve seconds; many athletes have had almost identical peak performance experiences. They call it 'being in the zone'.

My peak performance wasn't enough to match the skill and determination of 'Kash the Flash' Gill who, after knocking me down three times in the third, proved to be the more superior athlete and twenty years on still dominates his weight division."

"It was after that fight that I realised that I needed to move in another direction," recollects Bob. "I sat on a hill shortly afterwards and thought 'what next?' It was at that point that I decided to start my magazine, *Martial Arts Illustrated* – and I've never looked back since."

Commenting on my divorce last year, in 2011, Bob observes:

"It must be a horrible time for him. With people who are as independent and single-minded as Kash and myself, it takes a very special person to be our partners – someone who's on the same page as we are. I went through divorce, separation and heartache myself and lost a lot of weight too. All that stuff crushes you.

"You've got to be able to pick yourself up again. I'd gone from being a kid on the dole and within two years I was a martial arts champion. But there was something about the energy that I got from fighting Kash," Bob concludes.

I first met *UB40's* Brian Travers, at Howard Brown's party. I remember Brian and Ali Campbell going to one of my fights, then we all went back and had a party at Howard's.

"That's right. Howard was my neighbour; he moved in next door, then came round and said: 'Hi, I'm Howard.' I didn't know him before that," Brian explains. "We were mates after that. Howard was a *lovely* guy; my kids knocked about with his kids and had dens in the back garden. His kids were the same age as mine, so it was perfect. Because Howard was a boxer he'd invite me to the events, so I'd go because he was my neighbour. But that's how I knew Kash's name."

Brian and Ali watched me in one of my earlier, more minor fights... when I was on the Undercard. My book isn't just about the sport itself Brian, it's about the way I built myself up, despite the obstacles and got through some very tough times. The two of us have that in common; we've both reached the top of our field, from humble beginnings.

"That's very kind of you. That's the thing about this book and why I think Kash Gill is important, even though I'm not a fan of martial arts. My good friend Howard invited me. I was there to support Kash – not to revel in anybody getting their teeth kicked in. It became more of a social thing, because the people involved in this stuff are the people I came from; the kids or children that I grew up with. I knew this was their only way out, so that if we could help, by our fame – we were very famous in those days.

"It's tricky, this music business," comments Brian, "because the older you are the better you get at it, but it's for kids: seventeen-year-olds look better playing guitars than fifty-year-olds! But we turn up, civically-minded; to help the people we grew up with, or from similar neighbourhoods, to show that they're doing something positive."

When I was fighting abroad Brian – and I explained that I was from Birmingham, some people didn't have a clue where that was, but as soon as I mentioned *UB40* they made the connection – so that was like a universal thing.

"Sure, it was a big responsibility that we had back in those days. We sponsored a lot of sports, including a rally car guy, who became a champion, James Prochowski. He died of leukaemia, unfortunately, in early 2006. We sponsored his car – the car was painted up.

"We sponsored a Birmingham Boxing Gym, which they renamed *The Cauliflower Ear*, which I thought was a shame! So we sponsored sportsmen and football teams, boxers and rings and shows around Birmingham, giving them a break. Not necessarily because we supported the particular sport," Brian explains. "You're supposed to be a fan of the sport when you do that. But I'm a fan of people – I like people."

Round 9

UB40, ADIL RAY, CYRILLE REGIS, ET AL

Various friends and sports personalities, some having featured in previous rounds, are in conversation with Kash, during this Round.

Our two UB40 musicians are followed by Adil Ray, Wayne Elcock, Frankie Gavin, Dorian Yates, Peter Wilson, Cyrille Regis, and Dave 'Kwame' Barnett.

Brian Travers compares and contrasts his life experiences, career and the history of UB40 with Kash's, in company with their keyboard player Tony Mullings. This British reggae band, formed in 1978 in Birmingham, has placed more than 50 singles in the UK Singles Chart, and has also achieved considerable international success. One of the world's best-selling music artists, UB40 has sold over 70 million records.

The ethnic makeup of the band is diverse, with musicians of English, Scottish, Irish, Yemeni and Jamaican parentage. From the band's 1978 inception through early 2008, UB40's line-up was constant. In 2008 Ali Campbell left the band, followed shortly afterwards by Mickey Virtue, marking the first line-up change in the band's history.

Brian Travers, saxophonist, musician, songwriter and arranger, is a founder member of *UB40*. Most of the band attended Moseley Road Art School together, in Balsall Heath

"You had dedicated Art lessons every day," explains Brian. "We used to paint and sculpt. Artists sometimes become musicians, as in the case of John Lennon et al. Music is probably the most abstract of all the art forms: you can't touch it, you can't see it. But it can touch you and you can certainly feel it! It's one of the oldest as well, pre-dating painting, sculpture and the written word.

"We took the Eleven Plus Exam and then we had to take an art exam. There were a lot of artistically-talented people. Other group members attending the school were Ali Campbell, our former rhythm guitarist – his oldest brother was in the band and his other brother's in now; also, Earl

Falconer, our bass guitarist and Jimmy Brown, our drummer. Those group members who didn't attend the Art School knocked about with us in the evening, after school. We all lived around Balsall Heath.

"We were always going to be good, because that's what we demanded of ourselves, even though we hadn't yet played a gig. None of us could play an instrument – we all started together. But we had nothing else either. We had no chance of a job and we thought: 'We'll never have a car, we'll never have a house.' We were at our fittest, our strongest, the best soldiers are eighteen to nineteen years old, not my age, and we hadn't even got a job: the queues were a thousand miles long! This was in the mid-70s. All we had was confidence – and ourselves.

"We were confident because we loved music and we knew we'd get there. But we started off with no songs of course; none of us could play, so we learned these chords and how to tune our instruments. We started every day at nine o'clock in the morning. Me and Earl had to sign on at the dole every day, as well, because we didn't live with our parents: we lived in bedsits in Balsall Heath.

"Me and Earl lived next door to each other, at 118 Trafalgar Road. There was an empty cellar underneath that you got to from the outside of the building. So we nicked wood off building sites, nailed it all up, put a padlock on and rehearsed in there every day. A proper coloured Hell's Angel lived above us – patches and all that! We were nicking his electricity, because the wires came down. But he said: 'That's alright. You're sounding good!'

"All eight of us were rehearsing at that stage. For any poor kid it was sport, music or criminality. There's a very thin line between all three of them. We chose music.

"I love my background and I wouldn't change it for the world," Brian continues, "but there were very few choices for us... apart from winning the lottery or becoming famous!

"I've been doing this for thirty-odd years. Music appealed to us, because you danced with girls to it; it was the music we heard when we went out to discos; to youth clubs; to things that the Social Services would try to set up, to get us ruffians off the street – not that we were!

"The name *UB40* came from an Unemployment Benefit Card. Most of our band left school in 1975, to go on the Dole, because there were far fewer jobs in Birmingham, once the car factories closed. I got a job through the Irish building trade. Just as the West Indians look after themselves, the Irish had to do the same, especially after the bombings. I worked on a building site, making the tea, as an apprentice electrician. That only lasted for a year, until I got a saxophone."

What's really intriguing Brian is that you put up posters advertising your group, before you could play the instruments – that takes some nerve! Where do you get your inspiration from?

"It's what I do – I force it out; I sit there until something happens. I get a line and turn it into a couplet or I find some rhythm within the poetry."

My good friend Apache Indian sent us this email about you, while he was abroad:

Yeap Brian is a dear friend too, more than the other members of the group. I recorded a song with Maxi Priest for my first album and Brian made the video. He had a film company then, think he still does. Lots of love for UB40 – incredible! Came from the streets of Brum; proud of their roots and internationally respected. They inspired me all the way. Legends!

Brian and Chips Chipperfield, sadly now deceased, set up PMI in London, EMI's video division, in the early 1980s-83. But he was never at home with his family. So he did that for about five or six years, then set up his own film company in Birmingham, as Apache mentioned. Their Albert Street offices no longer exist, as the area's been redeveloped.

"When I set up the film company, *Brian Travers Associates – BTA*, the more business we got, the more successful we became, the less time I had to spend on artistic endeavours, on directing, which is the way I got into making films. I directed hundreds of Pop Promos and shot documentaries in Russia and America. It's part of our business, to sell records. People take it quite seriously – they don't just see it as a bit of film. I've been asked many times: 'The girls in that video, are they your girlfriends?!' 'No, they're dancers or actresses.' 'No they're not – that's your *bird*, isn't it?'

"But the longer I did it, the more successful it got, the less I was being creative and more like a producer, so I closed it down eleven years ago after twenty years.

"We went on tour in Africa, to Namibia, in February 2011. It was a bunch of gigs for an *Aids Awareness Foundation*, which is part of the *World Health Organisation*. It was all in one place in the Hope Village, to raise money for this charity. Our latest album includes one of Willie Nelson's songs, *Blues Eyes*.

"Academics just learn by rote. Self-expression depends upon you and how much 'balls', how much grit you've got to face up, if somebody doesn't like your idea."

But your music has inspired young musicians, all over the world, Brian, across cultures. I've been trying to inspire young people too, but in my case through sport.

"Well I don't think *everybody* likes our music Kash, but it's inspired us enough to go out and perform the songs. All of the group, individually, are very political by nature because of the times we were growing up in. I write love songs too, although they're the hardest songs to write. Everybody thinks that they can, but you try writing something that hasn't already been said," concludes Brian.

Tony Mullings' family are originally from Jamaica, but they came to England in 1959.

"I grew up in Kings Heath. I was born in 1961 and went to Queensbridge School. Everyone except my mom is musical. My dad plays guitar. He has always been my inspiration. He blew us all away as little children... he can play! It was all Gospel and he was a big fan of Country and Western and Jim Reeves. So my musical background is through Gospel music and Jim Reeves," Tony explains.

"My brothers and sisters all play instruments too. My mother asked me what I wanted for my sixth birthday and I said: 'Piano lessons,' because we had a piano in our lounge. My piano tutor lived up the same road. I have three brothers: Robert, Roger and Roy and then there's my sister, Janet. I'm the oldest of the brood.

"My brother Robert is a professional guitarist; he was on a recent *UB40* album: he did a session and played on twelve tracks. My brother Roger plays piano as well. He didn't go to piano lessons he just picked it all up himself! He's got his own recording studio, next door to Queensbridge School.

"I was involved in kickboxing for seven years. I did a lot of competition fights, so I'm used to being in the ring. I played the piano from the age of six; my first stage appearance was at the age of seven. I did my first solo at the Seventh Day Adventist Church in Camp Hill. My brother, Robert, and I formed our first band when we were eight and nine. My first gig was at

Digbeth Civic Hall, many years ago. I was eight years old and I played bass guitar. I used to sing tenor, but I don't sing any more.

"I play keyboard with *UB40*: it's a 'Korg', which is a brand name. I play the actual instrument and then Robin Hickman does all my programming and changes all my sounds. I've been in several Birmingham-based bands, including *Buffalo Soldier* and *Crucial Music*, which was with my brother Robert and Patto Banton originally and Jaffa (Jeffrey) Wright. My brother Robert was the songwriter; it's all predominantly Reggae music. *Buffalo Soldier* was a tribute to Bob Marley – it was one of his songs.

"I met Apache through Jaffa Wright, who's got his own sound studio in Trafalgar Road. He works with numerous West Midlands musicians. He's done a lot of tracks for Apache. It's been years now though since we've had any contact, although when you're little boys you're in and out of each other's pockets.

"I have six daughters and one son. Taylor, one of my daughters, wants to be a fighter – and she's a big fan of Kash's," observes Tony. "She wants to join Kash's gym. She can't wait. I haven't been able to take her there yet, because I'm always away, travelling, but as soon as I can I'll take her there."

There's a parallel to be drawn Tony, with *UB40's* thirty-plus record in the music business and my own career, which now spans thirty years. So to update people about what the band have been doing, at the end of 2010 you finished a UK-Republic of Ireland Tour, in which *Signing Off* was featured.

"OK. The *Signing Off* album was the first album that the band ever recorded. 50/50 songs and instrumentals; not all the songs on the album were written by themselves, but they managed. This is the classic thing about *UB40* – they can always pull out the right songs to suit the audience they're playing to.

"When it comes to picking songs the band do that themselves; nobody else has an input in that; but the biggest in-putter into the technical side of things is Robin Campbell. Robin's like a Headmaster, then next in line would be Brian Travers: he's the schoolteacher – very intelligent, very smart. They wanted to find a style that nobody else had. My favourite two are *Impossible Love* and *Kingston Town*. *UB40* are the best reggae band in the world. The only artist who's bigger, as far as I'm concerned, is Bob Marley.

"For the Namibia tour, in South Africa, we hired a tour bus, with built-in bathroom facilities; internet, live TV and so forth; laptops and beds," continues Tony. "Sometimes we can be very childish – we play pranks on each other! We can be up all night; these are grown men – fifty years plus! But we're still running around being silly.

"My dad, to this day, thinks all of his sons are 'off-the-wall'! Eventually, we all made it as musicians. It's not just my immediate family who are musical; the majority of my male cousins who live in the UK are all musicians... predominantly guitarists. I can play a bit of everything.

"Norman Hassan was a good friend of mine, prior to me joining the band. Norman suggested Duncan and myself to the band. We auditioned at the same time; we were both very nervous. Duncan is the lead singer. Robin, Duncan and Norman, Astro and Earl all sing for themselves – that's five members of the band who could take centre stage. While one person is performing, the others harmonise."

Thanks Tony. In 2000 Adil Ray joined the BBC Asian Network, and was doing the *Late Night Music Show*.

"Through doing that show I got in touch with Apache a few times and then met Kash again through Apache," remembers Adil. "We hadn't met each other since 1996. Since then we've been to Aston Villa together and we've watched games there. There's a funny story about the Villa boardroom.

"Doug Ellis was there. Kash and I went to see Portsmouth play. I was friends with the Chief Executive at the time," Adil continues. "We were waiting to be seated for lunch with the board members, when Kash looked at the seating list and said: 'Look, I'm sitting with that horse jockey, Richard Scudamore.' Richard was actually the Chief Executive of the FA, but Kash had confused him with his cousin Peter Scudamore, who was a jockey. So we were sitting at this table and Kash tried, a few times, to start a conversation about horse racing, to everyone's bemusement. Kash then says: 'None of these guys look short enough to be a jockey!' It took a while to explain.

"When we actually watched the game, Doug Ellis was sat behind me. He had his hands on my shoulders throughout the game: 'Come on son – we're doing it!' But it was an amazing time. We lost 3-1."

Boxer Wayne Elcock got into sport around the age of fourteen, the age when I began to take kickboxing seriously too.

"Yes, I was always scrapping in the playground at school. One of the kids said: 'Elcock, you might be tough in the playground, but if you got in the boxing ring we'd show you what it's all about!' That was at Sir Wilfred

Martineau School. So I took him up on his offer. This kid had been boxing about four years, at Lakeside Amateur Boxing Club, over at Kingshurst, but was a year younger then me. Although he knocked seven bells out of me," continues Wayne, "I stuck at it, determined to set the record straight.

"When I chose boxing instead of football my dad said: 'You won't keep that up son. Stick with the football.' My mom still doesn't like the fact that I do boxing but from my third fight onwards dad was always there at the ringside, all the way through my career. He was instrumental in helping me.

"Now I'm a Middleweight boxer, known as 'Mad Dog', but that title came later. I boxed as an amateur for quite a while. My trainer said that I'd done really well and that I should take a break from it; but that was the worst thing that I could have done," observes Wayne.

"After three years of dedication, at the age of seventeen, I went right off the track. Guys who were complete monsters wanted to be associated with me, but as you become more mature you can see the dangers.

"My uncle, Clifton Elcock, was a former kickboxing world champion, in the *Light Contact* category, but there's the discipline of getting up at four o'clock in the morning and going out training. I just wanted to scrap. He'd say: 'Not yet – not yet!' So I drifted away from kickboxing. But we were very proud of my uncle being a world champion."

Wayne continues.

"Getting a new place of my own was a positive move, but then I lost my best mate Leroy in 1995. I was gutted, but coping with these sorts of things made me a stronger person. Then in 1998 I had an even greater tragedy when my dad was killed in a car crash.

"By 1999 I'd won five Birmingham titles, two Midland titles and I was an ABA semi-finalist and finalist. My amateur career lasted ten years. I turned professional in 1999."

Wayne has an impressive list of professional victories: the British Lonsdale belt, plus Commonwealth, English and WBU and WBF World Middleweight titles. We met on the sports circuit.

"Yes, we just naturally got on – he's a fantastic bloke. I knew all about Kash at the time, and we kept in touch from that time onwards," Wayne recalls. "We had a lot in common because of our background and both being in the fight game. I'm a fiercely proud Brummie, so I'm interested in anyone involved in the city, especially in the sports arena.

"When I left school I got a certificate for 'The pupil who was most likely to be excluded, but to survive and improve beyond all recognition'! Being of mixed race at Secondary School was really hard for me."

That's what happened to Howard Brown, but he 'knuckled down' just in time Wayne. One of the things that attracted me to kickboxing is that, unlike team sports, you sink or swim by your own efforts. Is that what appealed to you about boxing?

"Yes. While I was still at secondary school I was in the newspapers, because of my boxing and I got respect from my teachers because of that. It was all about me, unlike a team sport. When I played for a football team the articles were about the team itself. I'm a team player, but I hate losing! A big part of the boxing was saying: 'Well at least my destiny is in my own hands. If it goes wrong it's my fault'," Wayne concludes.

Frankie Raymond Gavin, born 28 September 1985, is another British professional boxing friend of mine, from Birmingham. Whilst still an amateur, he won the gold medal at the 2007 World Amateur Boxing Championships, to become English Boxing's first ever World Amateur Champion. Shirley interviewed him in October 2010, at the *E57 Social Club*, Birmingham, where he and Wayne were presenting awards.

"This is the gym where I first started my amateur titles," Frankie explains. "I won a lot of titles here. Although it's not situated actually in Hall Green, it's a neighbouring area. The majority of the fighters tonight are from the Hall Green Club.

"I'm presenting seven different trophies and then there's a Leon Gorman Memorial Trophy here tonight too. I give that out to the best fighter. Leon got stabbed ten years ago; he lived just around the corner."

Frankie, who was born in a Hostel, has lived in Yardley all of his life.

"My next-door-neighbour used to box and I was always 'out-and-about' with him. Then one day I was at a gym with him," explains Frankie. "The trainer there said that I was good, and I just kept running, from that point. When I had my first fight at the Mirfield Gym, by the Meadway I was twelve years old. Later, in 2007, I became the first World Amateur Gold Medal Champion from Great Britain; David Hay got the Silver but he was the only other British guy to get to the final and I won the Gold in Chicago.

"In 2002 I won the Junior Olympic Gold in Michigan. I won European medals. I've never been to an international event and not won a medal! As a 'Pro' I've had 8 fights and knocked 7 out; one went the distance. I love football – I follow Birmingham City. One of my best friends, Craig Gardener, used to be a lead player with them."

Several of our contributors have links with Birmingham City in one way or another. Tom Ross, David Dunn, Andy Walker, Dave Barnett and Kenny Cunningham are just five amongst several others who are helping us with this book.

Frankie explains. "I used to watch Kash for years when I was younger. He'd kick really high. After a while we'd say hello to each other. Everyone was raving on about him and you'd see him in the paper, so I kept following him. I read that he'd had a record one hundred fights! He'd had fourteen losses; eighty-four wins and forty-three knock-outs.

"Kash became the Four Times World Kickboxing Champion, winning at different weights, which makes him very special. My boxing heroes are Pernall Whittaker: he was the best defence boxer ever, and more recently, Joe Calzaghe. I live in Manchester, so I have to travel back and forth."

Frankie won the Intercontinental Title in London, in 2011, against 'Young Mutley'.

Bodybuilding champion Dorian Yates grew up on a small farm in Hurley, Staffordshire. His mom was a horse riding instructor and his dad an engineer.

"We had a few acres of land; horses, dogs, ducks, chickens," Dorian recalls. "So I lived in quite a rural background. My mom wanted me to be a horse rider, but I was never really any good at that. My sister took to it and she still competes in British championships: in Dressage, and stuff like that, under her married name, Lisa Garland, she has a lot of horses.

"Funnily enough, my early interest in sport was martial arts. The Kung Fu-Bruce Lee movies came out when I was young. I did karate lessons when I was fifteen or sixteen.

"My father passed away when I was thirteen and my mom met somebody else. So we moved to Birmingham, to Castle Bromwich – and a lot more things became available.

"I did karate lessons at Peter Suzuki's gym in Digbeth, but it didn't click with me in the way that bodybuilding did, later on. So that's probably another parallel with Kash.

"When I was sixteen I left home and had to find a place to stay and a job, to survive. Another parallel with Kash is the Handsworth Riots. In 1981

I was unfortunate to be in Birmingham City Centre that night, a little bit drunk and disorderly. Me and my friend were picked up and given six months in jail, just for being in the wrong place at the wrong time; although having said that, I must have done something to justify the six-month sentence!

"When I went into the Detention Centre they had weights in there, that's how I was introduced to them, although I'd used them a little bit before, with my karate. I hadn't had any time to focus on it before that, because I was trying to make my way in the world. But being in this Detention Centre, with about four or five hundred guys and doing the weights, I found that I was stronger than everybody else, with a better physique. So this was something that I might be really good at.

"The prison guards used to tell us, 'If you don't change your way of thinking, you'll be in institutions for the rest of your life.' So that was a wake up call for me. When I came out I got a job and was determined to pursue my goal 100%... to compete and see how far I could go."

He started Body Building in the 1980s and began training around 1983. Dorian subsequently won the Mr. Olympia title six consecutive times from 1992-1997 inclusive.

"I'm still the only person who lived and trained outside of the United States, to have won that title," Dorian continues. "Kash is very well known in Europe, whereas it's the reverse with me: I'm well known internationally, so there's a bit of a difference, but the times are parallel.

"I completed my first contest in 1985. It was a Novice Competition, so it was about the lowest level that you could enter, to being in a major competition the following week. Although this was my first contest, the reaction from the judges was: 'You're one of the best guys that we've got in the country already!'

"They persuaded me to compete in the World Games championships the following weekend. I came seventh, but I'd only been training for a year-and-a-half and was already up against seasoned guys! To compete in a professional body building contest, you have to be the overall amateur champion in Britain or America, or wherever. It's very much an American-based sport. If you compete in one of those contests and win then you compete in Mr. Olympia, which is all the winners from across the globe, competing to find the best bodybuilder in the world.

"The first professional contest that I did was in 1990 that was the *Night of Champions* in New York. I got a second there; then the following year I returned to win that, then competed in my first Mr. Olympia, where I got a second. My first Mr. Olympia win was in 1992. That's the first time that someone *living* in Europe had won it. Arnold Schwarzenegger won it of course, but he was living in America at the time.

"When I started body building in the 1980s there were only about five gyms in the whole of Birmingham, with very basic facilities. Now you've got a totally different situation. I retired from Mr. Olympia in 1998, because of a serious injury, which made it impossible for me to continue at that level.

"There was always this synergy between kickboxing and bodybuilding. The *Temple Gym* housed us both at one time. I went to some kickboxing events with four guys, to see bouts involving Kash and Howard Brown, because the guy who used to own The *Temple Gym* was Mike Haig. He ran *Combat Sports.* Mike initially put the money up for the gym, because I was a young lad and didn't have any money. Paul Clifton mentioned him in an earlier round.

"We had a business relationship: Mike ran *Combat Magazine.* I wanted to open a gym and he asked: 'How are you going to fund it?' I told him that I'd got someone who was willing to pay for all the equipment. Our arrangement was very simple: I'd run the gym, they'd supply the money; we'd pay the bills and we'd split the profit.

"Mike said: 'Dorian, I've been in business many years and been ripped off so many times by people, but I know, by looking in your eyes, so I'm going to do this.' Later on, Mike let me buy him out and carry on with the business. Once I had my own gym I had a source of income, so I no longer had the stress of trying to look for work, balancing the income and so on. So that definitely gave me a 'leg-up'."

I was well supported by my father and brothers Dorian. Was there anybody who supported you in that way?

"There were a few people along the way. I have to say thanks to Mike Haig who had sufficient faith in me to give me a leg-up with my first business. I'm recently very happily married, in April of 2010. Gal is a world champion in her own right. Her full name is Glauce Ferreira.

"My sports nutrition line is dorian@dorianyatesnutrition.com. I'm heavily promoting that at the moment, travelling the world to the USA, Poland, I've just done two weeks in Russia. I go to Bodybuilding events,

Expos and stuff like that. I usually have a distributor in the country that carries my product, so I go to meet the fans and so on.

"But I'm still Birmingham-based. These days you can run a business from anywhere, if you've got a laptop and a mobile phone. We might go to Spain in the future, because of the weather... and we've got a lot of friends there. We'll probably split our time between the two," Dorian explains.

Peter Wilson is the Home Affairs Correspondent for BBC *Midlands Today*. He became Staff with the BBC in 1997, because he specialised in crime stories. I first met him in 2004 at a local *Virgin Gym*, which we both go to.

"I was the one who was either always swimming or lounging in the Sauna! I've never see anyone drip as much sweat as Kash," observes Peter. "I was introduced to him by a friend of mine, a retired police superintendent, John Plimmer. It seemed quite interesting to be able to chat to a former world champion.

"He agreed to let me come to his gymnasium in Handsworth, at Holte School. I approached him. He was trying to build bridges between different parts of the community. When I went to his gym, there were white, black and Asian kids all training together. I was able to talk to them about what was going on in the streets there; what was happening. Kash really came across as somebody who was able to bring people together. He was certainly very charismatic in the way he was inspiring people to train and also to excel."

Thanks Peter. I remember when Aston Villa were playing West Bromwich Albion. My brothers and me went up the Soho Road, to watch the fans walking to the match. We felt a bit nervous about walking into matches in those days, with so many white fans there, coming into a black area. A lot of Asians avoided football matches, for that reason.

When Cyrille Regis and Laurie Cunningham joined the Albion, the shops would close early, in case the white fans raided the bananas. Once Cyrille and Laurie got onto the pitch the white fans would be hurling bananas at them. Football has kicked a lot of the racism out now, but at the time it was no joke if you were on the receiving end!

Laurie and Cyrille were pioneers for black footballers. Before that time, black players had tried, unsuccessfully, to get into Premier League football. When he and Laurie actually made the breakthrough, it was the turning point for black players. Cyrille's professional playing career spanned nineteen years: he made 610 league appearances and scored 159 league goals.

Cyrille was born in Maripasoula, in French Guiana, on 9 February 1958. His parents are Robert and Mathilde Regis. His father moved to England in 1962, with the rest of the family, including Cyrille, following a year later. The family lived in the Portobello Road area of London, later moving to Stonebridge.

After leaving school Cyrille became an electrician and then a professional footballer. His first professional club was West Bromwich Albion, in 1977, where he remained until 1984.

In the early chapters of this book we describe my Handsworth childhood. It's interesting to compare that with Cyrille's London childhood.

"I lived all over London; mostly north-west London – Brent. My father was a labourer and my mother did seamstress piecework at home," explains Cyrille. "The usual typical first generation – immigrants coming over here; problems with housing; walking down the London streets with signs on the doors: 'No Blacks, No dogs, No Irish'. We had lots of issues with housing.

"I had an older brother and sister and a younger brother and sister. I was the middle child. We moved around north-west London; at one stage we were split up for nine months, then finally found a four-bedroom flat in Stonebridge, London. It was the first time that we had an indoor toilet, with the building situation in the 1960s. But this brand new home was in a high-rise block of flats, on a big massive estate, which notoriously became a 'no-go' area, with the drugs and guns.

"But when we moved there in the early 1970s, it was fantastic. The house we'd lived in before that, for about three years, had an outside toilet and a tin bath. My mom used to send us once a week to the local Baths, to have a bath.

"When I came to this country, at the age of five, I didn't know what a football was! But like most boys, you start playing around in the playground, with whatever is available; a plastic ball, a stone – whatever! We used to play out in the streets when I was younger. The house where I lived, in Barry Road, before Stonebridge, was a dead end. We had a factory at the top end but not many cars used to come up. So we played football, 'Wembley', absolutely anywhere, until all hours."

Our Asian fathers used to stress the importance of getting your own house Cyrille. But we're of a different generation – we want our kids to have everything. So it was a tougher time for our fathers' generation. Even though the cost of living has gone up, we're more educated and we don't have to work in foundries. We have to respect our parents for this.

"Absolutely, when I was young it was more like school football; organised football through the Church Group or Youth Clubs. My son was at West Bromwich for a bit, but he didn't follow it through," Cyrille explains.

David Dunn attended an academy as a young lad, but points out that few young footballers from academies become professional footballers; he's one of the exceptions.

"Yes it's very hard to focus entirely on football," Cyrille observes. "I first met Dave Barnett when he left Birmingham, to live in London. He's a friend of my brother, David, who's about six years younger than me. Dave Barnett didn't turn professional until the 1980s; he's about seven or eight years younger than me. Then he came back to Birmingham and we've been good friends ever since."

According to Wikipedia, 'Although not by any means the first black footballers to play professionally in England, the *Three Degrees* were an integral part of their acceptance in the English leagues.'

"Yes, there were three of us at West Bromwich: Laurie Cunningham, Brendon Batson and myself," continues Cyrille. "There was a sea-change in mentality about black players. Beforehand it was thought that we couldn't handle the cold weather; that we were 'flash'; that we had a lot of attitude; too laid-back; not enough 'bottle': enough courage. That was the barrier. It was prejudice because we were black; there was no doubt about it!

"The three of us, Viv Anderson, Garth Crookes and others, broke that barrier. We showed that we could play football well. But the history, like Kash, was that we had to fight prejudice and break the barriers. When youngsters saw Kash or myself they realised that they could do it too. Kash was the first in his sport. He opened the doors for lots of Asians to go into the sport and think 'Well if Kash can do it, I can do it.'"

Laurie Cunningham joined the Albion in 1977; Brendon Batson joined in early 1978. Did the three of you hang out together socially too Cyrille?

"Yes, football is a community game; one of the factors of being in a team sport was the socialising, the banter; the team spirit – the social dynamics that surround you. Viv Anderson was the first black guy to play for England's First Team. Viv was playing very well for Notts Forest and he was picked to play for England as a result, in 1979. I was in the England Under 21s from 1978-82; the England B Team 1978-1980 and the England 1st Team, 1982-1987. I played with the 1st Team against Northern Ireland, Wales, Iceland, West Germany and Turkey."

But nowadays you're a football agent?

"Yes, I work for *The Stellar Group*, probably one of the biggest football agencies in the country. I look after a load of players; some players from the age of fourteen or fifteen, all the way through to the end of their careers. I negotiate their contracts; find them football clubs; keep them going when they've been rejected; sort out their finances, cars, houses and generally provide a support system for them, as footballers. Basically, they have to make good career decisions."

And you're able to draw on all those years of experience, to help them achieve the best they possibly can?

"Absolutely, also to mentor, especially young players, 14-16; the mental strength needed; the lifestyle needed and the dangers that might stop you from fulfilling your dreams."

From the age of fourteen I was totally focused. People remember me running around the streets of Handsworth and going to the gym, with my black bag. Apache Indian would ask me why I didn't go out and enjoy myself more. Did you have a similar approach to football Cyrille?

"Yes, you have to. I had to make sacrifices too, to a degree, to achieve my goals. So when your mates are out partying on Friday, you stay at home, because you've got a match the following day."

Did you have a mentor to help you? In *my* teens I made a lot of mistakes with my training, because I had no one to guide me.

"Not really. Even as a professional, back in the 70s, no one knew about dehydration, injuries; recuperation; in fact, half of the footballers and 'tourists' would be drinking a lot. After a game you'd go out and have six or seven pints, which is the worst thing ever for you," Cyrille continues. "Alcohol is diuretic: then you get dehydrated and you can't function well. Nowadays you have ice bars, a glass of water; nutrition. There are Sports Psychologists to advise players too, so we can work it out for ourselves," concludes Cyrille.

Dave Barnett remembers, "Back then without a doubt, Brendan Batson, Cyrille Regis, Laurie Cunningham, Garth Crookes, all laid the foundations for the next generation. But unfortunately there was still institutional and open racism. It's how you dealt with it. Black players were not the norm that they are now. But you go through transitional periods, including the need for managers to understand black players; to bring on board the spectators too. Basically that's due to a certain amount of ignorance – and that's not Football's fault, that's Society's," observes Dave. "The bottom line is that nowadays managers understand and support black players much more; they have an educated grasp of the situation."

In the 1990s, Dave, when you were playing for Birmingham City, you snapped an Achilles tendon, so you were out of action for a long period. You did some kickboxing training, as part of your fitness rehabilitation regime, although you'd been kickboxing long before then. I took you over to Paul Sutton's Aston gym.

"That's right – you did some coaching and we did some sparring; we did all our fitness work together and had a good time. I was into Kung Fu at an early age, which incorporates discipline and also respect for the person who's teaching you."

In Round 14 we provide examples of people who lacked that respect – and the consequences that followed. Returning to your football career Dave, you had a brief spell at West Bromwich Albion, 1989-1990.

"Yes, that was an interesting period, but the time that gave me the greatest satisfaction was 1993-1997, with Birmingham City, under the manager, Barry Fry. I played under Trevor Francis as well. Imagine, you're a Handsworth lad and you get to play for your home town and the team you support.

"I was playing Centre Midfield as a schoolboy, for Wolverhampton, and non-league when I went to London. Then I suddenly filled out and grew about another three or four inches, so I became a Defender. When we're growing up, we all want to be the creative genius in front of goal! But it doesn't always work out that way, so I became a 'stopper'. But I enjoyed *stopping* people being creative – that's an art in itself!

"When we went to Birmingham City the team won a national trophy and I also played at Wembley: there were 97,000 spectators. We had some great times," remembers Dave. "We won that shield. We also played at Anfield – all the clubs that I'd had on my bedroom walls, as a schoolboy growing up in Handsworth... I was able to play in some of those stadiums!"

RAZZMATAZZ

Continuing the theme from Round 9, Kash is in conversation with Tom Ross, David Dunn, Andy Walker, Hudson Richards, Kenny Cunningham, Joe Egan and Phil Upton.

Tom Ross, who wrote the Foreword for our book, became Head of Sport for BRMB in 1993, and was then further promoted to Head of Sport for the Group in 2009. He still considers himself to be very much a Brummie, having spent his childhood in the inner city slums, on the Aston-Hockley border – 2/437 New John Street West, Birmingham B19.

"I was born in 1950," explains Tom, "and funnily enough, I lived on the 19 bus route! I went to Saint Chad's right the way through my schooling. The Infant and Senior Schools were in Brearley Street, but the Junior School was at the back of the Cathedral, in Shadwell Street. My upbringing was definitely on the 'rags' side of 'rags to riches'! Without any doubt I stared poverty in the face every single day.

"When my dad lost his job, we had no money coming in, at all. We had a really tough time at that point, because my mom wasn't working. All told, there were eight of us! As kids you go home for your tea, but you don't think about where it comes from. Inside the house, you had cold water only. When I was really small, we had gas mantles. There was no electricity at first then it was put in downstairs. There was still no hot water: you had to boil a kettle. There was a tin bath, in front of the fire, which was awfully embarrassing at times! We all used the same bath, so you wanted to be first in, that's for sure!

"My mother's name was Mary Agnes Sullivan; she married my dad, Thomas Ross. They've both passed on now, and I still miss them every single day of my life. My dad was from Glasgow; my mom came over from Belfast, with my Nanny and Granddad Sullivan.

"My mom was a legend. She went to the Rosary School, but got expelled, for knocking a boy out, who called her an Irish tinker! She ruled with an iron hand, that's for sure. After my dad got a job at *Fisher & Ludlow*, when I was about ten, things were *better*. My mom worked as a barmaid, at the *Britannia* pub, on the corner of New John Street West and Summer Lane.

"My dad was my hero and taught me three things: 1. Live your life by your own standards. 2. Never be ashamed to pick up your wages. 3. Never let anyone take the p**s. I have lived by that mantra and would think that Kash would probably say it's his way too.

"It was an amazing place to live though, with a pub on every corner. Perhaps that is why I am tee-total and always will be? As kids we used to go to the Saturday matinee at the *Newtown Palace* – the 'Flea-pit'.

"I stayed on at Saint Chad's and took my O Levels, then went into an office job, as an accountant: all of my family can do instant maths in their heads too – that came from my dad. I worked at *Gothic Electrical*, in Hospital Street, transferred to their Buying Department, for a while, because I'd got the 'gift-of-the-gab', and met my first wife there. Eventually I went to work for *City Electrical*, staying in Sales and didn't work for BRMB until 1981.

"I worked for Hospital Radio first. I was a Pitch Announcer for Birmingham City Football Club and I met a few footballers. Because of my connections I could interview people like Jasper Carrot, who's a friend of mine. I could get various footballers to come on the show. Hospital Radio, BHBN, Birmingham Hospital Broadcasting Network, had never really had those sorts of interviews.

"I absolutely adored my time at BHBN. It was based in the Birmingham County Cricket Ground, although they're not there any more. Les Ross, Jimmy Franks and many other people who got into radio learned their trade there. One famous voice I worked with was Alan Dedicote who is now the voice of the lottery draw. It was great grounding: you had to go to the hospitals and get the requests; you couldn't just be a presenter or a DJ. It taught you quite a discipline, for radio. That was during the 1970s.

"After Hospital Radio I then went to work for BBC Radio Birmingham – it wasn't RadioWM in those days. Tim Russon was the Sports Editor. We were broadcasting from the Pebble Mill Studios. Tim asked me if I'd like to do some games – and I was there for a short while. Then out of the blue I got a phone call from Tony Butler. He was the Head of Sport at BRMB: 'I want you to work for me – no ifs or buts!' So I went to work for him. He left not long afterwards, under difficult circumstances. I was then assistant to

George Gavin. Then in 1993, when George left, I became Head of Sport and in 2009, Head of Sport for the Group. It's been a fantastic journey and I have loved every single minute at BRMB!"

In the late 1980s you worked with George Gavin. I used to teach George Gavin's son. You've covered a lot of charity events. What's your favourite sport Tom?

"Football without a doubt Kash... my favourite team is Birmingham City. I know that you're a big Villa fan Kash. When my dad came down from Scotland he could easily have taken me to the Villa, because we lived equidistant to the ground, but my dad wanted to take me to Birmingham City, because they had a Scottish Winger playing – Alex Govern. I became hooked and I've been a fan all my life. However, I also love boxing, kickboxing and ice hockey: those are all my favourite sports – I just absolutely adore them."

Tell me about your radio shows.

"I do live kick by kick football commentaries, which can be any day or night of the week, from Sunday to Sunday inclusive, thanks to TV. There are also different kick-off times.

"I cover all the local clubs: Birmingham, Villa, West Brom, Wolves and Coventry and present the *Goalzone* programme which is broadcast across BRMB, Beacon Radio, Mercia FM and Gold stations whenever any of our teams are playing.

"Every Monday night I present the *Sports Bar*, between 6 and 7 with Villa legend Ian Taylor, talking about the big football issues, with a bit of tongue-in-cheek banter and humour. On Fridays I host the *Football Phone-In*, with Tony Butler, who was the first ever presenter when it started in the mid-1970s.

"There are loads of funny stories from my 31 years at BRMB, but one really funny story was from the Butler era, when one of the reporters, Tony Trethewey, didn't realise he was on air when Tony asked where an interviewee was and replied 'He's pissed off Tone!' Everybody listening to it at home was in stitches!

"It was 31 years ago that Tony Butler gave me a chance at BRMB, so when he was let go by the BBC a couple of years ago I offered him the opportunity to join me on Friday nights, on the football phone-in. He's seventy-seven now and semi-retired. He looked after me all those years ago, so it was only right that I looked after him now. He is a broadcasting legend and the pioneer of the 'football phone in'. I have so much to thank him for."

Do you have a favourite from my fights that you think we should put in?

"One of the things that I always remember about most of your fights is the psychological edge that you got, when the Bhangra Band led you into the ring. Apache Indian did a song called *Chok There*, which was a Chart Hit. He put different words to it, for you. I played it first, on BRMB, on the day of your fight; I've still got the original tape that we did – it's a cassette."

I enjoyed introducing all that Razzmatazz into kickboxing Tom.

"No one else had done that before; there was nothing like it in kickboxing. You grabbed kickboxing and had this wonderful ability to put bums on seats. If you were fighting, people wanted to be there.

"Yourself and Paul Ingram, the President of the WKA, combined together to make kickboxing attractive to go and see. It became a spectator sport. I remember the *Aston Villa Leisure Centre* being absolutely packed to the rafters when you were fighting... and the Bhangra Band came out. There was always a tingle when you came into the ring. As a boxer, you brought a lot to the sport, because you were entertaining. But outside of the ring, you made the whole sport attractive, sexy; put bums on seats; made it an essential sport to go and watch."

You make a point in an article about the actual kickboxing organisation needing to devise a marketing strategy. You wrote in one of my promotional magazines:

'This fantastic, exciting thrilling dramatic and yet too often under-rated sport should be available to a wider audience. The British kickboxing scene should be a regular on Sky TV; instead, we get foreign shows from all over the world. British kickboxing has to sort itself out, become proactive, and show the world what we have to offer here in Britain instead of the other way round.' How can we do that Tom?

"Well, sadly money is always the key to making these things happen and essentially through sponsorship. But I went to a lot of kickboxing shows, in year's gone by, which weren't yours, and there were badly-matched fights: the matchmaker hadn't done his job right. It was supposed to start at eight o'clock, but at nine o'clock you were still sitting there!

"You recognised that and tried to offer value for money. I remember saying to you: 'When you fought it was different. But kickboxing in this

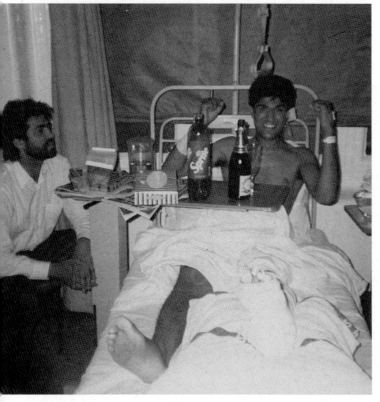

Above: Kash kicks off with a winner at the age of 16.

Left: Kash takes a break. A Scottish relative visits him in hospital. His ankle and foot were in plaster for ten weeks! Life is full of 'Dodgy Situations' but Kash remains undaunted.

Above: 1986: WAKO European Championships in France. Having struck gold, Kash then went for the British title on 4 October, held at Nottingham's Victoria Leisure Centre.

Below: Kash's second International fight, against Yugoslavian Buric Igor, in Birmingham City Centre. Kash won on points after five rounds.

Above: 1990: Kash becomes European Middleweight Champion, in Sicily.

Left: Public Weigh-in at Birmingham's Hyatt Hotel, Broad Street in 1991. Alex Tui from Australia versus Kash, for the WKA Light Middleweight Title.

Above: Alex – is he asking for the toilet?!

Left: Kash's trademark, the Nachdhey Hasde Bhangra Band, has brought glitz, glamour and live entertainment to the sport of kickboxing.

Kash, victorious after a fight at the Aston Villa Leisure Centre, is carried aloft by his brothers, Cougar and Gurdip, Master A in background right.

Above: 1993: Jules Evoule of France, for the ISKA World Light Middleweight Kickboxing Championship. Kash won on a twelve-round points decision at Aston Villa Leisure Centre.

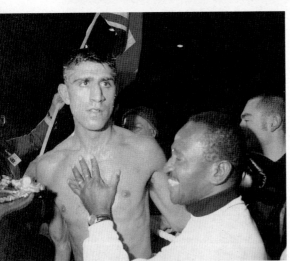

Left: 'Mr Handsworth' Hector Pinkney, congratulates Kash on his victory, at a World Event.

Below: 1995: Austrian Ronnie Hinterseer and Kash, public weigh-in outside Birmingham Council House, Victoria Square.

Above: Flash Promotions at Villa Park, 1995. Villa Park was a regular venue for promoting Kash's fights.

Right: Bitter rival Mike 'Cobra' Cole gets smashed by Kash at Aston Villa Leisure Centre. World Middleweight title defence. Mike was KO'd in Round Three.

Below: World Title Fight in a South African shopping centre, Johannesburg, 1997. Opponent, Richard Ndana. Kash lost on points, after twelve rounds - a hometown decision.

Above: Kash was never short on security! Leisuresec PLC provides the protection, Aston Villa Leisure Centre c.1995.

Below: Kash, a proud World Champion, with trainer of champions, Master Toddy, in black, and his brother, Master A.

Above: What a training camp! From left to right: Kash, Sot Chitalada, legendary former World Flyweight Boxing Champion, Thailand. 'Edge' Brown and his brother, Howard, complete the line-up.

Below: Kash with trainer and lifelong friend, Howard Brown. Australia 1991.

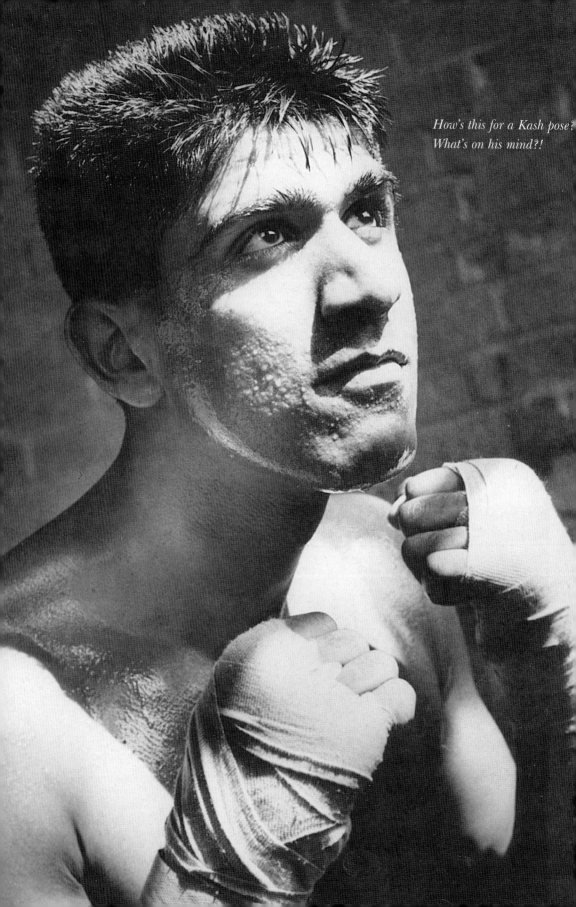

How's this for a Kash pose?
What's on his mind?!

Right top: 'Kash the Flash' parades his European Kickboxing Defence Trophy.

Right Middle: Kash at his Icknield Port Road Gym, surrounded by a collection of Championship Belts. He continues to train future champions and motivate students from all walks of life, through Gym Classes, Presentations and a variety of other events.

Bottom: Fosco's Flyers: Dave Nicholas, of 'Fosco Hayes', is second from right on the back row. After this match perhaps they should stick to printing?!

Above: Team Kash, instructors and fighters.

Below: April 2005: WWE Wrestlers Kane and Batista on back row with Kash. Front row from left to right: Simon Akufo, Bal Singh, Sunny Hira. Grant Lawley, centre front.

Left: Cyrille Regis awarding a raffle prize with Dorian Yates. Centre back, Bernard Chong.

Below: A big supporter of 'Kash the Flash', six times Mr. Olympia Dorian Yates presents a pair of boxing gloves to the raffle winner.

Above: Kash with loyal sponsors, Murria Solicitors. From left to right: G. Kang, Makhan Singh, Mark Reynolds, Harry Sangha and Makhan's brother, Kully.

Below: Flash Promotions – we only did it the Flash way.

Top: Bhangra Boxing!

Left: Is it Flash back or Kash back?

Bottom: Kash fights in front of 40,000 spectators, Kurdistan c. 1997.

country has gone backwards now.' You said: 'Well come and have a look at one of my shows.' And you were right – you'd made it better; you recognised the problems within the sport and put on your own shows. Matched the fights brilliantly and they were quality fights; on time, refereed well," Tom concludes.

During a radio interview, Sonia Deol told me: "We've got this e-mail from Sanje. She says: 'I would love to know how the Bhangra dancers bringing you up to the ring started for you and how did a non-Indian crowd react to all of that?'

They loved it. There's so much noise as well. It came as a surprise because nobody knew and to this day, I've not seen a better entrance than that. They're all friends of mine – and I helped them out as well.

BBC WM presenter Phil Upton recalls:

"I interviewed Kash primarily about his own achievements and then later regarding his coaching and his shows. The initial interviews about his achievements would have been in the late 80s early 90s. I've seen him fight a couple of times and then interviewed him subsequently for the radio, because of those fights."

My brother Gamma comments: "Kash's events are more spectacular for the audience than some of the amateur boxing shows. Sometimes sponsors would just offer goods such as cars, rather than money, but we'd turn them down. With hindsight, we probably should have accepted gifts like that. If you're fighting in a minor sport, why try to get bigger than that? You're only going to get a certain percentage of people interested in it, as well. You can grow, but it takes time."

Cougar agrees: "That's right, but when Kash got to the world title fight, that time that he got hit, me, Daljit and our old next door neighbour, Doris, were there. It was horrendous, but because of the bonding that we had as we grew up, we all helped him with the shows. I think it was amazing that Kash promoted these shows at the *Aston Villa Leisure Centre*, and fought in them as well. Kash took a B Tech National course at college, when he left school, to help him with his business ventures," Cougar explains. "But the night before he was fighting, Kash might still be matching up fighters, where someone had pulled out the night before.

"I've seen him coach his students, because I've trained with him," continues Cougar. "When he teaches, he can see out of the back of his head!

He can bring the best out in his students and motivate people. He's a fantastic teacher!"

"I'll be honest," Gamma admits, "I *hated* watching Kash in the ring. I enjoyed the sport, but that's your brother in there! I'd be leading the chorus, shouting for him, 'Kash, Kash, Kash!', but at the same time my chest would be pounding because he's my brother. Win or lose I used to find it hard. We'd jump in the ring and put him up on our shoulders and everything."

According to Resham, "Kash would determine the date for his fights. He would probably book the venue: somewhere like *Aston Villa Leisure Centre*. And he would put a lot of energy into trying to sell the tickets. We'd all have a meeting at my father's house in Grove Lane, to break the tasks down but Gamma would coordinate things, like equipment for the event and promotions.

"This was a high risk thing. Kash fought with an injured neck, but got the chiropractor in to give him treatment, just before he went out. Bear in mind, he had invested a lot of money in that show. If he wasn't fighting, then people wouldn't have come to see it.

"We looked at eventualities," Resham continues. "Sometimes his shows would be in November – what if it snowed? It would mean that he would lose money so there was always that risk. We had a whole team of people of unpaid volunteers, because all of us are very proud of his achievements and wanted to do our bit to support him.

"I used to prepare all the press releases," explains Resham, "trying to maximise media exposure so that it would increase the sale of tickets, mainly pre-fight. Kash has had some good support from some high-profile individuals. Now Hudson Richards has a good voice and a good presence, but people like Tom Ross and Phil Upton are professionals.

"The difference between Hudson and the other two is that I would do all the fighter profiles and write them up for Phil and Tom, whereas Hudson preferred to talk to the fighters himself," Resham reveals. "It helps if you've got an idea about your fighters when you're in the ring, but Tom has reached the stage now when he knows most of the fighters so he'll just go into the dressing room and look at how many fights they've won, how many they've lost; find out what their ambitions are. But to start with I did all of the research.

"Phil Upton was very professional," continues Resham. "If there were any gaps in the show, he was particularly good at thinking on his feet and ad-libbing. I looked after the VIPs at events. We've been very lucky: we've had a host of celebrities coming along: footballers, pop stars, et cetera.

"Kash won the Junior Championship, when he was sixteen. I got quite excited about that, because he appeared in the paper. I was working in Town and I bought a copy of the paper for each member of the family. My brother has a strong sense of who he is. Our family members enjoy celebrating those achievements too. That sense of celebration goes back to Punjab tradition, celebrating a successful harvest, for example," Resham concludes.

Shirley, my son, Mitch, and myself met up with David Dunn on Saturday 8 May 2010, at the Malmaison Hotel, Birmingham City Centre.

David was born in the centre of Blackburn, at Queen's Park Hospital and grew up in a town just outside, called Great Harwood. He started playing football in the streets at an early age and was selected for the town team when he was about eight years old. He was accepted into one of the new academies, when he was nine or ten; signed Schoolboy Forms, joined a Youth Training Scheme and then made his debut in 1998 for the First Team at Blackburn. After serving two years apprenticeship at the club, he signed a professional contract, at seventeen.

He got into the Lancashire Schools Cricket Team Under-15s, but could never play because it was always conflicting with football, so he had a choice to make. He used to be a keen golfer too, but football and cricket are his two main sports.

How did you come to play for Birmingham City Dave?

"I was quite successful at Blackburn – got into the team; made a few appearances for the club and was part of the Promotion Team for the Worthington Cup. My team qualified for Europe and that year I moved on to Birmingham City, for about six million quid. So around late 2004 – early 2005 I started playing for them. I had quite a number of injuries when I was there, which dinted my career a little bit.

"My main problem at Birmingham was my hamstrings. I had really bad problems; then I had a spine fusion as well, which was obviously a bit of a 'kick-in-the-teeth' – to be out of action for so long. But since I've got back I feel pretty good. You gave me a few stretches for ankle strain Kash and things like that, which was good."

We first got to know each other when you requested some tickets for one of my shows Dave. I met you outside the Hilton Hotel. We were doing a match at the Hilton Metropole at the NEC. You'd seen the 'flyer' about the show – hence the telephone call.

"Yes, I phoned you up and took a few of the lads down there from the Club; there were quite a few of us, including Damien Johnson, Stan Lazerides, Matthew Upson, and myself."

You gave me some signed football boots and a shirt, to auction.

"Yes, it was quite a funny match really, because it was full of Villa fans that night! So I think me boots went for two quid; the signed shirt went for a quid. The auction was a tough one, but it was a good night!"

Although you never watched any of my fights Dave, you watched some of my students.

"That's right. Steve Lahori, who'd got a bit of a boxing background, was fighting a lad from Liverpool who'd actually forgotten his gloves and was outside the ring, just casually walking around. You were in the corner and this lad's hamstrings were getting stretched and he was doing little moves. I thought: 'Yes, this lad must be a good'un like. Eventually, they found some gloves in the back for this other lad, he got them on; the bell went, but within seconds your man was spark out on the mat!

"He was on his back, with birds whistling around his head and getting stretchered past us within about thirty seconds! We couldn't really say that much: it's tough getting in that ring. I've got quite a few friends in the fight game," Dave continues. "It was an Amateur fight. I was talking about it the other week, with a friend of mine who is an ex-world champion arm wrestler from Blackburn: he was there! You've got to take your hat off to these fighters, because it takes a lot of guts to get in the ring to start with."

That show at the *Metropole* was in 2005. It was in the *Birmingham Mail* the day after. It was the same night that I was in a fight with Batista, which made headlines all around the world! We cover that incident in more detail in Round 14 – *Dodgy Situations*.

My brother Resham remembers Matthew Upson and David Dunn attending that show, plus someone from *RadioWM* and a famous Asian businessman from the East End. Murria Solicitors were sponsoring me. Resham was a Marketing Manager from 1990-2001, for *Birmingham TEC Ltd*.

Andy Walker recalls: "Kash stepped in and we ran the story about the *Metropole* fight as a big *Solihull News* front page. Being the PR-hungry machine that Kash is, he was delighted to see it there. The only exception that he took to our story was that we included his address – he didn't want a gang of big American wrestlers bearing down on his house!"

Andy always wanted to get into sports journalism, but was never good enough to be a professional footballer, so the second best thing was to get paid, watching it!

"So in December 2003 I got a job at the *Solihull News* as News reporter and Sports Editor," Andy continues. "The *Solihull News* and the *Solihull Times* were two separate papers, but they had one Sports Editor, responsible for the coverage, for both papers.

"I was there for three years and three months," he explains, "and then I went to the *Sunday Mercury*, just as a sports reporter. I did that for eighteen months or so before there was a restructure, which saw me working as a multimedia sports journalist, on the *Sunday Mercury* still, the *Birmingham Mail* and the *Birmingham Post*."

Andy joined the *Sunday Mercury* in 2007, worked for the two Birmingham papers right up until July 2010, but is now the PR & Social Media Manager for Birmingham City Football Club, managed by Chris Hughton under Chinese ownership.

"The PR side is helping newspapers to arrange interviews with the players and manager, but the reason I was attracted to this job is the Social Media side of it, which is Twitter, Facebook, Blogging – it's a thing that's really taking off at the moment. Birmingham City hasn't yet got a strategy for dealing with that, so it will be my baby in a sense: I can go in there and develop the way that Birmingham City deals with itself, through the social media.

"There are two coaches: Peter Grant and Andy Watson. The owner of the Club is Carson Yeung, from Hong Kong – a businessman. He took over in October 2009; which is another reason that I wanted to join – it seemed like an exciting time.

"From 14-28 July 2010 we did a Birmingham City Tour. We went out to China for two weeks; it was a historically-significant tour for the club, with the new Chinese ownership: they want to boost the image of the club in the Far East. So it was the most important tour in the Club's history.

"We spent four days in Hong Kong and played one friendly fixture there; then went to Beijing and played in the *Bird's Nest Stadium*. Then we went to Shen Yang for the third and final match, followed by a brief stopover at Guangzhou. We won all three. There were lots of Dinners, visits to shopping malls; the Forbidden City et cetera. Everywhere you went there were Chinese journalists," remarks Andy.

Former international footballer, Kenny Cunningham, grew up in Dublin. At eighteen he finished his schooling then had a couple of years of football training there, prior to leaving for England. He was very focused, not only on football but also on Gaelic Hurling and other sports. We first met at the *Virgin Gym* in 2002.

"Our paths first crossed that year, when I arrived in Birmingham, I'd just signed with Birmingham City, but the gym facilities at the Club, at that time, weren't particularly good," Kenny remembers, "so we trained at the new *Virgin Gym* in Solihull.

"A lot of local players were using the facilities there so our club did the same. Football players have something of a high profile around the area, so Kash probably recognised one or two of the players."

I'm an Aston Villa supporter Kenny, so I kept that very quiet!

"Kash was interested in what kind of training we were doing," Kenny continues. "Other sportsmen tend to be interested in your particular sport and how you condition yourself. Sometimes you can get small tips from each other, that can help you in your particular field.

"When I first met Kash, I'd just moved from London, and Birmingham City had just moved up into the Premier League.... it was all happy days. Steve Bruce was the manager at that time. He'd brought the club into the Premiership, so there was an air of excitement. They hadn't been at that level for a number of years.

"There were other new players in the team, like Matt Upson and David Dunn. Steven Clements came into the club; Emile Heskey... probably half a dozen or more, all arriving at the same time. It was a real challenge for us to keep the club in the Premiership, that particular year. In Solihull, where the gym is, it's predominantly a Birmingham area, sprinkled in with some Aston Villa supporters. Everybody was interested in the club and the players," Kenny explains.

According to Tom Ross I was particularly good at beating an opponent, because of the way I planned everything to the 'nth' degree. I'm a bit of a perfectionist Kenny, so I like to have everything just right!

"That's probably similar to a football environment where with video technology now, players have access to information. Some clubs will embrace it more than others; the majority of clubs will, to a certain extent. They'll look at the strengths and weaknesses of the opposition team. Obviously it's no guarantee, but if it does end in failure at least you can look within yourself and say: 'I covered all bases and prepared as best I could.'

"We went up to Sunderland, where I finished my professional playing career, before returning to our home in Birmingham, where we remain to the present day. It's handy for a lot of professional footballers, because of the easy access to Manchester and London," concludes Kenny.

Celebrity boxer Joe Egan had his first major fight at the national junior championships, with Steve Collins. By the age of twenty-four he had achieved over 80 wins, 7 Irish titles and was also a 'Golden Gloves' champion.

He was born, 15 November 1966 in Ringsend, Dublin, just a couple of months after me, so we're *almost* the same age. Known affectionately as 'Big Joe', he's a former Heavyweight Boxing Champion. Although he previously lived in Ireland, he has since made Birmingham his home.

Tell me how you first became involved in boxing Joe.

"My dad encouraged me and my brothers to box, because he felt that boxing first and foremost, gives you self-respect, respect for other people and the confidence to 'walk tall' and to stand up against bullies.

"My dad worked on building sites in England, so we came over to this country, as children. I got bullied when I came to this country, for having an Irish accent. Then when I went home to Dublin I got bullied, because I had an English accent! I had two front teeth knocked out, by the schoolyard bullies. In all my years of boxing, I only had *one* tooth knocked out!"

Your father was a former amateur boxer?

"Yes, he boxed for the Corinthians Boxing Club in Dublin and was trained by Maxie McCullagh, who won the 1947 European Gold Medal. I boxed at Heavyweight; when I was a Pro, at 15 stone 10. I'm 6 foot 1 and have always had broad shoulders.

"I had 105 amateur fights and won seven Irish Titles; two Under 19s; one Junior and four Senior Titles. I boxed for Ireland on thirteen occasions. I beat a Pole; beat a couple of Americans; a Welshman and an Italian. I lost twice to England, which is hard to take for an Irishman. But the respect amongst fighters is great."

To have achieved all of that by the age of twenty-four is quite something isn't it?

"Yes, because of my size, when I was sixteen I was boxing men. But you're not mature at sixteen; these guys that I was boxing were in their twenties. It's very difficult when you haven't got that natural strength and you're still a young boy. Experience comes with age, but I was strong and keen and I enjoyed boxing.

"I won the *Golden Gloves Championship,* in New York State, in 1985. I'm also known as the man who went the full distance with Lennox Lewis. I fought him as an amateur. But I was beaten in the New York City *Golden Gloves*. The guy that beat me was beaten in the American Championships. The American Champion boxed Lennox Lewis, just a couple of weeks before this particular tournament and was knocked spark out!

"I agreed to box Lennox. At that time I'd been sparring with Tyson, so I was so 'psyched' that I knew I could take Lennox Lewis's punches. And I went the distance with him. He was knocking everybody out; he was Number Two in the world at the time; he was Pan-American Games Gold Medallist. He'd won the Bronze in 1984, in the Olympics; he went on and got the Gold in '88. But I walked into the ring, a confident man. It's a great feeling: knowing that you're being punched by the hardest punch in the world – and you're still on your feet!"

Mike Tyson described Joe as the 'toughest white man on the planet', which he quoted later, but I think if I'd hit him with one of my leg kicks it would have been a "Big Goodnight Joe!"

You beat the WBA Champion, Bruce Seldon, in the *Sands Hotel and Casino*, Atlantic City Joe?

"Yes in 1988 – it was Ireland versus America. Bruce Seldon was the American Champion. He was being groomed for the 1988 Olympics. This guy was very special. He battered me in Round One, but I said: 'If I can take Tyson's punishment I can take anybody's punishment.'

"I went on to win a fantastic fight: I beat Seldon... and he went on to win the World Professional Heavyweight title, so I've shared the ring with a few world champions, which is a great honour.

"It was absolutely amazing! There were ten former great world champions in attendance: Rocky Graziano, Joe Frazier, 'Jersey Joe' Walcott, Sandy Sadler, and Billy Conn, just to mention a few. During the fight, Jake

Lamotta, the 'Raging Bull', was standing there throwing punches, because the fight was like a throwback, to when Jake O'Morrow was boxing. Raging Bull tripped and hurt his arm and cut his eye. I wasn't aware of what was going on outside the ring," continues Joe. "I was having enough problems with what was going on *inside* the ring!

"Even though I won, I had to go to hospital. As the adrenalin wore off I was in a lot of pain. Jake Lamotta, the 'Raging Bull', shared the same ambulance. He complimented me on the fight. That was in 1988, and we've remained friends, to this day."

In early 1984 Floyd Patterson encouraged Joe to join Mike Tyson's training camp in the Catskill Mountains, with the great trainer Cus D'Amato.

"Mike was smaller than me, a similar age and I really thought that I was going to beat him up! But he was just sensational," Joe exclaims. "The first day, I watched him knock out a couple of big, powerful men, before I got in the ring.

"I walked with him the day before; talked about Ireland; talked about Barry McGuigan. Ran with him that morning; had breakfast with him, got on really well with him, because unlike all of the other fighters in the camp we were the only teenagers.

"I got to the gym and saw the first fighter get knocked spark out. Mike knocked out all the other sparring partners that day, but I stayed on my feet. I wrote to people that day, saying, 'I'm training with the future Heavyweight Champion of the World.' Even though he was only seventeen I knew that he was special. I'd boxed older men, including an American champion, but I thought: 'This boy's just sensational!' He'd sparred with Frank Bruno in New York when Mike was just fifteen – and Frank Bruno was a great fighter. I did a Dinner with Frank, in Doncaster and one with Mike Tyson, but for a fifteen-year-old boy to do that, was something really special."

In one of the sparring sessions with Mike Tyson, he described you as 'The toughest man on the planet.'

"Yes, this particular day he had just four white sparring partners, which is unusual, because there would usually be some black sparring partners too. Mike knocked three of them out; I was Number Four. I got battered from pillar to post, but I stayed on my feet. At the end of the sparring session Mike Tyson said: 'Joe Egan is the toughest white man on the planet!' Well,

I was the toughest white man in the *gym* that day, but it was a nice compliment. That was all in the Catskills. I sparred with him for two years and we've remained great friends ever since: we've kept in touch and we've met often. I've been over to Mike's home and he's been to mine. He's visited my mam."

Joe became a professional boxer under top trainer Barney Eastwood's stable, but his dreams of boxing were cruelly shattered when he was forced to quit, following a serious road accident, on the night of his second pro fight.

"Yes, my second fight was fighting on Dave Boy MacCauley's World Title Bill, in the *King's Hall* in Belfast. I fought a powerful black guy called Carlton Headley, who eventually became the 'Gladiator Warrior'.

"I'd watched world title fights on the telly and fought other world champions but I'd never actually been to a World Title Fight before. So suddenly, I'm boxing on the Undercard section of a World Title Fight!

"Dave Boy MacCauley was fighting an American guy, Lewis Curtis. They were filming it, and then sending the tape to America. As they pointed out in the Press, if Dave Boy stopped Lewis Curtis, I'd a chance of my fight being shown on live American television, with it being relayed straight to America.

"Instead of boxing I got drawn into a fight and badly cut up. I had sixty-four stitches after the fight! It was a great win – but it wasn't a great performance. After the fight I travelled back to Dublin by coach, with friends and family, who had come up to see the fight. But a taxi crashed into the coach. My knee was injured and I had to have keyhole surgery; that put me out of action, for a long time."

I understand that you had a spell in prison?

"Yes. My ex-fiancée cleared off with Michael Flatley of *River Dance* fame. As a result I got into trouble with the police, of which I'm ashamed. I originally got two-and-a-half years in prison, but then the Crown Prosecution Service appealed and it was increased to four years, of which I served two years. If I'd stuck with the original two-and-a-half years I would have been out within fourteen months."

Your come-back fight was within six months of coming out of prison?

"Yes, I made a comeback after twelve years out of the ring. I had headlines in the *Boxing News*: 'George Foreman made a comeback in ten years; Big Joe Egan makes a comeback in twelve years'. To get mentioned in the same paragraph as George Foreman was a great honour for me."

You've living in Moseley and have been in the UK for about seventeen years?

"Yes, when I came to this country first, in 1995, I managed the *Dubliner* pub in Digbeth for two years, for my friend, Paddy Finn, a former Heavyweight Boxing Champion. A lot of ex-boxers went into the pub trade. Then I took over the *Lyndhurst* in Erdington, with former kickboxing champion, Thomas McGeough. It had a function room, where we ran boxing tournaments. We had that pub for four-and-a-half years. But on the 26 July 1998 I was shot by racketeers and came up against the police."

We were introduced to each other some time within the last ten years Joe. We'd meet at places like the *Tower Ballroom* and so on.

"Yes, although boxing is my favourite sport, I like all athletes, in particular fighters, so I'd been a fan of yours for years, before I ever met you. There were a couple of friends back in Ireland – Paul Lenihan the former Featherweight Kickboxing Champion. Dave Cowley was another – he'd kickboxed for Ireland."

Do you think had you not been injured you would have achieved even greater success?

"No, I don't think so. My dad would like to think that I had the ability to be a World Champion. I've always been a real trier. I've met fighters over the years with more ability than me, but they didn't have the dedication. But to be a World Champion you've got be that little bit more special."

I understand that you've taken part in a total of thirty films, including *Sherlock Holmes*, with Jude Law and Robert Downey Junior?

"Yes thirty movies in three years. Cass Pennant, who published my autobiography in 2005, had a movie made about his life, called *Cass*. He gave me the opportunity to be in the film. I played the landlord of the *Britannia* pub: a bit of typecasting. One of the stars of the film, Tamar Hassan, an ex-boxer, encouraged me to give it a go and introduced me to his agent, who put me in for a fight scene, in *Sherlock Holmes*.

"Guy Richie-Jones, the movie director for *Warner Brothers*, said: 'Joe, we've been trying to get you into one of our films for a long time!' I said: 'You're joking!' Robert Downey Junior said: 'Joe, you come with a fearsome reputation.' I couldn't believe it, Kash, these people even *knowing* me!

"Eventually they gave me a scene in the film, where Robert Downey Junior actually calls me 'Big Joe'. To get called your own name by an Academy Award-winning actor is amazing Kash!

"I did *Dead Man Running* with Tamar Hassan and Danny Dyer and *Jack Said*, with Danny Dyer again. I'm getting the parts of tough guys. I've done a film called *Freight*, bought by *Icon*, Mel Gibson's distribution company. It has big British stars in it: Billy Murray, Craig Fairbrass, Andy Tiernan and Danny Midwinter. It's set in England and I play a Russian gangster called Emile. I'm gradually getting more dialogue.

"*Dead Cert* came out in October 2010. I play an English gangster who gets bitten and turns into a vampire. The people doing the make-up are the same ones who do *Harry Potter*. It was great fun Kash! And the money comes in handy too… it's a nice bonus!

"With each role that I play I get more confidence. It's all exciting to me and there aren't enough hours in the day when I'm filming. I'd do twenty-six hours – no problem!"

Round 11

SPORTS COMPARISONS

We compare the personalities of those involved in team sports, as opposed to those who stand alone, in full contact sports. Contributors to this Round are Adil Ray, Wayne Elcock, Frankie Gavin and Bob Sykes; Dorian Yates, Cyrille Regis, Joe Egan, Gamma and Resham; Dave Barnett, Kenny Cunningham and Andy Walker.

One of the advantages of kickboxing is that opponents can use a variety of limbs, unlike boxing; also, compared with wrestling, where in certain cases, the match result can be, allegedly, a foregone conclusion, it seems far less likely in kickboxing.

"I think there's more skill involved in kickboxing," observes Adil Ray, "it's a bit more intelligent. Boxing's more a case of getting in there and punch somebody's face in, a very simple philosophy. But kickboxing requires more skill. There's a certain training required and a lot depends on the type of person you are too, which develops outside of the ring, which is also crucial. Kash is a great example of that.

"The thing about Kash is that when I've interviewed him, you wouldn't think for a minute that this guy's got it in him to go into a ring and beat somebody up," Adil continues. "But it's all really part of the same persona. If you meet a boxer, he normally has this 'macho' image about him, whereas with kickboxers there's a humility about them.

"One of Kash's former students, Sunny Hira, who I absolutely admire, is one of the nicest people you'll ever meet. He's a very confident young chap but you wouldn't think for a minute that he's got it in him to hurt *anyone*, but in the ring, that's what they do. He is good looking too. The sucker!"

When champion boxer Wayne Elcock turned professional, he was promoted by Frank Warren for a number of years, before deciding to go it alone. Frank helped Paddy Lynch to put on his first big World Title Fight, Pat Cowdell versus Azuma Nelson.

We asked Wayne about the different kind of personality types required for football, boxing and kickboxing, including whether you're a solo or a team player.

He commented: "There's a *massive* difference between all of them. Each sport has different sorts of discipline."

One of the things I really loved about kickboxing, as well as being able to use a variety of limbs, was the fact that I was totally self-reliant, so I sank or swam by my own efforts. But in football, if other players are having a bad day, the whole team might lose. I could never be part of that.

Wayne's fellow boxer, Frankie Gavin, feels the same. "There's a big difference: you can blame somebody else if you're losing; with boxing it's you and only you who is there to take the blame. If somebody else was having a bad day and we lost the game, I think I'd have a go at them, because if somebody stopped me from winning, unless they beat me on their own, I wouldn't be happy."

Martial arts expert Bob Sykes agrees: "I didn't like the responsibility of letting members of a team down, thereby letting *yourself* down."

According to bodybuilding champion, Dorian Yates, "It never crossed my mind that I wouldn't succeed. It was that 'do or die' desperation. That's the kind of drive that you need to have in order to be really successful, in any field, or business. I wanted to be the British Champion, then Mr Olympia; then I wanted to see how far I could go with this. I didn't want to be an old man, sitting in my rocking chair, thinking that I could have done a bit better. The only thing is that if I hadn't tried so hard, maybe I would have avoided a few of the injuries.

"Nowadays it's quite common to have a coach and a nutritionist, but in those days you didn't and that wouldn't have fitted in with my personality anyway – that's why I'm not a team sports player," continues Dorian. "I listen to people who I respect, but then decide for myself what works for me and what doesn't.

"In team sports you have people to support you, but if you're going in the gym you just do your own thing without any competition around you. Also, bodybuilding and martial arts are what I would call the 'Cinderella Sports'. The guys put in a lot of effort and dedication, but the rewards didn't really reflect that, although it's better now. In Mixed Martial Arts now the prize money is quite substantial.

"Kickboxing seems to be the most poorly paid of all the martial arts, at least in the UK. But you've got K1 in Japan: that's just kickboxing, not martial arts. The prize money there goes to several hundred thousand or so. There is no real professional bodybuilding in the UK. If I hadn't gone to America to compete then I wouldn't have a career," Dorian observes.

According to Cyrille Regis, "Another thing about football, which is different from Kash's sport, is that football is subjective. It's somebody's opinion, in terms of how you're rated, whereas Kash doesn't have that problem. Football's subjective in the sense that you have to appeal to a person. It's not a given that every manager or coach likes a player."

In fact, some of the most talented players have reputations for being quite difficult to manage, because of their independent spirit.

"Well yes – that's their 'character'," Cyrille points out. "Sometimes managers don't mind a bit of character. As a player it's a case of whether you fit the coach and manager's philosophy and his tactics: do you fit into the way that he wants to play football? Have you got the qualities that they are looking for? Do you fit in as a player? Are you fit enough, big enough, strong enough? Have you got enough football intelligence, to understand the game? So it *is* subjective; as a player you rely on the coach and manager to put you in the side.

"Kash is him – putting *himself* in the ring. He either wins or he loses; he doesn't care how he does it, although he can do it in a bad style or a good style. But there's not a third party, judging it."

I'm my *own* Third Party Cyrille! In a previous Round Kenny Cunningham described how players sometimes watch videos of opposing teams, analysing their tactics before a game.

"Yes, but that's more the manager's job and the coach's job, to analyse the situation and then pass the information on to us," observes Cyrille. "In my case I wasn't playing against their striker. As a centre forward I'd be playing against their defence, so it would be much more focused on what the defenders were like: are they slow; are they big; left-footed or right-footed? But then for ten or fifteen minutes you'd work it out within yourself, as a player, anyway.

"You can't be a centre forward without the personality for scoring goals; you need aggression and all those things, to be a footballer," Cyrille continues. "My special talents were Power and Pace; as a striker you need something extra to give you an 'edge'.

"Around the age of twelve or thirteen I found my position, as a goal scorer. There are good footballers, who never find their position, which will take its toll in later life, because you have to be good at one position, or else you can't focus your energy on it. Actual talent is a small part, of what makes a person; the rest is the mind and the emotion and Kash has bags and bags of that. There are loads of kickboxers around; there are better players around, but they don't always have the emotion and the motivation to take them to those heights."

Paul Clifton, the Martial Arts Magazines entrepreneur, described Kash as a 'Warrior Fighter', because he would pursue his goal, no matter what.

"Yes, that's his inner personality; not everybody's got that," continues Cyrille. "I see this all the time in football. Someone might have the *talent*; there are loads of players who have that. But if they haven't got the 'character', or they don't have enough love for the game, or they're enticed by 'wine, women and song'…"

Do you think the vast sums of money that can be earned in football can affect the quality of a player's performance too? This doesn't apply so much to kickboxing, because in this country, it's not well paid.

A friend of mine who's been an avid football fan for many years was comparing this year's England World Cup Team, with the team that won in 1966. In his opinion, it's become so money-orientated that the love of the game and total commitment to winning, which the 1966 team had in spades, has faded away. Added to which there's the fear of being injured during the World Cup, which might put a player's future livelihood in jeopardy.

"I don't really think it's the money," replies Cyrille. "The top players don't change. David Beckham, for example, is worth 180 million pounds. Once you get beyond a certain figure, the money becomes irrelevant. The players, intrinsically, are still the same. The majority of players *want* to maximise who they are as a footballer. Money is part of it, but it's not the 'be-all-and-end-all' of everything, because if you focus on the money, you won't realise your full potential. You've got to focus on 'I want to be the best that my talent can afford me to be.'

"Football is a more complex process – it's a team sport. I could study my defender who's playing against me and try to work it out, but if no one gets near the ball, if the ball's not coming to me, then all of that doesn't really matter.

"We've already talked about the character, the love, the attitude; the desire and sacrifice needed, to reach the top in any sport. I think kickboxing is more brutal and bloody. It's a single man sport and you have a totally different mindset than with a group sport. You love a single sport and you're good at it.

"To be good at a single event sport you have to be single-minded," Cyrille continues. "I've never tried the Martial Arts myself, although I used to watch Bruce Lee, when I was a kid. My friends used to go to Kung Fu classes, but it never gripped me. It was always football."

We asked Joe Egan for his views on the differences between the skills needed as a boxer and a kickboxer.

"Well, although I've got strong legs, I'm not much good at using them; with kickboxing you've not only got to be good with your fists, but you've got to be able to kick *and* keep your balance. It's a complicated sport.

"When Ricky Hatton tells his stories on stage, he says: 'I started my career as a kickboxer and tried to get close to my opponents, but because I've got such short legs I couldn't get near them to kick them!'

"That's one of the reasons why Kash has such a good advantage, because he's got such long legs," continues Joe. "It's a lot more difficult to block kicks *and* punches. It's difficult to put into words, but you've got to be more flexible.

"You look as some of the footballers, as they come out of the tunnel. You've got eleven men, all laughing, handshaking and everything else. It's nice to see, it's a sport. But you look at a boxer as he steps into the arena, he has his trainers and his corner men, but it's totally different, because really he's on his own – and totally focused.

"That walk to the ring, to me, is the hardest walk than anything you might ever have to do," Joe reveals. "There's a video called *Champions for Ever*; if you get the chance watch it. There are five great world champions in it, George Foreman, Joe Frazier, Muhammad Ali, Larry Holmes and Ken Norton, talking about their experiences, boxing each other. George Foreman talks about boxing Ken Norton. George is one of the greatest heavyweight champions of all time. He said he's looking across at this fine specimen of a man, because Ken had a fantastic physique. They walk to the centre of the ring, eye-balling each other. But George was hoping that Ken didn't look down, because his knees were shaking! People that don't fight don't understand what's involved."

No disrespect to wrestling intended, because there have been some great champions, but there's always been this innuendo about some of the matches being, allegedly, fixed, although very few wrestlers would ever admit to it. In kickboxing there's no predetermined outcome, other than the fact that some of them have the advantage of better coaches than others.

"Yes, some of the wrestling is stage-managed, but they're great athletes, I'd take nothing away from them," comments Joe. "Full contact sports are the hardest sports in the world. I'm biased because I'm a boxer, but anything where you're getting hit: full contact. It doesn't matter how hard you train, if you leave yourself open, you're going to get hurt. Training helps, because you can absorb more punishment, the fitter you are.

"It *is* savage, boxing and kickboxing: they're modern-day gladiators. The first Olympic Sport was boxing. The Greeks in Athens – that was their first sport. Years ago, in gladiatorial events, men died. They died in the boxing ring tragically too. But in the gladiatorial arena, the objective was to kill your opponent. When you got your opponent to the ground the crowd would decide whether he lived or died – thumbs up or thumbs down.

"Modern-day fighting doesn't include that killing savagery, but there's still controlled violence," continues Joe. "People want to see it because fighters are a breed alone. It has to be in you. You cannot take a child and say: 'We want to give you the courage to become a fighter.' That child has to have the courage in him, from the day he's born. Sometimes it's in your genes; sometimes it's in your own mentality, depending upon your circumstances."

While my friends were going out to clubs and so forth, I simply focused on my training Joe.

"Yes, that's why you became so successful, because of the sacrifices you made. But when you are part of a team you could be the most dedicated, but the other ten on the football team could be Party Animals, slovenly and not performing well. My dad used to say: 'The biggest fool is the fool that fools himself!' If you pretend that you're putting all your effort in, in the gym and you pretend that you're going to run hard today, you'll be found wanting in the fight. One of my trainers used to say: 'If you don't put it in, in the gym you won't have the stamina to win the match.'"

Shirley interviewed one of my former fighters, Simon Akufo, on the Sunday evening in 2010 when he'd just won the European Welterweight

Competition. Simon said that the difference between his success at that point compared to previously was that he's been training with me for about twelve years, and reached a stage when he thought he was fit enough; but he hadn't actually achieved the level of success that he'd hoped for. So I said: "Right, you've got to give up your social life now and just focus on your training." And that seems to have made the difference.

"Yes, you have to, otherwise you're going to be an 'also ran'," agrees Joe. "But if you've got the potential to be a champion, it's a shame not to fulfil it, because you haven't made enough sacrifices. I've seen it with so many boxers.

"Now my younger brother, Emmet, was Irish Amateur Boxing Champion; he could punch naturally; he was super fit. But he just wanted to do his running. He became a champion in the 1500 metres and the 800 metres sprint. Emmet had so much potential in the boxing, but he didn't want to hurt people.

"Fighters are a different breed of person and there are various things that drive them on. We strive for greatness for different reasons. Every boy wants to impress his dad, so if you're a fighter you want to impress him with your fighting. My mother never wanted me to box, but she would encourage me in whatever I was doing," concludes Joe.

As a professional footballer David Dunn trains Monday to Friday, followed by the game on a Saturday.

"We do a couple of hours a day but we do go on the pads now and again: mainly in the pre-season," explains David. "A lot of our training is technical stuff and tactical work. We do full fitness work at the start of the years and then we get ourselves as fit as we can. It's not like a fighter where you've got to build up and get yourself to your peak fitness, ready for a fight. We've got to maintain a constant fitness, all the way through. Whereas a boxer and kickboxer has got to peak at the right time – and get the right weight and whatnot.

"In an individual sport you've got to be that much more focused because you make a mistake and you *will* pay for it," Dave continues. "Whereas if I make a mistake on a football pitch, I've got maybe four or five people behind me, who can get the ball back."

Gamma observes: "What Kash *did* have was that he was very brave: even when he was badly hurt, he carried on; you'll see that on some of the videos.

That toughness goes back to our Sikh philosophy, which originated hundreds of years ago – there's a long history to it. It's like the Ghurkhas – they're warriors.

"It's pride but it's also when you cross the line and say: 'Well I don't care now if I get knocked out!' It's bravery, knowing that you'll continue no matter what," Gamma continues. "So where many fighters would decide to call it a day, once a fight gets really tough, something inside of Kash says, 'No, this is it now – no matter what happens!' That's not enough on its own of course – you've got to have the skill and the experience too, to hold it together.

"One of the things that I like about kickboxers," continues Gamma, "is that they're very humble; they're nice people. To go into the ring is one helluva thing to do, if you think about it... I couldn't do it!"

For whatever reason Gamma, I've always felt that I had to rely on myself and therefore needed to do everything myself. It can be a lonely existence, because it builds up tension within you, which needs to be released.

According to our oldest brother, Resham, most of our family are quite open about sharing our feelings. Daljit said that Cougar's quite an emotional sort of person; for example, he was crying when we were talking about our mom. He's also very family-orientated. But in my case, the reliability aspect is the thing; even in my sport I've never relied on anyone.

I prefer a solo sport like that, because it was my own determination that helped me to be successful. I trained very hard and was extremely dedicated. There aren't many people like me, to this day. I wanted to be the best and I wanted to stay my best, so I held my world title for eleven years. Thirteen or fourteen years is the record in boxing, but I've been in fighting for almost three decades: there are very few fighters who will do that.

My sport depends on the individual; I'm a very independent guy anyway. But as Dave Barnett points out, when you are injured and have to get yourself back to fitness it then becomes a solo effort.

"Football is both team and individual," Dave explains. "When you play the game you're working together, but you have your own particular position to bring the ball in, within the team system: that's a 'given'. But there are so many aspects that are individualistic. So the mental capacity to become a footballer is individualistic. You have be very talented at a physical level, but 70% of being a professional sports person is mental: can you discipline yourself not to go out late at night, so that you're training the next day? Can you be disciplined enough to say no, to some of the temptations along the way – drugs, women, alcohol? Can you respond positively to your coach and listen to what he's got to say, even though you might not agree with him, i.e. having the right attitude? Are you going to be able to socialise with your team mates, even though you might not be the best of mates?

"You have to get rid of some of the less mature attitudes that Cyrille's brother, Dave Regis and I had in our younger days, in order to become a better player. Generally speaking, players would rather break a leg, than snap an Achilles tendon," Dave Barnett continues.

"Now I snapped my tendon, so I had to use a great deal of determination to get through that. I'd inherited a lot of that determination from seeing my mother working very hard and being focused, while I was growing up. But also you draw upon your own experience and training. I had to get up at 5 o'clock in the morning; walk to the swimming baths; train there for two hours in the baths; walk back; then go into Birmingham City; do training for two sessions of two hours; back to the swimming baths in the evening, then get home at 9 o'clock at night!

"I had to do that for four months, for rehabilitation. But half way through my four months I ripped my Achilles again in an accident in a health club. So I had to go through the whole thing again! Kash put me through the training in the gym during this time – he was there for me when I needed help. Robert Codner, Peter Shearer and Simon were injured as well, so there were the four or five of us who went down to the gym for these vigorous training sessions.

"So the 'bonding' in team sports is a great help," observes Dave. "It inspires you to get up in the morning, to work with people you enjoy working with and to all have this desire to have fun, while you're working hard. Kash's sport is somewhat of a 'loner' experience."

Kenny Cunningham agrees: "Being in a team with the team dynamic is something that *is* very rewarding. You're depending on each other and yeah – you have those days when people underperform, but on the days when everyone's performing to their maximum ability then you end up achieving something as a team.

"My initial football training was just on a high volume: running back from school, then grabbing your training bag, between the ages of fourteen to eighteen; up until I went away. I pretty much trained every day of the week and played football on the weekends. I couldn't afford a gym, at that time. That's probably more rewarding than maybe on an individual basis. But I can understand where Kash is coming from."

Even though I've got a gregarious, sociable side to my nature, there's this other side of me Kenny, which prefers to be self-sufficient.

"Is that right? That's very interesting because you'll always come over and make yourself available – have a conversation with people."

As you prefer to be part of a team sport, it must be great for you to have been a professional footballer Kenny.

"Yes it is, without a doubt – I was very fortunate in that respect. In 1988 I played for two Dublin teams, Tolka Rovers and Home Farm, and then in that same year I had a trial with Millwall: it was only a one-year professional contract; there was no guarantee. But if it hadn't worked out in England I would have gone back to college in Dublin and gone down that particular avenue. But I got another contract with Millwall on the back of the first one and things took off after that.

"It's a bit like Kash I suppose: he's stuck to the one profession too," continues Kenny. "I stayed with Millwall until 1994, followed by Wimbledon, 1994-2002. Once you sign a professional contract, you pretty much dedicate yourself to one particular sport. Everything else gets pushed to one side; that's the way it has to be."

Did you have a Mentor over in Ireland, during those earlier years, who guided you?

"When I got into professional football, over here in England, Sports Science was in its infancy, so the onus was on the individual, to educate himself. Nowadays young sportsmen are fortunate that there are qualified people to give them that advice – there's no excuse for getting it wrong now!

"It's quite technical too, especially with Sports Science Degrees and the Hi –Tech world we're living in. For top level sports that's what it's all about... those very small margins which, when added together, give you that significant advantage over your opponent," observes Kenny.

According to Andy Walker, "As it's historical, I think kickboxing will be able to out-muscle ordinary boxing in British Sport. Abroad in some countries kickboxing is already the king, but certainly in Britain, *boxing* has always been. However, I've always found kickboxing to be more entertaining, because often, highly-billed boxing fights can just turn into two men pushing each other, for the duration of the fight. At least kickboxing gives you ways out of it!

"Closing this round on a sport that differs somewhat from kickboxing, football and boxing, the first time I witnessed Muay Thai was at a recent event in 2010, at the *Second City Suite* in Digbeth. I took a friend along with me who was actually into martial arts and knew about Muay Thai," explains Andy.

"There are certain rituals and costumes to it. The most distinctive thing is that a steady beat is played with the fight – a rhythm alongside it. That's a huge, massive sport, in the Far East. You wear a headband, called a 'mongcon', almost like straw: it's coloured. They take that off before they fight, otherwise there'd be a few lost eyeballs! So they wear a special costume and they also sit down on their hands and knees and speak a prayer before they fight. Both fighters do that at the same time, when it's done properly," Andy concludes.

Round 12

FLASH, BANG, WALLOP!

We begin this Round with Kash's two attempts at the World Thai Boxing Title, followed by his four successful World Title fights, together with subsequent fights where he was defending his title. A selection of additional fights, which were not for a World Title, can be found in Round 15.

Kash progresses through from Midland Champion, British Champion; European Champion, World Amateur Champion; World Professional Champion and eventually becomes a sports icon. His weight fluctuates between 10 stone 12 to 11 stone 6.

The first World Championship that he wins is in 1991, at the Aston Villa Leisure Centre, Birmingham, against Alex Tui, from Australia, in the Junior Middleweight division. Alex Tui and Howard Brown give their accounts of the fight.

A few months later, Kash wins his second World Championship, at the NEC. A Super Welterweight contest against Ronnie Deleon of Texas.

World Championship 3 is in 1992, in Liege, Belgium, against Bern Grau. Kash goes up to Middleweight.

Kash wins World Championship Title 4, in 1993, for ISKA, International Sports Kickboxing Association, becoming the undisputed champion, in the Light Middleweight division.

This is about the late 1980s and early 90s, by which time I'd already had a few Thai Boxing matches. Master Toddy had a big show over in London at Pickett's Lock; all the best fighters were there.

Normally I'm out running every night, but at that time I wouldn't take Thai Boxing seriously... but you live and learn!

'Superman' Osodsapa, as he's known as in Thailand, is 6 foot 1, which is very rare for a Thai: they're mostly 5 foot 2 or 5 foot 3. Superman was the Asian Games Gold Medallist Boxing Champion. It was live on TV over in Thailand as well. Master Toddy described this fight in a previous round. In the 1990s, the top Thais, like Superman, were very good fighters. I wish I had trained harder, because I would probably be the World Thai Boxing Champion!

I made a big name for myself in Thailand, because we continued for five hard-fought rounds. Superman dropped me after about 30 seconds and won the first two rounds, but the next three rounds were so exciting as I came back at him. If only I'd been fitter. Most observers thought I'd won the fight, but getting dropped early on was a decisive factor.

I was subsequently invited to go out to Thailand for six months, but I didn't have the time, due to my commitments here. The Thai mentality is that of a warrior... and I was a warrior. Had I gone, I would probably have performed at one of the main stadiums in Thailand – the *Rajerdamm Centre*. Looking back, I wish I *had* done six months here and six months there. My life would have been totally different.

My other Thai fight was against Jomhod Kitiasongrit, one of the biggest names. People still talk about him to this day, twenty or thirty years later. I fought him at his peak, when he had 285 fights behind him. I remember that fight well. It was at the *Aston Villa Leisure Centre* in my home town of Birmingham.

Before that fight, my friend Rob drove us up in a little Fiat Punto. We reached the stadium and parked next to Nigel Benn's Porsche, which was really comical! I took a big gulp of brandy, before leaving my house. Normally I would never do that. I said: "I'm going to have a sip of this Rob – a bit of 'Dutch Courage'" If my lads did that now I'd be so mad with them!

So we brought in another big name, another big crowd. Sunday afternoon, again, live on Thailand TV. People were still fighting Jomhod in 2009, but I fought him at his peak. He's an old man now. We fought five three-minute rounds. I went the distance, but didn't fight that brilliantly because fitness let me down. Again, it was experience for 'The Flash'.

Vinny McGrath was another tough fight. It was five three-minute rounds. My shins were really sore, because I'd just come back from a fight in Europe, but I won on points.

I won my first *Amateur* World Title in France. That was the start of my career. I remember it well. In 1986, Mike Tyson won his World Title against Trevor Berbick, in the first round. Mike and I are a similar age; just one or two days difference. I became the World Amateur Champion after winning four fights in one day! That same year I won the European Amateur Title and then I won the British Professional Title. So 1986 was a fantastic year for me.

Then in 1991 I said to my family: "Right – you can come and watch my fight," the first time that they were sitting at the front watching me.

I hate losing. It's very disappointing I go very quiet for three or four days – I don't talk. That applies to everything that I do. If we had a game of Monopoly I'd be going for the cash!

I've got such a career to talk about! Let's take a closer look now at that first World Title Fight, against Alex Tui, in 1991, at the *Aston Villa Leisure Centre*. It was the first World Championship that I won. Alex was a bit of an unknown quantity; what a tough fight that was! My weight then was 11 stone 2, which is 71kg.

It was classed as a *Junior Middleweight* division. I don't like that title, because it implies that we were under a certain age, but we weren't, it's just related to our weight. We were both exactly the same weight: you have to be, to fight for the title. I came in far too light, at 10 stone 12, so I was 4 pounds under weight, which is a lot; Alex Tui was bang on, 71kg. But I knocked him out in Round 6.

Alex has kindly sent us the following account of events, from his home on the other side of the world! We're just putting speech marks at the beginning and end of his letter:

"I'm of Tongan heritage, born in Australia, brought up in Tonga, then did High School in New Zealand. Began kickboxing in New Zealand in 1980. Lost my first fight but that started it. I wanted to do better.

I moved to Sydney, Australia and continued at Jin Wu Kwoon with Chan Cheuk Fai, where kickboxing started to grow. Started winning local titles, then national, South Pacific and Commonwealth, through the 1980s.

When offered a shot at the WKA Middleweight Title in early 1991 it was a surprise but an exciting challenge. Stopped by Kash, but then in a return fight, three months or so later in Sydney it was great to win against Kash in front of my home crowd.

I first met Kash in Birmingham in 1991 when we went over. He was very tall! He looked relaxed and confident. I knew I was in for a hard night.

The World Title Fight between the two of us, at the *Aston Villa Leisure Centre*, in 1991:

I was glad to get in the ring. The rest of the week I was in this cold, overcast and unfamiliar environment, where I never once saw the blue sky! It was hard to get my measure because of his unusually long reach. Where I thought I was out of range he tagged me! My effectiveness was getting in close, but it was getting in there... and out safely! I always went in to win – which was to do my best, so I always won!

The reasons for his becoming a four times World Champion are that he used his height well. He had good leverage and used that better than most tall fighters. He obviously doesn't mind a hard physical challenge and looked after and prepared himself well enough.

I live in Redfern, Sydney Australia. In the same address since I went to fight Kash in England in '91. I live in the 'capital' of Aboriginal Australia, a small neighbourhood called 'The Block'. I'm married with seven kids, plus a fostered nephew.

Have been doing the same job since '91, which is managing the local neighbourhood's Health Centre and Boxing Gym. I live across the same street as the Gym. Our Gym is named after Aboriginal Boxing Great Tony Mundine Senior, of the 1970s. Today his son Anthony Mundine trains here. He is already a multiple Boxing world champ with I think more yet to show.

After both our matches in '91, in Birmingham then later in Sydney, Kash and I had a good laugh, not to mention a good drink, at after-match parties, so I learnt that he had a similar basic attitude – train and fight hard then party hard, because at the end of the day it was only a sport. I didn't make heaps of money from fighting in my day. I enjoyed my sport and I think for me it was the same way I took to my rugby days in New Zealand at school, and briefly at club level.

I defended my title four times after winning the match with Kash, then retired in '94. Came back to the game in '96 for three kickboxing fights, two of which I lost; then for three K1 Max fights with two losses and one win, and then finally giving way in 2002. During my kickboxing career I also did some boxing, fighting professionally from 1983 to 1994. I had twenty-five fights winning and losing about half of that. That's how punching became my weapon to watch, which Kash survived – the first time! Cheers, Alex."

Thanks Alex. Howard Brown was my coach for most of my fights abroad.

"Yes, we went to Australia, the former Yugoslavia; we went to France, to Holland," Howard remembers. "Kash's rivalry with Alex Tui of Australia was absolutely terrific! What a fighter! Alex was trained by one of the greatest Thai Boxers ever known in the history of the sport, called Sakad Petchindee, pronounced 'Sagat'. He's a really fun guy... one of the greatest Thai Boxers;

his speciality is punching. He went into boxing afterwards and did really well, but he had to pull out, with a detached retina."

Just before the Alex Tui fight, Howard was on BBC *Midlands Today*. He said: "I think Kash will be one of the most famous kickboxers." The reason for that was that I would be recognized by a lot of people because I'm Asian. Asians never seemed to be in the fight game: they tended to be lawyers, doctors and so on. Looking back at Howard's interview, it's only now that we're doing the book that I realize that he was right. Being 6 foot 3 and a good-looking guy... and modest!

Paul Clifton comments: "If you tell anyone that they're great lots and lots of times and if that person keeps winning, there can be a downside. Tyson's probably a great analogy, but on a much bigger scale; probably not in terms of finances, but exactly the same in terms of that point in their lives and times. Kash appeared to become very arrogant, about certain issues and things. I think it took a little while to get through that; at least a year to eighteen months.

"It happened when he got the first championship," continues Paul. "It was kind of new, which is understandable; everybody adored him: he was fantastic, a champ and a winner. Then he won his second fight, which was more difficult. Again, because he was good at what he did, he started to believe in himself. Having been around a lot of fighters, over the years, it's the same pattern.

"But if everyone keeps telling you: 'Oh you're fantastic – you're a great fighter,' you start to believe your own publicity. And gradually you become 'a legend in your own lifetime'! It wasn't just Kash; everybody goes through the same experience, at that level. If people keep telling you that you're brilliant, fantastic and a winner, you develop that psychology – that mentality. By the same token you have to give credit to Kash as he made it! He put in the effort. He put his personal life on hold to be able to acquire the skills and ability to be a CHAMPION! You also have to understand that it is ESSENTIAL for a fighter to have huge confidence in himself, as without it he would have to enter the ring with defeat in his heart; it's a bi-product of the skill set needed to be a CHAMPION."

I'd have to disagree with you on that Paul. I've never become big-headed, I emphasise that to my own fighters too. So your comment about 'a legend in your own lifetime' is quite comical! I certainly became more *confident* in my fighting methods as I progressed, but my personality, as far as I'm aware, has always remained the same.

I don't think my sister Binda actually saw any of my fights live, because she was in Germany; she just watched them on video later. Resham didn't see my first three fights. When I fought for that first Professional World Championship against Alex Tui, Resham was in Scotland. I didn't want any of the family to watch me until I actually won something, but as Tom Ross confirms, some of my brothers ignored that agreement!

According to Resham, "My brothers went along and supported Kash. I remember being on the phone, to make sure that he hadn't been injured, but then I was highly elated when he won the World Championship. As part of his marketing Kash often did exhibition shows, with his students demonstrating their talents, in a shopping centre or a park, so I would go along and I'd usually be the MC."

When I won that first World Title, back in 1991, my dad arranged a party for me. He got all my friends down to watch my fight and we had a celebration there. Gurmej would bring at least thirty Asian friends to the fight, because I became a kind of legend amongst the Asians. He was very proud of me, but he would never show it, although after the fight he would give me £50, or £100, which was a lot of money. Dad was sometimes quite reserved, but he liked his beer and his whisky. If he'd had a drink, obviously he'd be more candid about his feelings.

I brought the Bhangra band in for that Alex Tui fight. It was a great experience to win the title in my home town of Birmingham. That was held at *Aston Villa Leisure Centre*, now known as the *Aston Events Arena*. David Webb and his wife were amongst my special guests.

The second World Championship that I won was later on, in 1991. I remember it well, because I went the full twelve rounds. It was at the *NEC*. Again I was 10 stone 12, which is only just above, which is the *Super Welterweight* division – kicks above the waist – still full contact. It was a full programme with Ronnie Deleon of Texas.

It was a Martial Arts Extravaganza: all the big names were there, including Americans. I stayed at the *Hyatt* and fought Ronnie, who was a Mexican. When he arrived he said: "Is that Kash Gill over there?" He looked me over... I was very skinny. He said: "I won't even need a stool!" meaning that he would knock me out in the first round.

However, we went the full twelve rounds. Luckily for him, the regulations didn't allow me to use leg kicks on him; otherwise I might have stopped him. But we went the distance and I won it unanimously. So that was my second World Title.

The third World Championship that I won was in 1992, in Belgium, against Bern Grau, I went up to *Middleweight*, which is 11 stone 6 – 72.5kg. I knocked Bern out in Round 6. He'd been over to England before and beaten someone else, so he was a dangerous fighter. And again, we were both a similar weight.

I moved out of Handsworth in 1993, because I was planning to get married and have kids so I wanted a change of environment.

My last World Title fight was in 1993, which was for ISKA, the International Sport Kickboxing Association, and I became the undisputed champion. I was 11 stone 3 pounds, which was the *Light Middleweight* division.

I fought Jules Evoule of France. He was a replacement for Frank Van Hoove, at only a week's notice, but he'd never been stopped before. We went twelve rounds. That was my fourth World Title Fight, again, at the *Aston Villa Leisure Centre*. In each of my championship fights I was fighting at a different weight. I fought at anything between 10 stone 12 to 11 stone 12, because I went up and down in weight.

For my first title I was at my lightest and I gradually progressed to heavier weights, as the number of title fights increased. I started off light, but was that same weight when I finished my career, so that shows that I could fluctuate between any division.

I fought a guy over in Germany. He was a 76kg. I was only 71kg. Going the distance with those guys takes some doing, because of the weight division. I'd got my height and reach, which helped, plus my experience. I was a warrior and a survivor!

Going back to 1993, Cobra Cole was very arrogant. The fight, which was a World Middleweight Title Defence, was billed on Sky Sports. I remember it well because Julie and me spent four months apart. We weren't married at the time.

So I just trained as hard as I could… I was like a man possessed! And I won the match, which was on a big stage at *Aston Villa Leisure Centre*. Julie phoned me at my hotel and said that she still loved me. I have an article that describes how many million people saw the fight, around the world, because it came on *Transworld Sport* as well, which covers Saturday mornings. My opponents often became best friends after we'd fought. Mike was the exception.

Apart from one fight in Kurdistan, in 1996 I took a year off, and then in 1997 I was offered a Light Middleweight World Title Defence fight, in South Africa. That was three years after the World Title fight, so I needed a big name. I weighed 70kg. My opponent had to go running beforehand, to lose an extra 6 kilos.

It took place in a Johannesburg shopping centre. They pulled the wool over our eyes. I thought I'd won it. I dropped him a couple of times, but unfortunately it was biased. It was screened live on TV in South Africa as well and he got the decision. In my opinion, they 'scammed' us. It went the full twelve rounds. I lost on points, but we didn't witness the weight loss weigh-in before the match, so we had no proof that he'd actually lost those 6 kilos.

I was really disappointed but came back in 2000 and fought Jean Louis Lacene. Went ten hard tough rounds. I remember sitting down, about Round Five, thinking: 'Why am I doing this?' But the hunger struck back in and I managed to win that fight unanimously.

Another fight was against Conference Johnson from South Africa. We went two rounds. I won that match. We went to a nightclub and he came to my house and we had drinks after that. He died very recently, with heart failure. I was really saddened by that because he was a lovely guy. He was probably about thirty-eight when he died but he fought me when he was at his peak.

I first met Tom Ross when he did the commentary for my first World Title, against Alex Tui, at the *Aston Villa Leisure Centre*, in 1991. Apparently, Tom still has videos of all the fights and recalls the pre-fight interviews with me, before the match:

"I remember him being unusually nervous," recalls Tom. "I've hosted two years of kickboxing programmes for Sky TV, as well as lots of Kickboxing interviews for the World Kickboxing Association. Unlike all the other fighters that I've interviewed Kash's family were always close at hand and I remember thinking: 'what a close family they are.' It's a bit like my own family, because if you take one on my brothers you take us all on. Kash's brothers were just the same, if you kicked one, they all limped."

On the subject of being nervous Tom, going into the fight and in the changing rooms, you feel as if you've got no strength or energy. It's nervous energy, but you feel like going to bed! When you walk to the ring it's *so* nerve-wracking. Even if you're as fit as anything and the Bhangra band are playing. But once that bell goes, the nerves just disappear! It's the same every time. I would say that if you don't have nerves there's something wrong. You can't do anything about it, but I think it's good for the lads to have that feeling; it's not being over-confident, as well.

"Kash was such a nice guy," continues Tom. "My first impression was 'You're too nice to be a World Champion!' You've got to be aggressive; you've got to be a bit nasty and he didn't come across as that. But I remember when the bell went, it was almost as if it switched him on; he became a different character.

"He epitomises what kickboxing should be like. Inside the ring you can be aggressive as you like, but outside the ring you're back to normal. He was a true 'warrior' for me, because he had that ability to turn on and off. He was a considerate man for his opponent as well. He knew that everybody he fought, whether he won, lost or drew, was a warrior, and treated them with respect and dignity. When the bell went he wanted to knock them out!"

Tom refers to that dignity in kickboxing in his article, in Kash's *Judgement Night* booklet, published 2008, comparing kickboxing with other sports.

'Kickboxing, like boxing, teaches you discipline; it gives you great confidence, a direction. Kash's technical ability is second to none,' wrote Tom. 'He can fight at different *weights*, which is amazing: he won world titles at different weights.'

"Kash's height, reach and leg length were a great advantage for him," Tom continues. "But you don't *do* what Kash did in kickboxing without having the utmost dedication – and I'm talking about dedicating his *life* to it. And I knew that. He treated his body properly and trained as hard as any athlete in any sport.

"The people who went on to become mentors, like Howard Brown, were fighting at the time, so you hadn't got that," Tom continues. "He's a great man, Howard. But the ring is the biggest lie detector in the world! You can kid your coach, you can kid your trainer, and you can kid yourself: I've done my road work, I've done everything – but the ring is the lie detector – it will find you out.

"But Kash *did* work and was properly prepared, every time that he went into the ring. As a result, he won't let anybody get into the ring who isn't properly prepared, which isn't true of *all* promoters and managers."

How would you assess the effect the film industry has had on kickboxing and the Martial Arts in general Tom?

"With Bruce Lee, they were always big, but when I was doing shows for Sky TV, on a couple of them my co-commentator, was Cynthia Rothrock, who was China O'Brien, in all the Kung Fu movies. She sat next to me and we did the fights together. She was sensational as China O'Brien. She was wonderful. She was a Kung Fu Champion, and was in loads of films and a top actor," Tom observes.

"But she wasn't an actor when it came to Martial Arts: she was a World Champion herself. And she was gorgeous as well – which helped!

"Paul Ingram and Kash brought this quality of people into kickboxing; from being a nothing sport, it was capturing the imagination and attention. They made that happen," concludes Tom, "because they brought a glamour and glitz to it – they made kickboxing sexy."

Cynthia came to a couple of my fights. She came over to the *NEC*, back in 1993 and gave an Exhibition there. Paul Ingram the President of the WKA invited her over, paid her air fare and probably paid her to perform. Paul was my co-promoter; he promoted some of my fights.

Obviously, that must have brought in at least one per cent of the crowd! She was well known in the movie industry. So who better to commentate with Tom Ross… it worked out really well.

NO FLASH IN THE PAN

Success did not come easily to Kash: conditions and training methods were primitive when he first began his career. Unlike today there was very little advice or expertise available for him to draw upon. Coming from the inner city, he couldn't afford smart sports equipment and training facilities. So conditions were tough, for many years.

In this Round we consider some of the problems that Kash encountered as an individual, followed by the decline of the Muhammad Ali Centre, which was a retrograde step for the Handsworth community where Kash grew up.

According to Gamma, "As Kash came towards the end of his career there were a couple of fights that I didn't go to. Partly, because of work commitments, but, although it's a hard thing to say, I think that he should have retired earlier than he did."

When Shirley interviewed Howard Brown, he said a similar thing. He was concerned that I might be suffering from delayed after-effects of the fighting; there can be a delayed action, for some time, before the signs become apparent. Although the two of us fell out over that, Howard said that he took that stance for my own good. However, to this day, I'm not aware of any after-effects.

Gamma points out, "I think only a fighter can make that decision, although we all hinted at it. But for me it was a relief when Kash retired. He said that he was going to, at one time, but then he came back again, after about eighteen months. That was probably about nine years ago. I can go to one of his shows now and enjoy it, because it's not my brother in the ring!"

Becoming a World Champion, in one of the toughest kickboxing eras between the 80s and the 90s, meant being a trailblazer. I fought for the love of the sport. And I still feel passionately about it now. I suppose you do need money to live – and all the time you're putting into it, you need some rewards. But one day it will come.

Howard Brown and myself eventually parted company, as my coach and trainer, in the 1990s. According to Howard: "I was busy doing other things... I was Head Coach of the World Kickboxing Association. Kash had a couple of tough fights. He was already a Four Times World Champion, had won goodness knows how many amateur accolades – and he'd done enough.

"What got to him was that he had a really tough fight at the *Aston Villa Leisure Centre* against Austrian fighter, Ronnie Hinterseer. Kash won the fight, but he had to have oxygen after the fight, at the ringside; it was just too much for him," continues Howard.

"I'd been training Kash since he was fourteen and at the time of the fight I'm talking about he was in his late twenties; but he'd done everything. He was like a brother to me and before that, he was like a son to me, because of the age difference. I was just so cut up after that fight that I said: 'Kash you've done enough – how much more!?'

"He had nothing more to prove, at all. He was a legend. But fighters are the last ones to know when to call it a day, so he carried on – but without my approval.

"Even when I was sent to jail he was still fighting. Guys were telling me about him. But I just wasn't interested. We talked about it later. We didn't speak for a while, because there was a lot of Chinese Whispers. A guy called Bernard Chong asked me why I wasn't training Kash any more. I said: 'This is the fight game. He's young enough – I don't want him to fight any more.'

"To me, there were signs of Kash's speech being impaired already. And I could tell myself, without anyone else telling me, that my own short term memory was affected. I'm thinking: 'We don't need this.'

"Bernard Chong told Kash: 'Howard says he's not training you any more, because you're turning 'punch-drunk'!' I never said any such thing, but of course, Kash was offended by that... who wouldn't be? If you're punch-drunk you can't walk properly; it's very rare nowadays. I haven't seen that situation in kickboxing but I've heard rumours.

"Muhammad Ali is a good example of someone who was badly affected by boxing, but he's not punch-drunk, he's got Parkinson's disease; all the body shots had affected him. So I decided that I wasn't interested," Howard continues.

"Eventually, Kash came to visit me, when I was in Rye Hill. I said: 'Listen Kash, even I don't know if I've escaped all the punishment that we've taken over the years, because it doesn't manifest itself straight away. We can be in our fifties or sixties before it shows up. You've got to stop – and I can't be seen to be encouraging you. The other promoters can get you fights, but they haven't got you in their heart, like I have.'

"So that was it. It's not something that we speak about a lot. We're affected, but not to a great extent. Let's hope, fingers crossed, that it stays that way. Again, it's just one of those things that you have to go through. You go through every facet: you go through the start of the training; you compete; all the camaraderie. But at the end you have to face up to the negative side. And there's a lot of that, because what you miss is the buzz, the training and the excitement; the fear; getting prepared for the contest. And you miss the thrill of victory... *nothing* can replace that thrill.

"You finish your career and you think: 'Well, what now?' You've been in the limelight all those years and then suddenly you're just a normal person again. That's why fighters find it hard to stop. It's something that you get addicted to. That addiction is very hard to let go of," observes Howard.

I went to Kurdistan in 1996. Unlike my fighters nowadays I was unlucky. People had gyms but I had to travel around to different places; I was on my own a lot of the time so it was difficult. I'm a slow starter. The Kurdistan fight was an Open Air Event. During the time I was warming up Dev Barrett was elsewhere.

Once I was ready to go it started to rain, which was the last thing that I needed! There were forty thousand people watching. This was an actual football stadium so there were lots of celebrities there: Cynthia Rothrock was driving around the stadium in a pink Cadillac! She was interested in kickboxing because she's done a lot of Action Movies. But she's also a very pretty girl, so she's got a big fan club.

As far as the fight is concerned I was very unfortunate because the guy I was fighting, Mikel Bervoshot, had already had three hundred boxing fights: he knocked me out in two rounds! When you're knocked out your senses are gone. I remember going back to my dressing room and all the crowds coming in... and me giving things away. The following morning I'd got no shorts and T-shirts!

It's a very strange sensation. When you've won, it's very different to when you lose because then you're on a 'downer'. I'd told my coach, Dev Barrett, that I'd like to go on to India, but we hadn't actually arranged anything. It would have been the next stage, if I'd won.

Kurdistan was followed by South Africa, in 1997. The experience of it was fantastic! The promoter Joe Villahorn, said, "Do you want to stay at a hotel or would you prefer to stay on my ranch?" He was a hunter. He said: "If you stay at a hotel it will be like anywhere else in the world. But if you stay at my ranch you'll remember it for life!"

The drive to his ranch was about a mile, all open, in the middle of nowhere. Dev Barrett was my coach for this trip; he took me out there. There were no lights; we had to use candles!

It was really remote. I went in the room and you could actually hear the lions roaring outside. It was a fantastic experience. As he was a hunter there were lots of animals there. Thank God I don't sleepwalk!

It was just like a small house, with a bathroom, toilet and sink, but very dark. There were no animal skins or anything like that, but it was an experience that I'll never forget. Joe was OK, but he was promoting the show, so he wanted his fighter to win. But I normally get on with other trainers and coaches because I've got that kind of personality.

There were some really nice places around Europe. Of all the places in the world I particularly liked Australia and Hawaii, but I always said I wasn't going back to Australia, because of the flight distances: twice I flew thirty hours; twice I flew around twenty-four hours. In Round 15 there's more about my travels abroad.

I had to fight without having a sufficient gap to recover from travelling, so my preparation always let me down. Winning the World Title there was very important. I was on my own in the gyms over there, for much of the time. I got all the training in, but the sparring plays a big part in it – that was my downfall.

According to Paul Clifton, "Kash went through a childhood when he was sometimes picked upon, racially abused. This is probably controversial and it's only my *personal view*, but all of us are bullied, whether you're white, pink, green, whatever colour. There are many ways that this happens: psychological bullying, physical bullying; associate bullying by being part of a group that's not part of you, or befriending a group that won't have anything to do with you. But bullying is a part of character-building. That competitive situation is normal.

"I'm sure that Kash fell foul of horrible words like 'Pakki', 'Blackie', or a myriad of other pointless expletives that were/are used a tools to abuse and denigrate, in the confusion of the early eighties," continues Paul. "I don't mean to be controversial, but it is. When I was at school I was a bit of a 'Porker', so I used to get called 'Fatty'. Those are the things that I find, personally, help make and create people and leads to success in later life. By the same token there are people who fall foul of that and feel useless, incompetent and incapable, or grossly overweight and there's nothing you can do about it. The teacher used to say: 'It's not what's on the outside – it's what's on the *inside* that counts.'

"But Kash and Howard Brown and people like them, who come through the trials and tribulations of childhood, it's the making of their character," continues Paul. "Sometimes it teaches you to fight back, sometimes it will teach you to stand your ground and other times it teaches you to be a decent human being, in the face of adversity."

Not only has my sporting life presented me with difficulties, on an individual basis, but maintaining suitable sports venues within my home area is a major problem too. According to David Webb, "When Muhammad Ali was going to come to the *Muhammad Ali Centre* in Handsworth, one of the people I tried to get in on that was Kash.

"Progress was halted because the council wouldn't fund it, for a start," David continues. "We wanted to throw it open to the whole of the community; getting backing from several different organisations, like we did when the Centre was first put up. We need a committee with a chairman and other posts. At present, about four or five different organisations want it and are prepared to finance it, but they won't let anyone else come in."

That tallies with what freelance journalist Poppy Brady wrote. Her original article about the Centre was published in *The Voice* newspaper, on 15 June 2009, but then reissued two years later on the Internet, in *Voice Online*, as the subject became more topical. Poppy has become well known and respected by West Midlands' readers over the years and is a former sub-editor of the *Birmingham Mail*. We are most grateful to her for granting us permission to include extracts from the article, which also includes further comments from David Webb and Del and Hector Pinkney – see Round 19.

DEMISE: The run down venue today, by Poppy Brady:

'Why Birmingham residents are battling closure of the base opened by boxing legend Muhammad Ali

ASK ANYONE over 40 from Birmingham's African-Caribbean community if they remember the day boxing legend Muhammad Ali opened a popular centre in his name, the chances are you will get a resounding "yes!" And if they're under 40, they will have heard all about it from their elders.

That day in August 1983 when 'The Greatest' came to town is etched in people's memories as one of the proudest moments for the black community in Birmingham.

The Muhammad Ali Centre, next to Hockley Flyover, was opened in a blaze of national publicity, and it flourished as a much-loved base for everything from youth clubs and karate classes to wedding receptions and funerals.

But the city council-owned building has stood neglected and derelict for more than a decade, following its closure in 1996. Now community groups are waiting to hear its fate after the city council ordered them to submit a 'robust and viable' business plan by June 5 to save the centre from demolition.

Council papers were signed in February allowing the centre to be demolished on health and safety grounds, following claims that it had become a focal point for drug users. A three-month stay of execution was agreed for the local community to come up with a rescue plan.

The centre was built on the back of public donations, and ownership was shared between a trust and the local authority. Community activist Maxie Hayles says: "It is the African-Caribbean community's legacy. We have no institution that is ours and this could reach out to young people in Hockley, Handsworth, Lozells and Aston."

Gerald Nembhard, campaign spokesman for The Infinity Community Development Foundation campaign group, said: "The centre's sheer geographical position, being on the boundary of a number of Birmingham postcodes, gives it huge viability, as it reaches out to young people from different areas."

The Dojo Community Project Ltd has campaigned to save the centre for the past 15 years, led by sister and brother Del and Hector Pinkney. In the 1950s and 60s, their mother Mavis launched Handsworth's first unofficial community centre for young people, by opening up her Leonard Road home. Mavis's funeral was one of the last big events to be held at the Muhammad Ali Centre before it closed.

"We still have a lot of questions that we haven't had answers to," said Del, who is passionately opposed to demolition and has organised a petition containing hundreds of names. "We're told the building is a magnet for drug users, but I don't know how they can even get in. It's a fortress now, where everyone is barred." Del added that she had written to the boxing icon's agent, but Ali's own personal battle with Parkinson's Disease prevents him from becoming involved.'

Poppy's article contained positive comments from Ayoub Khan, a Liberal Democrat councillor for Aston, and Karen Hamilton, Lib Dem parliamentary candidate for Perry Barr. She continues:

'Retired Handsworth police chief superintendent David Webb stepped into the ring in 2006 in a bid to save the centre. At the time, he said the city council should hang its head in shame for allowing it to become so neglected. Webb clearly remembers the day Ali arrived to open the centre, and he helped to show the three-times world heavyweight champion around Handsworth.

Many cannot believe that today doubt hangs over the future of the centre that inspired such pride when it opened. In Birmingham Central Library, the city's Home Front Collection features a large two-page photograph of Muhammad Ali stretching out his hands to greet the crowds who queued to meet him during that 1983 visit. The photograph carries Ali's words: 'I'm saying this from the bottom of my heart – I've been to Africa, Asia, China, Russia, and all over the States, and I've never had acceptance better than I've had here.' Perhaps Ali saw all those smiling faces greeting him on that hot August day and thought to himself: 'What a people – the greatest.'

So the jury is out on that situation at the moment. Let's see what the future holds for the Centre.

Round 14

DODGY SITUATIONS

Appearances can be deceptive. We look at a range of other difficult or dangerous situations that Kash has found himself in, over the years, during a career that has been by no means plain-sailing, as we learned in the previous Round.

Kash's willowy physique often lulled his opponents into a false sense of security... a prime example of never 'judging a book by its cover'! Incidents with out-of-control Bouncers visiting the gym; missing his brother, Cougar's wedding due to a 'road rage' incident – P C Tim Green offers invaluable advice; students challenging Kash, to prove their physical superiority, et cetera.

Kash rents out the Grove Lane house in 2007. Two men offer to rent the entire house, but it turns into another 'Kash 22' situation, just like the wrestlers versus kickboxers incident at the Metropole Hotel, NEC.

A potentially dodgy situation happened in the late 1980s-early 1990s, when I used to do my ten-mile runs, from Handsworth all the way through to Great Barr and Perry Barr.

Running through Great Barr I came up against some guys. They were shouting: "Pakki, Pakki," as I was running down the road. The one time I stopped... and almost had a confrontation with them. I must have been in my early twenties.

It was a group of white lads. I was the European Champion at that time. They came over and I remember dropping a kick over the door of the car. Once I'd done that they stepped back and I carried on running. They didn't harass me again. But it just shows you what *could* have happened.

I used to travel to a gym in Handsworth on the 74 and 79 buses. As a sixteen or seventeen-year-old kid I'd go upstairs on the buses and there'd be groups of black or Asian lads who'd look at me and there's be fisticuffs. Normally they were black lads who'd had a few drinks or were high on drugs and were looking for trouble. Luckily I could hold my own.

Sometimes we had a scuffle on the bus – a quick 'One, two three', let's get off the bus. Maybe two or three of them would follow me off the bus, but thank God, nothing really materialised, because I could often talk my way out of it. They'd find out that I was into the martial arts and pretty well known. Obviously I'm not saying that was always the case; there *were* fights sometimes, normally fisticuffs: if you hit one, the other two would back off. That would happen once every few months, when I was between the ages of sixteen to twenty. Once I became World Amateur Champion I avoided it completely.

I didn't have a car until I was about twenty-four. Whenever I had to travel on the buses, I always felt a bit uneasy. When I was carrying the pads and I was all loaded up, it was difficult to defend myself. But I had confidence in myself to cope with potential fight situations like that, because I'd been defending myself from an early age.

Regarding my experiences as a coach, in the early 1990s, I'd been teaching about a year-and-a-half and I was around twenty-seven. I was trying to demonstrate a really big side kick. I thrust my leg out and I hit a girl on the front row; she must have been about ten years old. She flew back several yards. I thought: 'I hope she's alright!' She was a bit dazed, but she looked up. I said; "Are you OK?"

Still on the subject of coaching, in 1992-93, when I was World Champion, a big lad, walked in to the gym. He was about 6 foot 6 and thought he'd make a really good fighter, if I trained him up. But some students reach a stage when they think they're better than the coach. He looked at me as if to say, "I could do that better than you!" I said: "Come on then." What happened in the end was that he wanted to fight with me. I thought: 'What do I do about this?' It was a difficult experience for me.

So I sat the whole class down and we had a fight, in the middle of the class. I actually gave him a hiding. I kicked him in the face. He went down but then he got back up; then I knocked him down again. The other kids were getting a bit scared. I told him to get up and I knocked him down again. The respect he gave me after that was so much different.

The amount of people who want to fight me, because I look skinny! I always say to people: "You never judge a book by its cover." Anyway, this guy left the week after. I bumped into him a year later, and he came and shook my hand. Sometimes, to earn a person's respect, you have to give them a hiding. My dad used to tell me that.

I've got many stories like that. Three bouncers walked into my Sutton Coldfield class. They were big burly guys and they wanted to do kickboxing. One of them was a friend of mine, so I said he could come in. But his two friends were bullies. They were beating all the guys up; roughing them up.

I said: "Lads, this is a controlled contact sport." In the end I had to put my gloves on. I was a lot younger then and more ignorant. I said: "If you want to do it like that, spar with me." I gave the first guy such a hiding that he ended up sitting on the bench. He didn't want to know after that, so he went away and said "Forget it!"

The bigger of the two bouncers now teaches martial arts himself. I gave him such a hiding as well, and he ended up on the bench too. Actually that particular Wednesday I'd gone to a pub for a drink, with my friend Rob, before this happened, which is really bad of me, because I was training all day. But I had a brandy. Alcohol is no good for the system. That particular night was when I had to fight the bouncers and also go for a ten-mile run. I was exhausted. I had to phone Rob, just about a mile from my house, and get him to pick me up. Thank God I was only five minutes from home!

Another incident happened when I was in the centre of Stratford-upon-Avon. You wouldn't expect trouble there, but a guy was bullying the ladies, at the club where I was teaching. He was being a bit rough so I tried to calm him down, but he wouldn't, so then there was only one solution – spar with the coach. I gave him such a hiding and I ended up kicking him in the face. I cut him and blood started pouring down his face. He stormed off.

Two or three days later a solicitor's letter arrived at my house: he wanted to sue me. It could have gone further – it could have been professional negligence on my part. But Muria Solicitors, who were sponsoring me at the time, sorted out the situation and thank God, it never went anywhere else!

We've not really talked much about the teaching and the fighting: I'm sure there's a lot more we can say about that. But now I'm at a stage where I've got a lot of fighters, so rather than me doing the sorting out, I'll wink at one of my fighters and say, "Rough him up, because he shouldn't be doing that." It's very rare, but occasionally you get someone who thinks that he can take the whole world on. It doesn't work like that, because what we teach is discipline and respect; we expect that from people. We don't accept bullies in our Association.

A friend of mine, a karate teacher, came into the gym one day and said: "Does that guy train with you?" The guy who he was talking about, who was in my gym at that time, turned out to be a taxi driver who used to go into the roughest parts of Lozells, pick up all the black guys, the heavy 'Yardies' and want to fight them.

My friend said, "Be careful of him Kash!" In the end, I read about him, on the front of the *Evening Mail*, because he'd killed his wife! He was one of my students, but at that point he'd disappeared for a year. So you don't know who's going to come in through your door! But in teaching you *do* meet people from all walks of life.

In the mid-90s when I was really active, a guy named Mark Weller, from Norwich, spent some time at my house in Grove Lane Birmingham. To reduce his outlay he stayed at my house and he did some training with me. The next morning, a Saturday, he was about to leave for his house, but someone had stolen his car from outside my house.

That shows you the area we are in – Handsworth. It was a new car, a Cavalier. He phoned his wife, almost in tears, and never did get his car back. He did his training with me, but I don't think he ever came back!

I took over the Grove Lane house in 2007. Julie spent most of the time decorating the house: that could have been the beginning of the downfall in our relationship, because I left her to do that all by herself. We had a few people look at the house, with a view to renting it. There was this one guy who said: "Let me know when your house is ready. I wouldn't mind taking the whole house," which was fantastic; he was a French – Chinese kind of guy.

He took the house on and he said that there would be two of them living there – two males. You read about it all the time in the papers now, but one day I walked past the house and the door had been kicked in at the back. I put a note through the door, asking the guy to contact me, as soon as possible. I kept phoning him, but couldn't get through. In the end, I went in and had a look.

I went to the first room. It was all messy and dirty, with chicken legs thrown on the floor. I walked upstairs and it was all blacked out. There were plants in all the rooms... the house had been turned into a cannabis factory!

Each room I walked into had great big plants up to here. So now I realized why the door had been kicked in! Really, I shouldn't have gone in, because those kinds of people tend to set booby traps. I couldn't believe it!

I went outside, found two Community Police Officers. They counted 368 cannabis plants. I suppose that was part of inner city life!

You read about it now, but in those days I wasn't expecting it, because it wasn't so rife. So since then I've put a range of different working people into the house, checked them out and kept them in different rooms, so that, fingers crossed, that kind of situation won't happen again.

According to David Webb, commenting in 2011, "In the newspapers this last month, in Handsworth and in Walsall, there are huge cannabis factories. They say that they're making enough cannabis to be able to export it to other countries! So it's never stopped the problem."

Gringo, the former Handsworth Beat Bobby, agrees with Dave Webb's view, that it's a far more commonplace situation now, in all the major cities: "Yes it is – it's progressive."

Another unexpected incident took place in Broad Street, which is the 'in' place to be and everybody goes out drinking and clubbing. After we'd been training we decided to go out and celebrate with a few drinks. I went there with my friend Levi, who I train with. Levi bought these brand new shoes.

We were walking down Broad Street, when a guy bumped into him. Levi has a very quick temper so he went to kick this guy with a high kick to the face, but ended up arse-down. I thought: 'Oh no, what shall we do!' Then all of these lads started putting the boot in. I hit one guy and the rest of them backed off. Thank God the guy got back up again, because I thought the worst! We were just going to have a drink. These guys were already a bit drunk, but Levi's the wrong guy to pick on.

When my co-writer Shirley was writing Pat Roach's three biographies with him, they included an episode about when Pat had to go to court. The judge described Pat's hands as potential weapons, because he was a trained wrestler. It's exactly the same, with me, because we're trained in the martial arts, so you train to hurt people. So I have to be really careful how I use my skills, because they can do a lot of damage.

Footballer Dave Barnett recalls a major incident at the *Aston Villa Leisure Centre*, involving Ricky Otto.

"Previous to that," Dave explains, "we'd been celebrating at *Liberty's Nightclub*. David Sullivan the Chairman had taken us all out, so the lads were quite hectic that night. The management there weren't particularly happy, because we were banned. *Liberty's* had a little bit of a reputation for not letting certain people in.

"The manager happened to be at the *Aston Villa Leisure Centre* boxing match later. I'd had a chat with him, saying, 'I can't understand your policies,' basically, they weren't letting black people into *Liberty's*. But Ricky started having a real go at him. The manager went back to his seat but then Ricky went over and knocked him on the back of his head. So that triggered all sorts of things.

"I wasn't involved in it personally," continues Dave, "but Ricky was threatening to send people over to sort him out. This was all going on during Kash's fight, so I had to get in touch with people who could sort it out.

"It got very heavy at one stage, so here we were. I was playing football in Birmingham, supporting my friend, Kash, then the opposite of all that was that people were threatening Ricky, so I had to get the support of people I know, to make sure that it didn't happen. It died down eventually, but we weren't too welcome at *Liberty's*, although we weren't really bothered about that."

Regarding the incident that Dave's talking about, at *Aston Villa Leisure Centre*, Ricky Otto was a record signing for Birmingham City at that time – about £800,000. Ricky's a nice kid, but he had a bit of a troubled background. He wasn't happy that the manager of *Liberty's* was refusing entrance to black players. He slapped Simon, but Simon's got good connections with a Birmingham gangster, because Simon was running all the Birmingham doors for him.

Thank God Simon didn't ring him up, because he could have really 'kicked off' at my promotion. It could have really messed the show up and I was fighting for my title. So luckily it didn't go any further than that!

We close this Round with the ultimate in dodgy situations, which happened to me totally 'out-of-the-blue'. It's related by my good friend Andy Walker, whom you've met earlier in the book. As you can see this article was written by Andy, several years ago, for the *Solihull News*. Andy has kindly granted us permission to print the whole article.

Fight show ends in brawl shame
April 29 2005 By Andy Walker, Solihull News.

AS a four-times World Kickboxing Champion, Kash 'The Flash' Gill is used to battling it out with opponents in a ring but on Sunday he found himself brawling with American wrestling superstars in a hotel foyer.

The Buryfield Road resident, who has lived in the borough for 12 years, was holding one of his regular kickboxing charity events at the NEC's Metropole Hotel.

But as another successful show drew to a close just before midnight, WWE wrestlers arriving from a show at the NEC clashed with the leaving kickboxers in a 15 minute brawl. "One of our guys bumped into one of the wrestlers as he was leaving and apologised," said 37-year-old Kash. "But the wrestler said 'you will be sorry' and it just kicked off."

However as Kash came out to calm down stars including Chris Jericho and Kane, the Handsworth-born fighter was set upon by the 22st giant Dave 'Demon of the Deep' Batista. "When I went out this Batista grabbed me, so I shrugged him off and just went for him but five guys held me back. It all calmed down after a while but there was blood and ripped shirts over the floor," said Kash.

The big-hearted fighter raised £1,500 for the Evening Mail's 'Why My Child' appeal but now feels that this incident has over-shadowed the charity event. "With the amount these wrestlers are getting paid, they should take things like this with a pinch of salt. It's a shame because now people are talking about this incident rather than event itself," added the father-of-three.

West Midlands Police confirmed that they were called to the Metropole and that no arrests were made.

MORE FIGHTS & FLASH PROMOTIONS

Although Kash is best known for his four World Championship titles he also had many fights on the UK Circuit, particularly near the beginning of his career. Despite having a few losses he considers that these made him a better fighter, because it was like serving an apprenticeship.

In the first half of this round we describe time spent abroad, having already mentioned a few of the trickier times in foreign countries, in Round 14, 'Dodgy Situations'. We also cover a range of Kash's later fights in the UK, from the 1990s onwards.

The second half of the Round contains additional information about his company, 'Flash Promotions', which we introduced in an earlier Round.

When I travelled to various fights, as a fighter, there wasn't much time to look around, but I saw some lovely parts of the world, which I would otherwise never have visited.

I started off in Europe: went to Holland, Germany and France. As a fighter, you see the hotel; the arena, airport and so on, but it's a bit disappointing because you don't see that much of the actual country. However, when you go coaching abroad, taking fighters from the UK, you're able to see more. I've been to Australia four times; twice as a coach. You get looked after and taken out to smart restaurants.

Australia was in 1991, just before Hawaii. I took two fighters there, as a coach, Lawrence White, the Heavyweight Champion and Tyrone Herod as well, from London. It was just after my fight at the *NEC* with Ronnie Deleon. I was very tired when we arrived in Sydney, after that twelve-rounder with Ronnie, followed by my flight from Heathrow Airport, the morning immediately after the fight.

I coached twice in Australia: Sydney first and then I took Lawrence to Melbourne on that second occasion… what a lovely place! Melbourne, after

Athens, is the second city most populated by Greeks. They had some good Greek fighters too. People were really friendly, so we went out to some good clubs and restaurants. The quality of the hotel depended on who was doing the promotion.

I remember Sydney well. We were supposed to be going to Melbourne but were delayed there for a couple of days so they took us to the *Sydney Opera House*. People talk about it on TV and radio but I've actually got some pictures of us being there. We had dinner at the *Opera House*, at the bar; it was a really good experience. One particular reason why I thought that I'd love to live in a place like Australia was the hot climate.

We went to Hawaii in 1992. I took Lawrence White again. He was fighting Dennis Alexio. They had an audience of seven thousand people. If you've ever seen the film *Kickboxer* with Jean Claude Van Damme, his brother's played by Dennis Alexio. Dennis is a big name in Hawaii. He's got adverts on TV and on credit cards.

We went to the beach, where I met lots of people and was able to relax. The people in general, when they found out we were from the UK, were very hospitable.

We stayed in one of the top Five-Star hotels in Honolulu, by the beach and were buying all these T-shirts. Whenever I travelled abroad I always tried to bring some kind of memento back.

As a coach, I'd put the fighter to bed, make sure that he's OK, then one of the hosts might take me out. Sometimes I'd go out on my own as well. I wasn't married at this time, so I met some lovely girls out there – and had some fun.

In 1994 I lost my world middleweight title in Australia, against Ian Jacobs: I still communicate with him; he's a lovely lad.

To get my world title back I decided to get more rounds under my belt by doing Eliminators. One of these was with Ronnie Hinterseer, an Austrian. It was supposed to be an easy come-back fight, but as Howard explained in Round 13, it marked the turning point, in terms of his concern for the long-term effect of my injuries.

The guy was a bit clumsy. In the seventh round he came back with a spinning back-fist, which caught me and broke my nose... it also broke my heart! It's billed now as one of the greatest comebacks ever. Tom Ross of BRMB says, "Without question it's the best kickboxing comeback there's ever been." I came back, knocked him out in Round 9 and disappointed him, that's also on YouTube.

Cyrille Regis watched that fight against Ronnie, in 1995, which was particularly gruesome.

"The fight was at the *Aston Villa Leisure Centre*," Cyrille remembers. "I'd never been to a kickboxing fight before. It was awesome and just very bloody! But I have a lot of admiration for anybody who does a full contact sport. I don't know how long it lasted, but Kash looked as if he was doing very well, although I couldn't actually judge the fight. What happened was that this lad elbowed him in the face. He split Kash's nose.

"Kash went down, but then he came round. I can still see it now! It was unbelievably brutal – blood everywhere. I'm thinking: 'He's gone!' But the pain and the resolve!

"Kash came back two or three rounds later, and won the fight – honestly! I've played football, I've been in pain. I've had a thousand operations, but I've never been hit. I've been knocked out... and the brutality – and yet the mental strength. Being a player, I understand what would be going on inside his head: there'd be a soul fighter in there... The pain threshold you need to have and conquer; the desire, the fear, the motivation, all those things – to get back up and win the game. He must have had it in *bucketfuls*!"

There was a situation quite early in my career, where I had to go into a fight, despite having flu. That was my first and only *regular* boxing fight. To make matters worse, I didn't go into the ring until midnight. I was really tired. My promoter should never have asked me to do that.

According to Tom Ross, "Kash won't let any of his fighters into the ring unprepared, because he realises how dangerous it is. All the things that he learned from his kickboxing days have made him a great manager and promoter, because he looks after his boxers. As a young fighter, technically he was sensational; he'd got it all.

"The fact that Kash is totally focused on his sport has always helped him," Tom continues. "He's a very intelligent man and always put in meticulous preparation, before each fight."

I left it to my opponents to watch videos – and do the worrying, Tom! I had the same Game Plan all through my career: to never get hit and just give, don't take!

"Kash was brilliant at exploiting an opponent's weakness, whilst using his own strengths," remembers Tom. "He was a past master at it. I watched in awe. I watched him fight bigger, stronger and more aggressive people – and he saw them all off!"

I am known as a slow starter, so the first round is a warm-up for me. Normally I don't use tactics, because I train so hard, I'm conditioned really well and I'm ready to go twelve rounds. The Tim Izli fight was a classic: it's on YouTube now.

In 1995 I had the privilege of fighting at the *NEC* again, against Tim, which was a big grudge match. He told the big UK magazines: "Kash is avoiding me." So in the end I said: "OK then – let's get it on!" All the top martial arts names were there. Tim and I headlined it. I brought a big crowd with me and my band... great entertainment!

Paul Clifton explains how the show came about: "Paul Ingram wanted to get in on the Martial Arts; I wanted to do a big 'Shop Window' event. In 1991 I organised and created an event called *The Martial Arts Extravaganza*, with Paul Ingram. I then did *Combat 95*, which followed in 1995, which was a bigger, better, slicker, more experienced-based production, for a martial arts show, staged at the *NEC*. So I asked Kash to come and fight Tim Izli, as the big fight of the night.

"Kash brought a Bhangra Band along that night. It was his audio announcement, because everywhere Kash went, the Bhangra Band went. It was fantastic and it set the pace for the evening – very loud! He had the flashy dressing gown too: it was all golds, pinks, greens, proper showmanship," observes Paul.

Coming from an Indian background I thought to myself: 'Bhangra is on the 'up', so why not bring a Bhangra band in?' So from 1991, for all my World title and European title fights, I had this Bhangra band following me. For the 1995 event it was a great experience for them to perform in front of ten thousand people. They'd already performed in front of thousands, at local fights.

Tim Izli remembers:

"My fight with Kash was a really memorable night in my fight career. The fight was set in the Birmingham *NEC*. Kash was the best middleweight in England; I was the best light middleweight. We both were confident young men. We both had good records. We both had fought on the world circuit.

"For me it was a big challenge. Kash was the weight above me. Everyone was asking the question who was the best. I thought I was going to give Kash a boxing lesson. I knew I was a better boxer. But this was not just boxing... Kick-Thai boxing is different.

"My tactics were to get inside and work his body. Anyway, I did the fight the way I planned and got some great shots off for a couple of rounds. But Kash was strong for his weight and with that bit extra he nailed me with a big right. It was a great shot. I took it but went down.

"I will never forget that night, as I was up and OK to fight on, but the ref counted me out. I take nothing away from Kash. He pulled a great punch out of the bag. We have remained friends and both run successful gyms. We both went on to become champions and I know people who were at our fight who say that we were both great champions," concludes Tim.

As you know Tim, our *Combat* 95 fight was billed for seven rounds, as a 'Grudge Match'. On YouTube it's headlined: 'Nothing to gain, everything to lose'. But because it was on a big stage at the *NEC* in front of a crowd of 10,000, it was worth doing.

So Tim, I'll give you the first round, because I'm a slow starter, but when I hit you with that right hand and you fell on your face, I knew you were never going to get back up!

"I had a personal interest in the Martial Arts, not just from a publishing point of view," recalls Paul Clifton. "In the 1980 and 90s, there were some fantastic individuals who had a certain amount of flair. If you go back in the old days, twenty or thirty years prior to Kash, there were people like Steve Babbs: an articulate man, but a very quiet, very capable Kung Fu fighter. He would have given Kash a run for his money, without a shadow of a doubt," observes Paul. "He was a cerebral warrior too, but from an older generation, about fifteen years before.

"There was Frank Lynch. They were all people who had come into the Martial Arts Industry, in the wake of Bruce Lee; so they were people who had character, like Bruce; who had a desire to be successful and desire to be flashy, individual and different. Kash wasn't really one of those, to be honest. He was the kind of guy who worked damned hard – that's why I respect him.

"If you take a martial arts artist today, who trains hard and has a professional training regime, then you've found something very special," continues Paul, "because few of them do. The *MMA* side, the *Mixed Martial Arts* now, has been going on *successfully* for the last eleven years; *UFC* have just sold 10% shares in their company for a hundred million dollars. It's the ultimate fighting challenge, from America. That's what should have happened to kickboxing but never did, but America actually went into the *MMA* straight away."

I finished my career in 2002 against Sophanie Allouche, which was really disappointing because I got stopped in about three rounds. It was such a big hype-up, but I came back and my hunger and drive had gone. I had three kids. People who witnessed that fight would have thought 'Kash wasn't really that good,' but I should never really have been in the ring. After that fight I hung my gloves up – and never came back!

I'd already formed a company called *Flash Promotions* because I wanted to make kickboxing events a better performance: better organized and fast-flowing. There were too many gaps in previous shows. It needed to be a proper entertainment. So I thought: 'Let's gather a *mixed* selection of fights, not just Birmingham fighters,' although I was Birmingham-based myself.

I'd built up contacts over time, in the fighting world. I had good friends, in Nottingham, Leicester and London. My shows were becoming well known for their glitz, glamour and good crowds, so coaches knew it was a good place to put their fighters on display.

After doing all the leg work I'd go to Gamma and say: "Look, I'd like you to do this," and Gamma would come up with all of the promotional ideas: "What about doing a promotion at Villa Park?" We did two demonstrations there.

Gamma had done a marketing course, so it worked well. He got in touch with Martin Jones, the manager of the *Pallasades Shopping Centre* in Birmingham. He was always coming up with new stories, like 'Kash has gone off to Holland to train,' and things like that. Gamma was looking for different angles all the time – the press always want new stories. It was always a headache for me when fighters pulled out, but thank God most of them were reliable.

So there are many sides to marketing: you're getting all the promotional stuff, but you also have to solve the problems that accompany it. There's the financial side as well. Can we afford particular fighters? Do we have to pull out and get someone else? It's the kind of business where you can fall out with people very easily.

In my thirty years, I've fallen out with a lot of people. Much of that is finance and mood swings, because your mood can change when you're fighting. People don't understand that, if they're not in the fight game. It's very stressful. You may have been friends with someone for twenty years, but then you can fall out with them – over a phone call! It's very sad, but it's part of the game.

169

Becoming a promoter also meant developing my skills as a presenter. During my fighting career I didn't always build myself up as much as I should have done. As a Four times World Champion I should have been selling myself more.

I do it without any trouble on behalf of my own fighters: "Look at this guy – he's fantastic!" I'd have trouble selling my own car, but if it's *your* car I'd have no trouble. So it's a kind of modesty, about myself, it's the way I am. I've always been like that. It's only *now*, in the last 12-18 months, that I've realized the need to tell people about my achievements, because they haven't 'caught on'.

We've described how my brothers lend a hand to support me, when I'm staging a fight. Gamma explains the process of establishing my company:

"Kickboxing is more of a minor sport and there isn't a lot of money in it. It's the same for any minor sport in the UK. Even in football at the amateur end there isn't a lot of money, so they all struggle. Kash was getting quite a lot of fights, but different people were promoting them. It became very frustrating, because he wasn't getting much money. So he decided to promote a show himself," Gamma explains.

"Howard Brown couldn't be there a lot of the time, but Kash had the benefit of brothers who all had different skills. He has a lot of friends in the martial arts world who helped; his brothers had friends too, which meant that we could involve a large group of people in the promotion.

"Kash used to get the opponent to fight him and other fighters, who would take part in the show: that was his side of it, but I did all the promotional side of it and who was going to be doing what job. I used to write the press releases. The *Birmingham Mail* and other local papers all said how impressed they were with the standard of the releases. That was a big thing and quite a learning curve. But once we'd done one show, it was easier to do the others, including designing the larger posters and the smaller 'flyers'; designing tickets and getting them printed.

"When we were checking the number of tickets sold, at one stage it might be thirteen or fourteen; this is where Kash had the nerve because he then had to set about promoting the show. He made it quite spectacular with the Bhangra bands, Apache's music – all the glitz and glamour. So he made a name for himself which put bums on seats," Gamma continues. "That's why it was so special, because when we put the posters out, printed the tickets and did all of that side of the promotion, we grew in confidence. Kash became known all over the UK, not just as an Asian, but as a kickboxer with a 'do or die' style.

"On the day, the shows were always packed: we're talking about three thousand people; for kickboxing, which was brilliant! Birmingham was always known as the centre of kickboxing: Howard Brown did it first, then Paul Ingram.

"Paul Ingram started as a student with Kash," Gamma continues. "He's a wealthy businessman. Then he went from being a student to getting involved with promotions. Kash probably thought: 'I'll do alright here, because he'll promote the shows and he'll look after me.' But a rift emerged, because the amount that Kash wanted for a promotion and the amount that Paul was willing to pay were different. We had to make sure that we didn't lose on the promotions," Gamma concludes.

I sometimes give Hudson Richards, a hard time!

"Kash is not subtle and if he thinks you have a weakness he might play on it. You might be subject to intense loads of 'ribbing'," Hudson comments. "Like when I do any MCing. I've got to be the last person who is naturally suited to it; I just don't have that flamboyance. But he always gives me a grand introduction: 'And our MC for today is Hud-son Rii-chards!' And I'd feel about 2 foot three... "Hello!!"

Hudson has MCd many times for me now, in the Birmingham area. Venues include the *Custard Factory* in Digbeth; the *Second City Suite*; the *Cadbury Club*; also the *Q Club*, in Corporation Street.

"I'm honoured every time I'm asked to do it," Hudson continues. "Kash puts a lot of thought and planning into his shows. His drive and his zeal and his organisational skills come together, although people will sometimes ask: 'When did you find out you were MCing?'... 'Oh, yesterday!'

"But over the years, every single show is better than the last one, in terms of organisational stuff. I don't think that it was his natural bent, when he first started, but he has got better at it. Certainly by the time I turn up for a show," Hudson concludes, "he knows what everyone is doing and brings everything together, with all the contacts that he has."

Andy Walker, PR and Social Media Manager for Birmingham City Football Club, has attended four or five of my events.

"I usually take friends along, who're into the martial arts, so they get quite excited about it. The first one that we went to was at the *Metropole*, at the *NEC*. That was at the tail-end of 2005," explains Andy.

"Just as we arrived we noticed a helluva lot of people outside in shock blankets. A fire had started somewhere nearby in a hotel bedroom, just as Kash's big show was about to start, so they had to evacuate. We wondered what the hell was going on. After a further half hour or so they had to say that the event was being cancelled. That was the first one that I went to. Kash was absolutely mortified!

"It costs him a fortune to stage these events too. He's staged a total of four events, at the *Metropole*, but his concern was more to do with Kash as a person," continues Andy. "He'd promised all of these people that an event was taking place, not just the fighters themselves. The fact that the event was unable to go ahead... He was straight on the phone the next day. I remember saying: 'Look Kash, it's not your fault. You can't help a fire in a bedroom that's nothing to do with you!' Eventually, about six months later, it went ahead at the same venue.

"I saw a show around February 2010. It was at the *Second City Suite* in Digbeth. Again, I went along with a couple of friends," Andy continues. "We were at one of the front tables. Unexpectedly, I get halfway through, enjoying my nice dinner; enjoying the evening, when there was a tap on my shoulder. Without any warning: 'In two fights time, you're going to present the award to the winner!' Suddenly I lost my appetite. I went up there and had to pose; shake hands with some sweaty, out-of-breath fighter! The trophy that I presented was for the most outstanding fight of the night, so that really stands out in my memory. I had a great night.

"Although kickboxing has been described by various people as the 'poor relation' of combat sports, it's really entertaining because you have no idea who's going to win. Kash's events are also interesting because he presents kids and adults. So you can have a thirty-two-year-old man who's never stepped in the ring before, or a thirteen-year-old, in the same position. It's fascinating to watch. It *can* be quite brutal, but obviously it didn't do Kash any harm.

"Another thing that he does, which is a hundred per cent professional, is that he holds a press conference before, which is unheard of in kickboxing," Andy continues. "He hires out a restaurant. The most recent one was when he hired out the Thai Edge Restaurant in Brindley Place in Birmingham. He put on a bit of a spread for the journalists who turned up. His fighters were there, all dressed in their tracksuits. There were Sponsorship Boards in the background, he did it all properly.

"He introduced all of his fighters, said his speech. There were about five or six journalists: a couple of local ones like myself; a guy from an Asian magazine, based in London, and journalists from fight magazines. But you don't see that usually in kickboxing; you might see posters and tickets on sale in a gym, but Kash was trying to attract people walking by," Andy continues.

"For his next event, his 2010 European Championships, he had a Bhangra Band, with their drummers, walking through the centre of Birmingham, in traditional dress. Unfortunately I was covering a football match but I've seen the pictures. You've got all of the shoppers on them, wondering what's going on! The parade went down Broad Street, then through Victoria Square, onto New Street. His fighters were all dressed in yellow tracksuits. There were placards, with posters advertising the event. But aside from Kash, that's unheard of in this country, for kickboxing."

My brothers and I put up posters around Handsworth, advertising the shows; we did that unofficially of course. Even at a Handsworth café where I sometimes go for lunch, I have small flyers there on the table, advertising my show. So I get in wherever I can and explore all the angles.

"Kash is very hot on his PR," observes Andy. "He knows how to plug an event. Then it's just a matter of keeping his fingers crossed and hoping that he gets the turnout that he deserves. I'm friends with Kash on Facebook: he posts pictures up on there, of a wide range of events that he's involved in."

Phil Upton went along to one of my shows, to see what all the fuss was about!

"I went to see Kash at *Aston Villa Leisure Centre*. He fought an American guy. It was a World Title Fight, but the thing only lasted for about three or four rounds tops! He'd hardly got a kick on him; he was all over him," recalls Phil. "But the thing I remember, having never been to a boxing fight, was the atmosphere... and how quickly you get swept along in that atmosphere. I was out of my seat, bawling him on. It was very much a matter of animal instinct: you can see how people get swept along into that, because I know I was!"

According to my co-writer, Shirley Thompson, "When my husband Dave and I went to Kash's 4 July 2010 European Championships I felt exactly like that too. But those young kickboxers all desperately wanted to win, so it was anybody's fight."

UB40's Tony Mullings first heard about me when he got involved in the martial arts himself. He saw at least one of my championship fights at the *Aston Villa Leisure Centre*.

"I would have seen Kash in a tournament fight, without realising that it was him. I'd heard of him, but didn't know him by sight, at that time. I had a girlfriend whose brothers trained at Kash's Gym, her brothers used to tell me about Kash and they showed me some footage of him," explains Tony, "so after that I went to see him for myself.

"The first time I saw him fighting, to be fair, he was losing," Tony recalls. "But then he came from out of nowhere. Some people might call it a lucky punch, but if you're throwing it, it's not lucky, because you intend to do it. And it was just awesome!

"Throughout his career Kash has been synonymous with being down, but coming back from it, that's why he's so infamous! He doesn't look like he can hurt someone. It's like he's got loads of body mass and muscle. I'm light myself so I've got that advantage too, because it means you're so much faster," continues Tony. "You stand more chance of winning against the big guys. The last competition fight I had was against a guy called 'Rhino'. He was twice my size, but I beat him because he was too bulky."

We explained in an earlier Round that in 1995, comedy star, writer and broadcaster Adil Ray, a student at that stage, had three month's work experience at *Radio XL*, while he was attending university and that's where we first met.

"It was a very small Asian radio station in Bradford Street, Deritend, Birmingham," remembers Adil. "It was quite a nightmare situation to work in, pretty dire working conditions. After three months I left and went to *Choice FM*. But I made sure that I got some great content into the shows.

"Interviewing Kash in 1995 was one of the highlights, when I look back on it: Kash Gill, Wasim Khan, who played cricket at Warwickshire, one or two examples: people who hadn't been given the recognition that they deserved. I couldn't believe that someone like Kash, who at that time was into the championships; potentially going to be a world champion; fighting for serious belts, albeit in a sport that wasn't quite so popular, but still being a very local Asian, hadn't been given greater media coverage.

"Certainly the Kash Gill interview and going to the *Aston Villa Leisure Centre* was one of the highlights of my time at *Radio XL*. While I was working at that radio station, I also met Tom Ross, who's written the Foreword for this book.

"So I saw Kash fight at the *Aston Villa Leisure Centre* in 1995. Michel Silviera was his opponent. I remember him going into the ring and probably, like a lot of people, I was seeing him fight for the first time. How in the hell is he going to beat anybody? He's so skinny! To be a boxer of any kind he needs to be really muscular, well-built et cetera.

"But I loved it – it was absolutely amazing! It was like a new world for me, seeing the amount of people there and the way they really got behind their fighters and knew their stuff. I thought it was great!"

As you know Adil, I went the distance in that fight, but lost on points. I was attended by paramedics at the end, because I was dehydrated.

Martial Arts instructor Tony Whitehouse has been very supportive in a number of ways.

"We've always been part of Kash's team. It got to the point when he needed to do other things," explains Tony, "so he had to be able to rely on people to cover for him, do various classes and so on. Whatever's needed we just band together and help out.

"I teach martial arts classes here at Kash's gym during the week and I'll sometimes help out and cover classes on Saturdays. I've got my own clubs in Northfield, Small Heath and Bromsgrove. I'm generally teaching at some point on a Sunday so it does get a bit hectic, but it's what I've always wanted to do.

"We teach predominantly the Freestyle syllabus of the *IFA*," Tony elaborates, "but when it comes to the bits regarding self defence, within that, some of us teach slightly differently. I'll teach some self defence, some kickboxing. Some days I'll go in and say: 'I have no idea what I want to teach today. What do you guys want to do?!'

"In the earlier days, after we'd taught a class, Kash would take me back to Grove Lane. His dad would be there watching television. Gurmej was quite a character!"

In 1999 I suggested that a group of us should form the *IFA* – the *International Freestyle Association*.

Round 16

DEATH AT A WEDDING

In January 2003, Kash's father, Gurmej, returns to India, for a wedding, but sadly dies. Kash and other family members describe this traumatic event.

The family were all stunned, so Binda's husband, Satnam, played a crucial role over in India, in coordinating everything. He had always played a strong advisory role within the family and had been a 'tower of strength' to Gurmej. So when the time came to light the funeral pyre Gurdip, Gamma and Satnam lit it together.

Our father was the most important part of our lives, when our mom died. However, most of us moved out, because my dad was very independent: he didn't want to move in with any of us; he was quite stubborn. Gamma decided that would live with him in our family house, in Grove Lane.

Occasionally I'd go down on a Friday morning to get my dad and take him back to my house, because Gurmej loved my kids. Mitchell was only little, so I'd leave him with my dad, while I picked up the other two kids from school. My dad loved that.

Lighthorne Road was my first house in Solihull, in the West Midlands. I moved there in 1993. Dad came to Buryfield Road too, when I moved there later. He used to stay the night. It worked out well because I was teaching at *Handsworth Leisure Centre* the following day, so I could drop him back home.

Cougar recalls: "Whenever dad had a grandchild, he'd throw a party in a pub: there was food for all of the Irish; all the Jamaicans. He loved a party – any excuse to celebrate! When Daljit and I got married, my friend owned a pub. He said: 'Cougar, you need to tell your dad to stop that, because he's still celebrating a week later!' When our son Kietan was born it was the same thing.

"Dad had an ulcer in his leg. Kash and me used to bandage his leg. You could actually see through the cut, where his ulcer was," continues Cougar.

176

"If he showed it to anyone they wouldn't let him work, so he covered it for years and went to work like that. He didn't want to lose money, because he had to pay the bills. His leg would be swollen sometimes."

"The first Christmas that we were married," remembers Daljit, "dad sat on the chair, when he came home and started to cry. I was quite intimidated by him, initially. But the ice broke very quickly and that was the turning point for me and dad. I sat next to him and held his hand. He said: 'Your mother would have been really proud of the fact that you and Cougar have got married. I wish she could have been here to see it.' From then onwards, we got on really well," Daljit recalls.

Our father went to India and there was a wedding going on. He had a few whiskies the night before, because he liked his whisky, but he died in his sleep. My dad always used to say that's the way he wanted to go. So when you think of all the good things, it's the best way to go. A couple of extra years wouldn't have gone amiss, but before that he was in good health.

When he retired from work, like other people, he wanted to enjoy himself, so his lifestyle became more social at that point; he did a lot more eating and drinking than before and he wasn't getting as much exercise as he had in the foundry. As my dad turned seventy, it started to catch up with him. He put more weight on: you could see it in his face.

According to Cougar, "Gurmej's last words to me were 'Don't throw a party until I come back.' But then I had a phone call at three o'clock, to say that dad had passed away, so I phoned Kash. He and Julie still had our kids, so that we could go to the cinema. It was that night that we got the news, but because of tradition, not only did I not have time to grieve, but you have to think, 'Well tomorrow, everyone's going to be coming to the Grove Lane house'.

"I got the white sheets out and put them across the floor, at six o'clock. Everybody would be coming and Daljit was heavily pregnant, as well. So it was a really difficult time for us: Gian was born and my dad died. Then a few weeks after that, Daljit's brother died."

Daljit explains, "When Gian came along, he kept us sane. Cougar having recently lost his dad made it even sadder, just knowing how happy Gurmej would have been, to see his new grandson. Then when I lost my brother, we were both in grief again, so we had a *terrible* time. My mom gave up at that point; three years later she passed away; she couldn't face losing a second son.

"When Gurmej passed away it was a really sad time, for all of the brothers and sister, because he was the only surviving parent: he'd been mum and dad to all of them. I think they all grieved in their own way. He was only seventy-three when he died.

"Cougar often expresses himself emotionally, but with Kash, that was the first time that I'd seen him distraught – and I'd known him for about fifteen years prior to that. I'd never seen him cry that way before, the way he broke down," Daljit recalls.

According to Gurdip, "Dad had been ill for a couple of days before the wedding. He died at 5am on the morning of the wedding."

"It's hard, because you've never really said goodbye. Half of the family went out to India and half had to be here, because that's a hard part of Asian culture, the way that they all come to the house," recalls Cougar. "But life is a rollercoaster and you've just got to ride with it: you either cope with life, or go under, which a lot of people do."

Gurdip explains: "Within the next three days, once people knew that dad had died, hundreds of people came to the Grove Lane house to show their respect and to share their stories about him.

"Although it was only six weeks before Gian was due, I said it was fine for Cougar to go over to India if he wanted to," recalls Daljit. "The actual funeral was in India. Gamma, Binda and Gurdip went there. Kash, Resham and Cougar stayed here, to look after things. When everyone came back from India, we had a three-day ceremony at the temple. Their dad kept everything together for them: he was a central point, so his death had a massive impact on all of them," Daljit concludes.

Resham elaborates: "Whilst all of this was going on, Gurdial and Satnam's brother, Onkar, were both receiving the male visitors in one room at our Grove Lane house. In the other room were the aunts, receiving the female visitors. This *Paying of Respects* lasted over a fortnight."

"When we lived at Grove Lane, Kietan was the only grandchild. Dad would hold him and give him a kiss, before he went off to bed," remembers Cougar.

"For all that he gave us as kids, we gave him a lot back; because of the moments when Kash put him at the forefront, when he was in the ring. And the fact that the whole family were saying: 'Oh Kash, he's done us all proud – he's done the Asian community proud!'

"The only other time I've seen my dad in tears is when Kietan got a serious skin infection," Cougar continues. "Dad was at the Children's Hospital and then Kash came to visit. Kash just slid down the wall, because it was such a shock to see his nephew like that. He put his head in his hands. But Kietan pulled through and built up his immune system again."

Gurdip recalls, "When our father first returned to India, I remember going to the airport with my own children, to say goodbye to him, because he thought the world of my children and they of him. He went to the toilet, because he used to get nervous. He was very 'chesty' so I bought him some *Locketts*. I think, with hindsight, he may have had an idea something was wrong, but he didn't say anything about it."

That particular trip to India, when Gurdip dropped him at the airport, happened before my father's death. On his return he looked much better, because of the hotter climate. It did him good; that's probably why he was so happy to make a return trip.

Gurdip continues: "On that second trip, Kash took Gurmej to the airport. Unusually, they hugged each other, as dad departed. It was the coldest January for twenty years in India, so that probably had something to do with what happened. You can't just put your central heating on in those buildings over in India, and it's only cold for a six-week period.

"Gamma, Binda, my two nieces and myself went over, to lay him to rest. He went quickly; he didn't suffer. He had always said that he didn't want to have to rely on us to be his carers. Also, when he walked through his village, this is where he started and also where he ended. So in a way, it was nice.

"I think there were times, as our dad got older, when he really missed our mom, especially when he saw the grandchildren; he got quite emotional," Gurdip continues. "I remember him sitting in here on Saturdays; he adored the grandchildren. He'd say: 'It's a shame your mom's not here; she missed out on all of this.'

"When my children's granddad died, on Jan 5th 2003, they really took it badly. My youngest was six and the oldest boy was almost ten: he took it particularly badly. He managed to play in a Cup Final... but granddad wasn't there. He told me afterwards that as he was saving a penalty, he thought of granddad. Even now he wears a 'dog-tag', like the soldiers do, but he wears it in memory of his grandparents. He always keeps that with him in his glove, when he goes on the pitch," Gurdip concludes.

Resham comments: "Kash's son, Mitch, has got a lovely, cheeky smile. Because he was the youngest of all the grandchildren, dad had special time for him; he told me about every single thing that Mitch had done, when he came over to see us on Wednesdays. We always have a soft spot for the youngest don't we?"

Since then, Cougar and Daljit had Gian, but Gurmej died before he was born. Gian's middle name is Gurmej.

Above: Cougar and Daljit's wedding day July 1989. Photo taken outside the family's Grove Lane house. Binda, in the turquoise dress, her husband, Satnam, in the light grey suit, helped Cougar to tie his turban. Gurdip, standing with his back to the wall, is flanked by Gurmej and Gamma. BY KIND PERMISSION OF COUGAR & DALJIT GILL.

Left: Kash and his daughter, Elliesha get down to the serious business of reading the morning papers. You're never too young to start! 'Ellie' was born in May 1995.

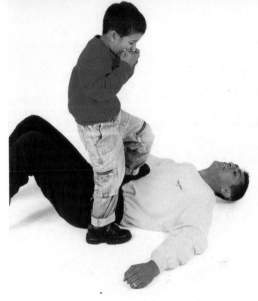

Left: Kash is out-for-the-count. And the winner… in the red top… is Kallan Kash Gill!

Right: Kids always want everything – including my belts!

Left: Recent photo of Kash's three children, Kallan, Mitch and Elliesha.

Above: Kash goes back home, to Handsworth Leisure Centre.

Right: Kash Promotions, Victoria Square.

Top: Kash, broadcaster Nikki Bedi and Adil Ray.

Middle: When the Lord Mayor Councillor Chaudry Rashid JP visited Kash, Apache was there too, as a guest.

Bottom: Island Pursuits - Kash's loyal instructors, Isle of Skye coach, Anthony Davies and Paul Murphy.

Top: Kash's Annual Demo in Handsworth Park, for the Vaisakhi Mela Festival.

Bottom: Apple and sword, in Handsworth Park.

Top: December 2011, Kazakhstan. Cage pictures of Kash with world-renowned movie star, Don 'The Dragon' Wilson, USA.

Middle: Kash, Don, Cynthia Rothrock and Oliver Gruner, (Hollywood Martial Arts movie stars).

Bottom: Hector Pinkney receives his MBE from HRH Princess Anne at Windsor Castle, Thursday 3 November 2011. He received the award for outstanding service to the Handsworth Community. BY KIND PERMISSION OF HECTOR PINKNEY.

Top: Kash, fighting politics.

Bottom: This is no cop-out!

Top: Apache Indian – Kid Milo. Boxing Clever, at Kash's promotion, Aston Villa Leisure Centre.

Bottom: Kash was honoured to be invited to 10 Downing Street, for Wednesday 13 April 2011, together with the BBC's Tommy Nagra.

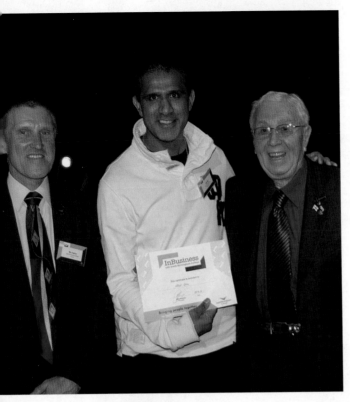

Left: Wednesday 25 April 2012 Kash appointed as a sports ambassador, official launch InBusiness with South Birmingham College, Digbeth Campus, Birmingham. Pictured here with guest speaker Sir Doug Ellis OBE and College Principal Mike Hopkins. BY KIND PERMISSION OF VINCE THOMPSON FOR THE HARP NEWS.

Below: Ready to surprise Hector! Kash, Amanda Lamb and Apache, You Deserve A House Like This, Channel 4, 7 April 2012.

Top: Kash, Frank Bruno and
lifelong friend Hugh Ford.
Hugh fought with Kash on
the regular circuit, in the early
years. He went on to win the
British & Commonwealth
Featherweight Professional
Boxing Championships.

Left: Kash was admitted to
the illustrious Hall of Fame,
in a Saturday evening
ceremony on 26 November
2011. Also pictured at the
event are three legendary
martial arts guys from
America: the late Joe Lewis,
Jeff Smith and Bill
'Superfoot' Wallis.

Round 17

NEW CHAMPIONS

In 2006, three years after Gurmej's death, Kash meets John Holcroft at St Theresa's Gym on the Holyhead Road and gives kickboxing classes there until 2008.

This Round features the most successful champions that Kash has trained and the raw talent that he is presently nurturing. He opens a new gym in 2008, after years of coaching at other gyms. On 4 July 2010 he stages the European Championships at the 'Second City Suite'.

His successful champions to date include: Paul Murphy, Kash's first European Champion; Paul 'Iceman' Collins, his first World Champion; Tyler Shakespeare, Junior World Champion; Sunny 'The Hit-man' Hira: three times World Champion; Richard Waller and Simon Akufo, European and World champions respectively.

Kash's on-going aim is putting something back into the community. Students Stuart Nicholls and 'Balogun', from entirely different backgrounds, describe how Kash has helped them.

Following my success as a fighter, and a few years before dad died, my next ambition was to become a top coach and produce some championship fighters.

My first champion was Paul 'Iceman' Collins. Although he's a lot lighter than me I predicted that Paul would be World Champion one day, an ambition that he achieved in 2005, just three years after I'd retired myself, from professional fighting.

Prior to that, I trained Paul Murphy, who became *European Champion*. I've produced several British Champions as well. My Junior Champions include Tyler Shakespeare.

I've produced Sunny, 'The Hitman', who is now three times World Champion. He came to me as a ten-year-old kid and is now in his late twenties. He's won three times but he's had less than thirty fights. But I had a hundred fights, so that shows the difference. Because kickboxing in my era was a lot busier, it shows that I'm a genuine World Champion. I'm not saying that Sunny isn't, but the era I was in was a lot harder.

Nowadays, when people say 'World Champion' you have to take it with a pinch of salt, because it's not as difficult as it used to be. I was at the tough end of it!

My European Kickboxing Championship promotion was held at the *Second City Suite*, on Sunday 4 July 2010. The first few fights were just novice fighters. Later fights featured Simon Akufo and Richard Waller, who both won their European Championships against Spanish fighters.

John Holcroft recalls the kickboxing classes that I gave at his gym, from 2006 until 2008.

"Kash came in about three times a week. He had his Mercedes by then," remembers John. "Nowadays we have children doing work experience with us for a week, when they're leaving school. If we can get them young, turn them away from the knives, then by the time they're sixteen or seventeen they're not going to be in a gang then are they? They're going to have a bit of sense and be learning things. That's why I like what Kash is doing."

Hudson Richards comments: "I found him to be a really good instructor. One of the standing jokes at my club is that you have to listen very carefully to what he's saying: he speaks loudly but also very quickly, so you're sometimes not quite sure what he's saying. When he's teaching, his demeanour is quite different, because he has to get the stuff across. His normal manner, in a one-to-one, is quite laid-back, but because he's very kinaesthetic when he trains, sometimes you have to listen very carefully, to get the instruction."

When I'm giving a talk or a grading I say: "I know I speak very quickly – but you want to see me fight!" Hudson became one of my coaches. He teaches at the *Bordesley Centre*.

"When I met Kash, we were training and fighting for *ECKA*, which was the *English Full Contact Karate Association*. Kash then formed the *International Freestyle Association* and I came and joined him. He was the actual founder of that," explains Hudson.

Hudson continues: "A group of instructors came across with him, but Kash is the front person: Kash *is* the *IFA*, in effect. If he hadn't instigated it, we would probably still be with *ECKA*."

Paul Collins, Paul Murphy, Sunny, Tyler, Simon Akufo and Richard Waller are six of the champions that I've produced. Sunny went over to

Ireland and Germany and mainly in the UK, because I bring fighters over here as well. Sunny was beaten in one of his German fights; otherwise he'd have equalled my title!

Paul Collins won in Reading. Now we've got Richard Waller, who won the World Light Welterweight Championship in New York, on May 1st 2011. We've got some young up-and-coming kids, between sixteen and eighteen; they'll either go one way or the other: avoiding clubs and pubs, or otherwise.

When Shirley interviewed Simon after his European Championship fight on 4 July 2010, he said that the main reason for his current success is that he took my advice about giving up his social life seriously. But even the fighters now, like Richard and Simon, two months after a fight, they're still celebrating. I'd be back in the gym the next day! So it's all relative, although you *could* argue that they've got to have some leisure time.

I always tell them that they'll never be another Kash Gill, although that probably sounds conceited! I was self-motivated, which is very hard to do. I became a World Champion in one of the toughest kickboxing eras, between the 80s and the 90s.

Over the past two decades the various branches of self defence have acquired a much more glamorous image. Tom Ross discusses that aspect:

"As well as the legendary Cynthia Rothrock more recently we have had Jackie Chan and Steven Segal, who have done a lot of big box office movies. This has added to the sexiness of the sport and made it easier to attract youngsters into the gym. So yes, martial arts have definitely become much more sexy; however, Kash also encourages youngsters to use it for discipline or keeping fit.

"I've seen some of the youngsters that he's brought on and I'm sure that had it not been for Kash, they might have taking the wrong turning at the crossroads," continues Tom. "Kash has put them on the right road. Society should thank Kash for that alone."

Phil Upton saw me fight a couple of times.

"I've witnessed him in two fights and done one evening for him. The only other time that our paths have crossed was when we went to film him once, when he was in the middle of teaching the kids, so we went along to one of his lessons. That would have been seventeen years ago, when I was filming a piece for *Central TV*, at the Gym in Harborne."

According to Dorian Yates, "Kash has invited me to various events over the last few years but I saw him fight back in the late 1980s and I presented a trophy at one of his 1995 promotions. I remember thinking how unusual it was to see an Asian guy in a contact-combat sport... that was why Kash stood out – with his personality, the gown and the hair... and all that stuff. Later on my son, Lewis, started training with him at John Wilmott School, in Sutton Coldfield.

"He's got a Black Belt as a result of his training: he's had that since he was twelve. Lewis started training with Kash around the age of nine or ten. He only took three or four years to get his Black Belt, which is relatively quick," observes Dorian.

Adil Ray has seen me at a range of promotional events and also in connection with my fighters.

"Yes, I presented a TV show called *Desi DNA*, from 2006, so I did some interviews for him then."

That was for BBC2. It was a 7-minute item, which was quite something, considering it was BBC2. I still have it on DVD. Tommy Nagra mentions it in Round 20.

"I've seen Kash both as a fighter and a promoter," Adil continues. "In 2008 we made a documentary about John Holcroft and the Handsworth Centre." Adil now stars in his own BBC1 sitcom *Citizen Khan* set in Sparkhill, Birmingham.

Stuart Nicholls, a civil servant for over twenty years, is just five years younger than me, so we're almost contemporaries.

"I grew up in very white-orientated, working class neighbourhood," explains Stuart. "I had quite a few friends, but my main problem when I was growing up was my deafness. My parents tried to make sure that it didn't affect me doing things, but obviously you're singled out as a target at school.

"I suppose in some respects I did quite well at school, but kickboxing was a great confidence-booster. Initially I thought it was a bit beyond me, but it helped me to accept things and realise that I could do it: it had that 'feel-good' factor. I was a bit depressed, but after doing kickboxing for a year I lost weight and became a different person. Eventually I started to make a name for myself as a fighter, so people wouldn't mess with me.

"I particularly noticed the way that Kash commanded the attention of his students. You could tell that he was a World Champion, just by looking at him," Stuart continues. "But he was down-to-earth at the same time; he listened patiently to what people had to say and advised them to do things a certain way. He corrected people, but not in a condescending way. That prompted me to join and I eventually got my Black Belt."

Balogun, another of my students, had a really tough start in life and continues to have certain issues. He was born in Winson Green, in 1975. Shirley interviewed him at my Gym, in July 2011.

"I've got six brothers and a sister, although I don't speak to them that much," Balogun begins. "I had a tough childhood: a loving mom, but a father who didn't really 'get' me. If I cried about anything he'd slap me, which didn't do much for my self-esteem. I went to Handsworth Boys' School, but I was considered a troublemaker, so I was kicked out of there.

"After that I got in trouble with the police and was sent to prison at fourteen, in Oxford. It was a horrible place – the worst experience of my life. There were about sixty-eight people in the whole prison. Most of them were white; there were just three black lads: one Indian lad, one half-caste and me.

"I eventually came out of there, but got into trouble again. It all went downhill and I started smoking 'crack'. I won't even say it was horrible, because for me it was 'normal'.

"I started beating myself up – I can't do this, I can't do that. I can't take drugs, so I took drugs; I can't drive a car, so I drove a car. I just thought: 'What the hell!'

"I heard about Kash because my mate trained with him. When I first met Kash I didn't have a role model, as such, because my older brothers had all grown up as tough guys, but I wasn't really into that. Kash is a tough guy but he uses his strength in a positive way. I kind of admired that.

"If he spoke I listened, the first person I'd ever done that with. My dad never listened to me. I listened to my mom but out of the love and respect side. When Kash said 'Do a hundred press-ups,' and I didn't moan, that's because I respected him.

"When I first punched a pad and it came off Kash's hand, he decided to put me in the ring. He started noticing little things about me that no one had ever picked out. Obviously my mom *would* say things, but when Kash made positive comments about my ability it really meant something."

It's important to remember that you can't just pick someone off the street and turn him or her into a Kickboxer. They've got to have certain skills already in them. It takes quite a while to train somebody up to be a competent Kickboxer.

"I loved the challenge that Kash gave me," continues Balogun. "It was the only thing that I was any good at. I found it easy to win a fight. I was no good at sport at school because I had no one encouraging me. But with kickboxing it was different. I loved the energetic part of it – the feeling that I was getting somewhere when I was training. I actually enjoyed sparring and the pain when I was hit! You feel alive with every punch! Going to prison was not *existing* for me, but this situation, when Kash put me in the ring ... I had a goal. I used to look forward to it," Balogun recalls.

"The first time I ever went in the ring we had a competition and I came second. It was the first thing I'd ever won in my life! That was an inter-club thing, in Halesowen. I was so used to being put down, so it was an incredible achievement. I carried on training with Kash and getting awards every year. I won a trophy for 'the Most Gifted Student' in 1997. I remember being really nervous. I often used to internalise my achievement, but that one I really celebrated. It was all 'part-and-parcel' of the journey I was going on.

"I always had my demon, my epilepsy, lurking in the background. But I didn't tell Kash about it because I was really good at kickboxing. In six weeks I was sparring with Black Belt people. Telling people about my epilepsy and stopping the kickboxing would have really killed me. I was fighting as a Light Middleweight. I've had seven fights altogether, including three in Birmingham, then in Leicester, Telford and the Halesowen one.

"My first fight, in Birmingham, was a 'wake-up call'. Kash said: 'You've got to run; you've got to do this, you've got to do that.' I was going, 'Yeah, yeah, yeah!' thinking that because I could go a round, I could win a fight in the ring easily.

"It's different, because on the pads there's no sense of panic, you don't have to control your breathing and so on. But when you're fighting someone and he's punching you back you've got panic; you're breathing's all over the place! You're not thinking the same. Everything's really fast, you know what I mean?

"Then at the end of that first fight, in '92, I got my second wind and actually won it. All the things I'd learned, I was throwing all these techniques without realising it – and knocking him over. The kid was on the ground."

Magazine entrepreneur Paul Clifton pointed out, earlier in the book, that fighters often reach a stage where they may become quite conceited, thinking that they can do anything. They get a bit 'above themselves'. But Balogun doesn't have the kind of background that would make him like that.

"No, Kash used to get quite frustrated sometimes, because I'd be fighting and I'd trained well, but during a fight I'd just turn my back and look away. He'd told me that I was exceptional, but at the back of mind I didn't have that self-belief. If you've always been told that you're no good at anything, that's a hurdle that you've got to get over. I'd close my eyes in a fight as well, but my opponent would be on the floor! Getting that kind of mentality out of my head was impossible – I couldn't get rid of it.

"I've never watched myself fight, never watched myself train. Never saw my own abilities, but everybody told me that I was really good. I believed them, even though I didn't witness myself fighting. In the one video that I *did* have, I could see that I wasn't believing in myself. I was just turning away and punching like a girl. That held me back a bit.

"It must have been frustrating for Kash because he could see that I was really good, but I was like a wounded animal, which prevented me from progressing further. It may have been a defence mechanism, because the better I was at kickboxing the further I went, the more danger I would have put myself in. And my epilepsy was always there in the background."

We've got a wide range of fighters in the book, all coming from different backgrounds, with different starts in life and approaches. It's great to show the different sides of sport – what you're up against and what you have to combat in order to achieve success.

"After my last fight what scared me the most was my reaction," recalls Balogun. "I got really mad. I was pacing up and down the ring. I was really angry. Since then I've been living in limbo. I've gone a full circle, but I've started training again. But I lost my girl; my relationship broke down, all sorts of stuff. It all happened at once. I didn't have an outlet for my aggression... no way of kicking or punching."

Kash has been going around schools for some time now Balogun, trying to get young pupils to channel their energy in a positive way, rather than getting into trouble, joining gangs and so on. So it's really important to get that out message to young people isn't it?

"Yes, it's the role models they're lacking. If their parents are hopeless they've got to help themselves."

If you were talking to a kid who is in the same situation that you were in, what would your advice be to him? Without sounding sanctimonious or preaching to anyone what would you advise him or her to do?

"Stop and think, which I never did when I was younger. If your parents can't help you, you've got to try to find a role model. There's bound to be an adult who can just stop and evaluate your situation. It won't be the other pupils in your class because they'll probably have their own issues."

Quite a few of the guys in our book came up against similar problems, getting into the wrong company. In some cases they were fortunate to have a father who kept them straight. Dorian Yates was in a similar situation to you Balogun, in that he went to prison. But fortunately they had a Gym there and that was the turning point for him. He suddenly realised that he was good at weight lifting, it was something he could do and it was confidence-building. So whatever sport it is, it's good to channel all of that adrenalin in a positive way.

"Yes, because I had too much to burn up. Kickboxing helped me to channel it and to change my aggression into something that I could use and not get into trouble with.

"When I did my training and my pads, I was really aggressive, but I wasn't arrogant with it. Some people can change when they do kickboxing and walk round the Gym like a Rambo – and be really arrogant. I've never been like that! When I was a kid I was a 'Crack-head' and a criminal," continues Balogun. "If it wasn't for sport I would have still been going down the same road. If Kash can turn someone like me into a half-decent kickboxer, then he can do anything. I was really mixed up. Training in any sport, as long as he enjoys it, can change a kid's whole character. Although a lot of sports don't work on your character, the sports that involve fighting do.

"When I watch some of the kids nowadays a lot of them aren't working on their mentality when they come into the Gym. I see some of the kids in the training and their half-heartedness and complaining about this and that and I think to myself: 'What are you complaining for? At least you get the chance to go for your world titles and your belts and that. You take my life, I'll take yours and we'll switch. You don't know how lucky you are!'

"But I'm not the sort of person who's going to stand there and say stuff like that. It's frustrating that you complain but you get the opportunity to fulfil a dream, which, to be fair, you're not *that* good at. Yet you're able to do all of the stuff that was a *dream* of mine. Stop complaining. It's annoying me! So you've got to do twenty more press-ups. Just be thankful that you can go and do all of that. But they haven't experienced the pain that I have, so they don't know what it's like. That's why I don't say anything.

"I'd love to be a coach," Balogun continues. "I keep going away then coming back and thinking that I'm going to do it. It's annoying. I'm thirty-five now and I'm still doing the same thing that I was doing when I was eighteen. I'm prevented because of my illness, so I'm still a bit bitter. They've got me on all sorts of medication. One sort that they were giving me was making me dull. It's a mood-stabiliser but when I'm training it doesn't help.

"I'm probably the one that *could* have been, if it hadn't been for my illness," Balogun concludes wistfully. "I can't help wondering what it would have been like."

Round 18

THE GILL FAMILY: ANOTHER 'KASH 22' SITUATION!

Everyone goes into marriage with the best of intentions, but cross-culture marriage can sometimes prove more difficult, because our cultural heritage defines our basic notions of 'love', and 'relationship'.

In May 2010, I interviewed Kash's immediate family. Date-wise, although the particular months are different, Ellie was born on the 24th; Kallan the 25th; Mitch the 26th; his former wife, Julie, the 1st and Kash the 2nd of the month! Talk about coincidence!

This Round differs from most of the others, as it contains extracts from my four interviews, interspersed with comments from Kash, as opposed to his normal role as Principal Narrator. Before Julie's interview, we'll begin with some opening thoughts from Kash:

It's Thursday Night. Just travelling back from the gym and I've been thinking about Julie today. We split up in May 2010. It went to court in October 2010, where a Decree Nisi was granted, in our absence. The final divorce was in June 2011.

I was just thinking about where was the demise? Where was the change? I remember when Julie's sister, Lisa, used to come round with all of her friends, about five or six girls. They were all 'dolled up' and ready to go out on the town. They kept saying: 'Julie, are you coming?' The first time I don't think she really wanted to go. I said: 'It's up to you. You don't see your sister very often.' But she said: 'No, I won't go,' but I left it to her.

But they came again, about two months later, so Julie probably thought she'd see a bit of nightlife. With hindsight I think she did settle down too early. Then she went away with my sister-in-law Daljit, so she was getting a bit more freedom, which was good, because the kids were growing up and maybe that's

what she was missing out on? I was a young star: I wasn't a rebel, but I did get a bit more social life after the fights. I still see that as a decisive factor.

OK, we had our problems but people get through their problems if they love each other. But obviously the love died. Over the years to come, I think she may regret it... sadly.

Kash and Julie first met on December 20 1990, at *Burberry's Nightclub*, Broad Street, Birmingham.

"It was three months prior to my World Title Fight. We'd just had a Christmas Party at the club. I'd been going out with another girl, for five years. That particular night, after the party, Rob James and I went to *Burberry's*. That's when I met my wife, Julie. I thought: 'Who's that good-looking blonde over there?'

"She was with her girlfriend. I could only dance to the one song, which is *UB40's Red Red Wine*. Julie lived in Stratford-upon-Avon. I visited her there every other night. Sometimes they were foggy nights, so it was hard to get home.

"But I was scared to stay away from home, because I had a strict father. I was twenty-four, but still concerned about my dad. If I'd been white I probably would have had my own place, but we were the extended family and we stuck together; it's definitely a different culture.

"On Boxing Day I told my other girlfriend that I was fighting for the World Title in March, so I'd have to give up everything."

Julie recalls: "The girl that I worked with, Dee, short for Denise, had a passion for the *Burberry's* DJ, so we'd gone there so that she could see him. It was a quiet night at the club. I hadn't noticed Kash, but then he came up and asked for a dance. I think he was trying to get his friend Rob to ask Dee for a dance, but Rob was completely drunk!

"We danced to *Red, Red Wine*, well... Kash jogged! Then we left, after I gave him my phone number. He didn't make an instant impression on me. To be honest, in the very early parts of the relationship, there wasn't anything compelling; it just gradually grew.

"I was twenty-two and managing a shop in Leamington. Kash was two years older. When we first met I was living just outside Stratford, at a place called Bearley, sharing a farmhouse with two other girls. It was great during the summer, but freezing in winter! From there, we moved to an apartment, close to Stratford town centre."

When Kash and Julie were dating they'd sometimes meet midway, in Shirley, near the *Plough*, because Kash was teaching in Birmingham and Julie lived in Stratford. At other times they'd meet in Sutton Coldfield; since 1986, Kash has run a club there, at the John Wilmott School.

When the couple moved to Lighthorne Road in Solihull in 1993, Julie continued with her hairdressing job in Stratford, at *UK Barbers* and Kash would visit her at the new house. He makes the point: "When Cougar and Daljit refurbished a house, dad gave £10,000 towards their property, which is fantastic, because it had made him happy, their having an arranged marriage.

"When my younger brother, Gurdip, got married to Jan, who is also an Asian girl, dad gave him between £7-£10,000. When I got married he gave me £250! I thought: 'What have I done wrong?' So it was strange. Normally Asian parents will contribute if you want to buy a property, but no one helped me out. Resham didn't need any help because he was quite well off anyway, but the rest of us *did* struggle."

"We *gutted* the Lighthorne Road house," Julie continues. "Kash knew people who could work on it. We had it painted from top to toe, before we moved in.

"I was managing the Leamington shop and Dee was managing the Stratford shop. Then she moved to Dorridge. A children's clothes shop in Stratford was being converted into a hairdresser's. She agreed to rent it off the owner, if I would go with her.

"Initially, Kash said: 'No, it's not a good idea,' but I stuck to my guns and thought: 'Yes, actually, I do want to do that.' We hadn't got children at that point. This was before we were married, around 1991-92, because the shop's been open twenty years now.

"So I moved there and it was fantastic. We were really busy. Dee and I managed it jointly: we both rented a chair. Then I left to have Ellie and Kallan, so I didn't work for about four years. During that period, the shop owner sold it to Dee, who was still working there. So she's the owner of *Snips*, in Stratford and I rent a chair off her. When I go back now, on Tuesdays and Fridays, Kash has the children."

"Julie and I built up a strong relationship, had a little break in 1993, but went on to get married on the 2nd December 1994 in Antigua. There was a particular reason for that," Kash reveals.

"Yes, because of our family background, where we lived and my family living away, we wouldn't have known *where* the best place was to get married," explains

Julie. "With not having my mum around it was more of a personal thing between Kash and me, so it was a private wedding. When we got back, my family held a big party and we also had a few drinks at the house, with Kash's family.

"Our Antigua wedding was near the beach," Julie recalls. "It was absolutely beautiful. We didn't know anybody out there, but we met a couple named Karen and Terry: they were our witnesses. Then about two or three years later they got married and we were *their* witnesses."

Julie is one of five children: she has three brothers and one sister: in age order, Tony, Barry, Chris, Julie and then her younger sister, Lisa. Her brothers and sisters live within two or three miles of each other, in Wisbech Cambridgeshire, on the border of Cambridgeshire and Norfolk, about thirty miles from Cambridge itself.

But Julie's rural way of life was totally foreign to Kash, as he was accustomed to towns.

"He totally hated it. If you have ever lived a village life, it's like stepping back in time. But I think that more of it is because we are a very close family. If we get together, everybody gets together, so there are about twenty of us at a time, for dinner, or whatever; everybody just chips in and does their own thing. He found it very hard to be in that environment – just relaxing; sitting down, having your dinner and so on," Julie remembers.

Kash points out: "I used to visit Julie's side of the family, maybe a couple of times a year. Christmas was a time when we were all cooped up in the house. Her brothers used to come down to Birmingham when I was promoting shows – they would sometimes help me out.

"Like I've said to you before, my way of life is always training, running, being active; a lot of the kids up there, were just eating all day long. I had to go out for a run early in the morning, or mid-afternoon, then come back and have an hour's kip, because my body was used to doing that. That was my routine, but hopefully people didn't think badly of me for doing that.

"I remember one time, about eight years ago, when a particular couple were splitting up. Julie said, 'Well people do fall out of love.' I said: 'Well that won't happen with me and you.' But it made me think about it – why would you say something like that, in that context?

"Looking back, as the kids got bigger, she must have fallen out of love with me. We were sitting outside *John Lewis* one day in Solihull, having dinner. Julie said to me: 'I'd never change my life for anything. I'm so happy.' So it's really strange, in view of what's happened now. But I suppose it's part-and-parcel of the job. You ask a footballer: you love football; you fall in love your wife... but can you love both?"

According to Julie: "I don't let things bother me... or get on top of me. I just take things as they come. In that respect you could say that Kash and myself are opposites."

"Julie came from a big family, like I did," Kash explains, "you very rarely met someone who did so we hit it off straight away. She was quite close to her brothers and sisters. It affects the way you mix with people, so Julie and I were similar in that way too."

"But I think that probably has its own shelf life!" Julie comments. "The marriage was good, but it was a case of I was very lucky, that I was able to give up work. I remember having a discussion with Kash, before we were married. He said: 'Obviously you'll give up work to look after the children.' At the time it was what I wanted to do. Mum died when I was twelve but I remember her always being there, during my very young years. Kash's life hadn't changed, from when I met him to his being a father: he had been able to do exactly what he wanted, when he wanted, because the children were mainly in my care. Since the divorce however, he spends more time with them."

"It's interesting too," observes Kash, "that we both lost our mothers at an early age, although I was nine when I lost my mother. But prior to that, mom was always there to look after the family."

"I don't think that you realise that you're doing it, but a lot of the time you tend to mother your husband, as well as the children," continues Julie. "It's easier to do it all at the same time! But then as your children get older, they still need you as a mother, but they're not so reliant upon you. And you think 'Where has the relationship shifted?' Rather than being man and wife, you feel like mother and son.

"It also depends upon whether you're parallel, in bringing up the children, jointly, or whether it's very one-sided. If one of you is just carrying on as normal with everything to do with their career, but suddenly, as a woman, you become a mother, you see things differently. And I think you reach a point where you think: 'Actually, I don't know whether I like your world... and I don't know if I know *you.*'

"As the children get older, you look at your own interaction. In the closing stages of our marriage the only interaction that we had together was when Kash was talking about himself. He would say: 'How's your day?' But before you'd had a chance to answer, he was telling you about his day."

Sadly, in many cases it seems that one can't be an ultra-successful person, and maintain a balanced family life... something's got to give.

"I think everything is OK until the woman or the wife thinks: 'Well what am I getting out of this? What about my feelings?' I've never liked the kickboxing macho thing from Day One, but I've supported Kash, because it was what he wanted to do, but I don't particularly like going to a show. And sometimes you feel like you're being 'wheeled out': 'Oh this is my family and these are my children,' as if you're in a box. I hate anything like that – I hate the publicity," Julie continues.

"I'm proud of Kash, for what he's achieved, but it didn't necessarily mean that I wanted to be part of it. I think sometimes that's what he didn't understand. It's not that you're not proud of him, but I don't like to be in the limelight. I've said it quite a few times at Sports Awards: 'You're better off taking the fighters.'

"It's when you're not aware of other people around you, or if you think that other people are there solely to help you, that it's a problem. I don't know whether it's because of us, or his age, or a lot of other things, that he feels that he needs the appraisal, to make him believe that he has still got it.

"I don't mean this in a bad way although Kash would probably disagree... his fighters have achieved what they have because they've had a good coach. And so he's getting the appraisal from that as well. He never had anybody behind him in that way, so I think he's determined to be there for his fighters. He probably goes over and beyond the call of duty, to achieve that, even though he's got a family. I remember for some of the kids' birthdays, for shows and things like that, to prove that it can be done and that he's the best, sometimes he's put the fighters first."

There's the self reliance aspect too Julie. Kash is the first to say that he doesn't feel that others can do certain things relating to his sport, as well as he can and he therefore prefers to rely on himself as much as possible. Kickboxing of course, is a sport where you sink or swim by your own efforts, unlike football, for example, where you have to rely on the other players giving an hundred per cent too.

"Yes, he isn't a team player: he's very competitive, even in very small things," agrees Julie. "If he was to wash up, then I've never washed up as well as that! If he was to hoover – we've never hoovered under the settee. Everything that he does has to be better.

"Sometimes with Kash, he doesn't think that he has any limitations – that he can achieve exactly what he wants to achieve, which in a way is a good thing: that's what got him his four world titles. But there's no leeway: he's very controlling, in the sense that no one can do it better; whether that's self reliance or controlling I'm not sure; I think it's very close."

I'm not necessarily relating this to Kash, but I've found with *some* of the high achievers that I've interviewed for biographies, over the years, from all walks of life, that it's a fear of failure that drives them; there is no way that they can allow themselves to fail. But again, that's probably how some of the greatest names in history have felt!

"People have different ways of showing their emotions," observes Kash. "For example, my particular way of showing my emotions on live radio was to mention my divorce. I'm not saying 'Come and get me – I'm single!' I wanted to announce it on live radio, during my interview with Sonia Deol, because my personal life is very important to me. I'm doing a job and it was a way of releasing my personal emotions at the time. It didn't feel like I was putting myself out for another relationship, because I don't feel as if I want to settle down again."

"He does say a lot of things without actually thinking about them; whereas some people will think about what they are saying first," comments Julie. "Sometimes that's a good thing. But sometimes the way that he says things can be very cutting. I don't think that he means to do that, but if people take it in the wrong way, he ends up having to explain himself. Rather than saying: 'Well, I didn't really mean it in that way,' he can't do that, because that means he would end up having to say sorry. Sometimes it can get him into a bit of trouble. But then he's very stubborn as well.

"Kash is very precise and organised in terms of his professional life. The shows that he does run perfectly, but in his personal life, his office for example, he's quite untidy."

"It's an organised mess," elaborates Kash, "because in 90% of cases I know where everything is. Making time for my children is more important than organising things."

"I've had a good marriage and a very fortunate life," Julie acknowledges. "One of the things about marrying Kash was that I felt I could trust him:

he's going to look after me. Life's going to be rosy. I've never had to worry about money and I've had everything that I wanted – basically.

"I have done a lot of it on my own, as with the children: Kash would just join us occasionally. I just feel that it's a new phase starting now, and if I'm perfectly honest, I think he deserves someone who will love him for himself – and everything about him.

But I just can't love him in that way, any more. I think that trust is everything."

Resham was the first in the family to marry a white girl. Kash feels that, had *he* been the first to marry a white girl, he would probably have had more difficulty persuading his father. However, Julie disagrees:

"I think that he could have done anything he wanted, in his dad's eyes, because of what he'd achieved in the other parts of his life. Obviously, his dad was very proud of Kash's achievements, so he could have married a pigmy or any other kind of woman – and it would have been absolutely fine!

"The fact that Resham *did* open the path for him probably helped. Looking back on it, I don't think Kash could have had anybody telling him: 'You're marrying this woman.' It had to come from him; but at the time, I didn't know that," Julie explains.

Kash was telling me that Ellie was born on 24 May 1995, although it was supposed to have been the 17th. The 13th was the day of his fight, so he turned up in quite a state, at the maternity hospital!

"Yes, on the birth pictures he's got two black eyes," confirms Julie. "There was a guy in the next cubicle who'd fainted and therefore had stitches on his head. So he was visiting his wife with stitches in his head and Kash was visiting me, with two black eyes!

"When Kallan was born, on 25 February 1997, he was just perfect: perfect head shape. He was a very good baby, but it was hard work because there was only twenty-two months between the two babies and at this stage, Kash was still going all over the place with his fighting, so you did feel as if you were on your own, quite a bit.

"Kash cut the cord when Kallan was born, but when he was due, my dad and my stepmother came down to look after Ellie. I was in contraction, from about two o'clock, on Tuesday afternoon. At five o'clock Kash was teaching a kickboxing class, in Halesowen, so he decided to go there – and ring me if the contractions got any worse. About seven o'clock on that Tuesday night, they took me into hospital. He then joined us at the hospital and we came back together after Kallan was born."

Kash comments: "I thought it best to stay out of the way. Why have *two* people panicking!"

When Mitchell was born, on 26 October 2001, everybody was 85% certain that it was going to be a girl.

"Yes, even when I was giving birth, the midwife was saying: 'Oh, she'll be here soon!' It was very rushed at the end, because he came out with the umbilical cord wrapped around his neck. They didn't realise that was the case until he was actually coming out of the birth canal. So at the end there was a lot of panic, a lot of doctors and nurses were running in. I remember looking at Kash and he'd gone white! I was saying: 'What's the matter? Is he OK? Is he OK?!' Then everything was fine. But even after that, they tested him on the ward, to make sure he could see properly," recalls Julie.

"At the time Kash was saying it would be a boy, I thought he was doing so because he wanted another son, so I remember saying to him: 'Don't be too disappointed. We *know* it's a girl.'"

As a result, Mitch came out of the hospital wearing a little sheepskin jacket and a pink hat!

"Kallan wanted to call him Woody, or Buzz, as in Buzz Lightyear, because he'd been watching the *Toy Story* film," Julie continues. "The kids have a say in everything and I remember going through lots of ideas for names, with them. When I was in hospital having Ellie, a friend of mine had twins called Ellie and Mitch. I loved the name Mitch, so he is a Mitchell, but we've shortened it to Mitch. If he grows up to be a surfer or whatever, Mitch is fantastic; but if he becomes a banker, Mitchell will sound more sophisticated.

"We found it quite hard finding names that fitted both cultures," explains Julie. "Ellie was going to be called just that, but it was Kash who wanted to put the 'sha' on the end. Kallan can easily be an Indian name, as well as an English name."

Kash explains, "Part of me still loves Julie, although she's told me that she doesn't love me. But I still feel something for her… shame!

"Our first daughter, Elliesha, was born in 1995. Those were really good times. Elliesha is a mix of English and Asian, but she likes being called 'Ellie'. She's very independent and very bright at school. She's a hard worker; into ballet. She began at Greswold Primary School, just down the road from our house," Kash continues.

"She was a fearful child when she was young. I remember going to her school. I was carrying the Olympic torch for the Peace Run. She was frightened because she thought that her dad was going to burn! I'm very close to Ellie. As she's the first child I spent a lot of time with her. I used to take her for walks in her buggy and take her to the park – 'Daddy's little girl'. But as she's grown up she's become a lot closer to her mom; she and her mom are best friends now. She's very polite and sensible.

"She's good at Art – like her mom. Ellie's a perfectionist; she likes storytelling as well, which is similar to me. She'll write pages and pages, like I used to do. She's very pretty too, just like her... dad!"

On 24 May 2012 Elliesha was seventeen years old. She elaborates on the Olympic torch story.

"I used to be scared of fire and fireworks, so when dad walked in with the flame I got really upset about it," Ellie recalls. "I was only young at that time. It was for a charity event that started at my school."

Ellie currently attends Stratford College and is taking four A Levels. She has been interested in fashion ever since she was ten years old. She loves shopping and enjoys being the oldest child in the family, with the extra responsibility that entails.

Ellie, what's it like having Kash as a father? How has it affected you?

"He's always taught me to stick up for myself. He's encouraged me to learn self defence, although I never actually have. I've always been into more girly stuff. I started ballet when I was about four, in a very small group, then I quit when I was five, but started again later, about four years ago, at a school club."

Getting back to your dad now, does the fact that he is famous sit easily with you?

"Yes, because I've never know anything different. He's the main part of the show when he's in the ring, announcing everything and being comical. He's very confident; he's the one who puts it all together. I've never actually seen him fight, although I was born before he retired from it. I wouldn't like to see him fight while it was happening, but while you're watching videos it's alright, because you already know that he didn't get hurt!

"If I went around telling people who my dad is, they might think that we've got a lot of money, but it's not like that... and I don't like boasting."

"I didn't have a lot of cash for us to go on summer holidays, although I would love to have taken the kids abroad," explains Kash. "I took Ellie to Holland, but even with Julie, we didn't have any beach holidays, apart from our wedding in Antigua. Because of the expense of running the gym it's not been easy. I was teaching all the time and finding time to take holidays was very difficult. Maybe that was one of the reasons why Julie and I split."

We're asking all the contributors to this book the same question: If your dad *does* have any faults, what might they be?

"He likes to get his own way and he likes things to be done his way, even if someone disagrees," observes Ellie.

Do you have any of his personality characteristics?

"I'm competitive, in little ways; even if it's just a game of *Nintendo* I like to win. I think I'm a bit of a perfectionist too: my writing has to be very neat and I don't like to do crossings out, so I don't rush," Ellie concludes.

Ellie and Kallan were included in a Kash interview for ITN in 2002, when they were very young. "They showed all my trophies, because it was my final fight and win, lose or draw, I was going to retire. I *did* lose that last fight. During that interview Ellie was asked: 'Your dad does kickboxing. How do you feel about that?' Ellie went: 'It's good, because nobody robs the house!'

"She's really embarrassed about it now, but she had this fear that someone might rob the house, when she was a young kid. I said: 'Look, no one's ever going to rob this house because they know that your dad's a world kickboxing champion!'

"Kallan, my eldest son, is fifteen years old in 2012. He's a great kid. I taught him to play football, when he was little. As a father, you need patience. I love my kids. Kallan's a good kid; again, very polite," Kash continues.

"When I told dad that I'd got a daughter, he said: 'Never mind!' The Asian way is to have sons, because of the old dowry system. But I was happy, because my child was healthy and I was more westernised. Within my heart I really did want a boy. You don't say that, but you want to be able to take them to football matches and all that.

"Kallan is very tall and willowy like me – he's had a growth spurt. Ellie was rather shy at first, but Kallan is 'happy-go-lucky' and makes friends easily.

"I've taken him down to Aston Villa and he's met all the Chelsea team, on two occasions, and had pictures with the top players. He's aggressive, which is what a fighter needs. He'll be able to hold his own, so I don't really worry too much about him. He's into fitness and he likes his football. I try not to put too much pressure on him."

Shall we begin Kallan, by you telling me about your dad playing football with you?

"He used to get annoyed when I picked the ball up instead of kicking it. He played football competitively with me, when I was quite young. If he'd let me win, there would have been no point in doing it. In football I like to win.

"I went to watch Villa, because my dad had got tickets from someone that he knew there. It was six years ago, three or four days before my birthday. We watched the game then met the players afterwards and had our photos taken with them. I used to have a bedroom wall full of Chelsea photos, before my bedroom was redecorated."

Kash said that you tried the martial arts about three years ago?

"Yes, I used to go with my friend, and then he left and I carried on for a bit. Then I went to another one on my own: the *Layca Centre*, at Lighthall School, in Shirley. That lasted about a year. I quit for a while, but then I decided to do Thai Boxing at my dad's gym. I prefer that because you can use more moves and body parts. I did alright with that but then my brother had football on the same night, so I couldn't do it any more."

What's it like having a famous dad?

"He's really organised for the shows and everything. He can talk on the microphone for ages, without people getting bored. I've seen him in his kickboxing classes. He explains everything clearly."

Do you talk about your dad much to other people?

"No. He plays football with me and my brother," Kallan concludes.

Kash and Julie's youngest son, Mitchell, aka 'Mitch', was born, on 26 October 2001 and was eleven in 2012.

"At one stage, he had a choice of football academies," explains Kash. "West Bromwich Albion really took a shine to him; Coventry wanted to sign him up, so did the Man United guy. But he chose Birmingham.

"Mitchell's a completely different character: very outgoing; really good-mannered and 'happy-go-lucky', but an ultra-perfectionist. He's versatile; good at art; gifted and talented at school. Recently he's done very well in PE. If Mitch has got the same genes as me, he'll go all the way!

"Kallan's helped him more with his football than I have, because he's had more patience with him. He's tried to educate him and be more aggressive with him. When Mitchell's played against him, Julie's always said let him win. But I said 'No, no, he needs to improve.' So me and Kallan have 'roughed him up' – and it's brought him on!

"There was a big article in a Birmingham paper, about how relieved I was that Mitchell was trying football rather than the fight game. I don't really want my kids going in the ring. Mitchell has left the Academy now and plays for 'Shirley Town'," concludes Kash.

The following interview took place when he was eight years old, but we've added some updates at the end of this section.

First of all Mitchell, I have to say that you seem very mature for your age: when we went to the *Malmaison Hotel*, for the David Dunn interview. The average eight-year-old might have been 'thrown' by the occasion, but you seemed to take it all in your stride.

"I was a bit scared."

You did exceptionally well to gain a place in the Birmingham City Academy, at such a young age. Has your dad's coaching helped you in that respect?

"He's taught me skills and encouraged me to use my left foot more. I play in the centre of the field and you do most of the running really: you have to run back and you have to run forward.

"I enjoy tennis, swimming and boxing. Art is probably my best subject, next to PE. I get loads of sheets out of my dad's office. I'll search on the Internet for a picture, and then I'll just copy it. I do collages – everything really.

"I like IT too. We were given this situation where crop circles suddenly appeared and we had to explain why they had appeared. Then we had to wait to see what had really happened.

"Dad's a really nice person, although he shouts at us a bit sometimes, if I argue with my brother or my sister. He takes us swimming at *Virgin Active*. I go if Kallan can come too, because dad goes in the Sauna."

You had some photos taken when we went to the *Malmaison*, didn't you?

"Yes, dad's got them on his computer, so he can just print them off. I kept their signatures somewhere special as well. Dad sent one of the *Malmaison* photos to *Match* football magazine. My brother was in there once, with Frank Lampard.

"We went to a Mercedes garage, because I'm into really fast cars! I said: 'Dad, can you get me a Mercedes SLK?' We picked up a flyer for this really quick one – the SLS. But I think it cost something like a million pounds! But I don't think I'll ever race cars – because that's kind of dangerous!

"My dad said he doesn't want me to go in the ring really, because I might get hurt. He got hurt a few times. He broke his ankle on the night of his brother's wedding. He had a street fight didn't he?"

Yes that was Cougar's wedding. Well, that's absolutely brilliant Mitch. Just to finish with, what's it like being the younger brother?

"Well it's kind of good, because everybody cares about you. But my brother and sister are stronger than me, so if they pushed me I'd fall on the floor!"

Kash's brother Cougar comments: "Kash is like me in a way: when his kids were born he was bringing them to my dad's house, changing nappies and feeding them. Although he's been away more than me, he's done more with his kids than me. He's very dedicated to them."

Cougar's wife, Daljit, confirms: "Julie and I had a weekend away in Chester and spent a day at Chester Races, which was lovely. Kash and Julie are both really nice people. We were devastated when we found out what had happened."

"My dad used to say it's always best to marry within your own culture," Cougar continues. "But Julie and Kash had some brilliant years together. They're both very dedicated to their children and no one *ever* expected them to split up. Kash has always been very happy in his marriage. But the life that he has to lead, has taken him away from her a lot.

"But Kash is gutted – he *has* got emptiness in him," Cougar observes, "because he's always been for family; take his family away now – and having to look for an apartment… I've put myself in his shoes and no matter what you say, he's still going to miss that family atmosphere.

"Julie's lived on her own before she met Kash; Kash has never done that. He'll come to terms with it, and he *will* move on, but it will really cut him up. But he's now thinking: 'How can I channel my enthusiasm into my children?'

"It's a shame about what he's going through now. It's the loneliness, the emptiness and the darkness that will be hard, no matter who you've got to lean on. He can come here, but it's never the same," concludes Cougar.

Kash's younger brother, Gurdip, comments: "It's a shame, because they've got three wonderful, well-mannered children. When he phoned me to tell me I said: 'I hope you can sort things out.' But you can't interfere – it's a difficult one. Kash is a very private man: he doesn't show his emotions, but when our dad passed away, I've never seen Kash cry like that. I see Kash as a fantastic father – he's very proud of his children."

Resham adds: "Kash doesn't want his children to follow his career path. He wants them to get a good education and progress. Hopefully he's laid the foundations for them to move on to better things."

Dave Barnett observes: "For as long as I've known Kash, he's been really family-orientated and his wife and children have always come first. I've always respected him for that."

Hudson Richards echoes that feeling: "One of the things that I respected about Kash was his wife and children. I haven't spent that much time with Julie, but she seems very special too. They have these awesome kids.

"The first time that I met her, I wondered how they'd met, because they seemed quite different from each other. But I think people do that with my wife too, because she's white," Hudson observes. "I've been in love with the same woman for twenty-one years. I love her to bits. I don't give a rat's 'hiney' what anybody else thinks. When we're walking down the street people look. You know what? We are here… and we are together… and you don't scare us."

Cyrille Regis makes the point that in the sport of football 60% – 70% of players have been divorced. Kash has devoted a huge amount of time, not only into training new champions, but also promoting the sport.

"It can be a very selfish existence," Cyrille observes. "You've got to strike a balance between your work – your passion – and your family. The pressures of achieving, the pressures that are put on you by publicity… media demands. But that's not the sport's fault. It's the character traits in the person who has the temptations around him."

Joe Egan acknowledges: "A sportsman's lifestyle can place a great strain on a relationship. You need the support of your partner in everything that you do, but especially in a sport where you're going to be getting hurt. If they're not with you, it's very difficult." I explain that Julie and the children are actually helping us with the book. "Ah – well that's nice," Joe concludes. "It must be an amicable breakup then."

As Julie, Kash and the children enter this new phase in their lives, we wish them all the very best, for their future happiness.

In the next Round we return to our normal format, with Kash as the Principal Narrator.

Round 19

FLASH FORWARD: ROLE MODELS

It's the second decade of the New Millennium, and as the Media reminds us daily, the need for effective role models has never been greater. With the recession continuing to bite ever deeper, young people, especially those from less privileged backgrounds, find themselves in increasingly lengthy dole queues, or on the wrong side of the law.

Since the middle of the last century public-spirited individuals have worked tirelessly in youth clubs, sports clubs and within communities, to help less fortunate youngsters, often with little public recognition.

During the late 1980s-early 1990s, Hector Pinkney, aka 'Mr Handsworth', tutors Kash and Apache, sports and music-wise. They subsequently contribute to the Birmingham and international scene, in various ways, combining their talents, for the benefit of young people, when time allows, through school presentations, talent competitions and promoting fitness.

Kickboxing students and university graduates, Emma Fitch and Jay Sokhi, credit Kash with their high level of sporting achievement. Poppy Brady, Hector, Apache, Hudson Richards, Brian Travers, Wayne Elcock, Peter Wilson, Tom Ross, Kenny Cunningham, Joe Egan and Phil Upton feature in this Round. Also, Holyhead School staff members, Leslie Edlington and Ross Trafford.

In her July 2007 article, *Nothing Can Stop Us Now*, Poppy Brady summarised Hector Pinkney, aka *Mr Handsworth*, in the following way:

'Hector has nurtured and empowered people of all ethnic backgrounds to improve their quality of life through sport, health and fitness. The *Dojo Project*, run by Hector, has members aged two to ninety across Aston, Perry Barr, Ladywood and Handsworth. Hector, who organised the run, explained: "We train our people to make a better life for themselves and for others, by giving them the key to self discipline."'

205

He most certainly helped to inspire a young Kash Gill too, back in the day, when he was aspiring to win world titles. To his considerable credit, many other youngsters encouraged by Hector went on to become famous sportsmen, musicians, doctors, lawyers, et cetera.

Hector arrived in Handsworth in 1962, from Jamaica. His parents, Mavis and Rudolph Vincent Pinkney had been living there since the 1950s.

"My father was a cabinet maker. He worked on the Panama Canal before coming to England. My mother, Mavis, is from Panama. My parents lived in Leonard Road, Lozells and my father ran workshops for young people at his house," recalls Hector. "My mother was a foster mother, so she was involved with the community."

Hector has continued Mavis's tradition by 'fostering' many young Handsworth-Lozells people, for most of his life

"It was important to keep the unity within the community. My father donated a tray to The Pinto Collection in Birmingham Museum," Hector continues. "A lot of his furniture is still at our family home in Leonard Road; it's never been exhibited.

"The *Dojo Community Project* has its roots in the 1960s, when it was set up as the Nightingale Project by my mother, Mavis Pinkney. The door is always open at our house for people of all ages who are in need. When my mother started the *Project* there was nothing to help people within the community."

Hector was featured in *You Deserve A House Like This*, televised on Wednesday 7 April 2012, by Channel 4 and hosted by Amanda Lamb. As two of his former protégés, Kash and Apache were on hand to surprise him!

Hector and his son were taken to a luxury weekend hotel, while his house was secretly decorated, as a reward for his years of work, helping others. During the programme Apache and Kash explained how Hector, a role model and go-between for people in the Handsworth area, had contributed to their success.

Hector first met Apache Indian when Steve was around seventeen years of age. At that stage Steve used to carry Hector's record boxes for him and served an apprenticeship, watching him set up the wiring for the discos and so on. Terry Brown, a school friend of Apache's would also help.

He ran roller skating sessions at the *Handsworth Leisure Centre*, which Apache, Terry Brown, Patrick Palmer and many others enjoyed. Hector also ran discos twice a week at the *Weld Community Centre* in Heathfield Road. His DJ name is *Captain Boogie*.

Hector first met Kash before he had won his first championship belt. He was already into the martial arts himself, particularly karate, and was able to give Kash a few tips at the *Handsworth Leisure Centre*. Hector didn't use pads, so when he asked Kash to kick him it felt as though he was wearing metal-tipped boots, although Kash has never worn them in his life! Hector, who also trained with Howard *The Hawk* Brown, could tell from the quality of Kash's kick that he was championship material.

Hector is multi-talented. In 1979 he won the *Midland Disco Dance Championship*, run by the Arthur Murray School of Dancing. The eventual UK winner appeared in a film with John Travolta.

In Hector's opinion the 1981 and 1985 riots arose out of a social need but the 2011 incidents were born out of greed. He recalls walking down to Lozells, when the 1985 riots were taking place, accompanied by a TV news reporter, but was attacked, en route, by a policeman with a truncheon, who simply saw him as a black person. Luckily Hector was able to defend himself and, due to his karate training, push the policeman away. He received a head injury but it could have been a lot more serious, had he been unable to defend himself. That same year, *Mr Handsworth* was interviewed by *Ebony* for a television documentary, giving his perspective on the riots.

He equates the martial arts with life. "You find a centre point in the martial arts: it's about balance, coordination and timing. And it's the same in life."

Hector has received several awards. In 2005 he was a *Chamberlain Award* Winner and also won a *Stay Healthy* Award. Mark Gough of Central TV interviewed him at the time of his *Chamberlain Award* and came up with the title *Mr Handsworth*.

He has a three-point proposal for improving the Handsworth situation. A subsequent book on the area would enable us to discuss this in more detail. He works for Birmingham City Council, as a Security Officer at Handsworth Library, but in terms of the extensive unpaid work he does he is also a Community Liaison Officer.

On Thursday 3 November 2011, *Mr Handsworth* travelled to Windsor Castle, to receive an MBE from HRH Princess Anne, accompanied by his eldest daughter, Marsha, his son Kyle and his sister, Dolores. He received the award for outstanding service to the Handsworth community.

"It's on behalf of the community. This honour is issued to me *for* the community," he explains. "The people want me to go and everywhere I go now Asians, Blacks, Whites, they are congratulating me, saying: "It couldn't have gone to a better person."

"I was working in another library, over in Weoley Castle and a lady pulled out a small paragraph in a book, which said:

'Hector Protector went to see the Queen
Hector Protector, he was dressed in green.'

So I hope that was a kind of prediction that I was going to get this award! The Lord watches over those who watch over those. Whatever happens in the community, people will come and let me know."

Hector, who exudes a *genuine* love for his community, continues to organise many events in the area. These include a weekly running club and exercise classes for the *Soho Elders Group*. He has set up a karate club and organises benefit nights. As a youth mentor, he helps the library hold talent competitions and live music events.

By 1991 Apache Indian aka Steve Kapur was already on the road to success when *Island Records*, a branch of *Universal Records,* signed him.

Those first three number one records in three years was a quarter of a million pound deal – the biggest thing ever, at that time! During 1992 his career really took off, with the next record called *Arranged Marriage*: it was Number Sixteen in the British Charts. He appeared on *Top of the Pops*, touching both the Asian and Black communities with his music.

"My hero was Bob Marley," explains Apache, "he died on my birthday, May 11th, so every May 11th I'd get up and play some Bob Marley. Now I was signed to his record label, *Island Records* and the first thing they did was to send me out to Jamaica. They said: 'Right – you need to go and record in the Bob Marley Studios!'

"I introduced the new hybrid sound of bhangra ragamuffin, also known as 'bhangramuffin', to the world, with my first album *No Reservations*, recorded in Jamaica and produced in 1993, by Simon & Diamond, Phil Chill, Robert Livingstone, Bobby Digital and Sly Dunbar.

"The second single that I ever recorded, *Chok There*, was adapted, with lyrics that I wrote for Kash. It was centered on his career; the fact that he was 'Number One in the Boxing Ring' and so on. It's a ragamuffin style. Still, to this day, it's a very big tune. *Chok There, Number One in the Boxing Ring, Chok There* ... and so on. It's an Indian phrase, it means tearing the house down. So I'd be shouting out "*Chok There*" between the lines," Steve recalls.

Apache was in the local chip shop on Grove Lane, when I walked in, just after my fight with Alex Tui, in 1991. I said: "Apache, I used your song, over in Australia. My opponent asked me who was singing it." It was from his first track *Movie Over India*. I said: "Apache, you've got to put some lyrics together for me." Within weeks, he was on the case. He put these really good words together for me. So from 1991 to this day, we've still been using them!

According to Apache: "Kash and myself try to help, through music and the community. I've always supported him and he's always supported me. He asked me to go in the ring at some of his shows and sing that song. He loves that. And he's proud of me too – we're both from Handsworth; I know his family; he's got his boxers and they know me, so I've kind of supported his whole movement, as well as him."

There's a real parallel between our two lives: both born in the same area; both knew what we wanted and were determined to reach the top in our chosen field; both entrepreneurs – and so on. Apache and me got closer around 1991. We had a bit more time. He was often touring the world, but he came to my fights. So we kind of built it up.

His big hit was *Boom Shackalack*, which charted very high. Apache writes all his own lyrics, although he has done some cover versions. He's very laid back – a modest guy. He's done very similar things to me. Wherever we're kickboxing around the world, music is always on the go. He's been to America; Japan; Jamaica; Germany. His family are from the Punjab, like myself – that's what made him so different; he's not West Indian. When he's singing you'd think it was a black person. Being brought up in Handsworth he learnt all the patois from the black kids.

We both went to Handsworth School and to Rookery Road in 2010, to do presentations together. At that time he was busy with his bar, then in 2011 he toured abroad, but we're trying to make time to do more things together. *Apache's Bar* was inspired by my gym.

"I thought: 'Wow, this is a celebration of all of the work that he's done; it's a source of inspiration.' He's got pictures and posters up, so a kid comes here and he has a look. You get such a vibe when you walk in. I thought: 'This is his landmark,'" explains Steve.

"I had it in mind to do something, but when I saw the gym I thought: 'Right, beautiful. Set up a platform like that; where's he's got kickboxers I've got dancers and singers. Young kids in schools can have the chance to sing and perform' so that's what I did.

"As I'm abroad quite a lot, *Apache's Bar* is temporarily closed. There's still a lot of demand for the music business – so off I go again! My album, *Home Run*, was released by *Universal Records*, Christmas 2011.

"Kash and I have been working even closer together, like when I was asked to go to Handsworth Grammar School, so I called him. I said: 'This school's opposite your house!'"

I joked with the kids about that: "I've lived there all that time and never even knew that the school was there!"

"That's right," continues Apache. "So we were standing there together, with all these kids in front of us. I said: 'We were these kids in here – years ago!' Just to have those two role models in front of them – I *know* it makes a difference. It's almost like a duty. We've had so much … now we can give something back.

"I'm still shy as a person, but over the years, being an artiste I've had seven Top Forty Hits; I've been round the world five times in twenty years. In 2009 alone, I visited twenty-seven countries!

"My songs have been featured in eight Hollywood movies: *Dumb and Dumber, Scooby-Doo 2: Monsters Unleashed*. So still, to this day, I've achieved more than any other Asian music artist. That's why I've got a lot of respect. And from the Reggae aspect, I've had more chart hits than any other Reggae artist, from this country.

"I have just recorded another album in America, in 2012, called *It Is What It Is* or *IWII* for short. The first single is on radio doing very well," Apache concludes.

Thanks Steve. I've been giving presentations at a range of Birmingham schools over the last three or four years, encouraging pupils to do the academic side of their schoolwork, but also to channel their energy into sport or the martial arts. I always advise them:

If you want to do something in life aim high: dedicate yourself to it; work hard for it. Once you're in the ring in the fight game you're on your own. It's in your own hands; you can't cheat! So whatever you want to do good luck to you.

Hudson Richards works hard as a role model too, encouraging young people. He teaches at The *Phoenix Hall* in Bordesley, every Friday.

"It's a very mixed class," Hudson explains. "When I originally set it up, we had a lot of young people running around Bordesley Village, with problems, trying to set up gangs and what-have-you. There wasn't much happening in the village at that time.

"Some of the gang members did come, but couldn't stick the training – the discipline and what they were expected to do. It's one thing for you to be hitting somebody in the face when you're mugging them; it's quite another when they're actually hitting you back! It was a whole new experience for them," Hudson observes. "There was a 'quid pro quo' arrangement, which some of them found a bit un-nerving.

"My interest in martial arts has much more to do with the self defence element rather than the competition aspect," continues Hudson. "Kickboxing offers a set of realistic tools and competences that are effective at both, although I teach my students that education and learning are the best form of self defence."

Emma Fitch has been a student of mine since she was about twelve years old.

"I was a really active child and I saw something going on at a gym in Saint Faith and Saint Laurance Church in Croftdown Road, near Court Oak Road, Harborne, where I live," recalls Emma. "So I walked in. Tony Whitehouse, whom Shirley's also interviewed for this book, was the first trainer that I met. I went the following Monday and I've been doing it now for seventeen years.

"When I first met Kash he was very strict, because that's the way you need to be in martial arts classes. I went to London University and started my own kickboxing classes on campus, when I was nineteen years old. I'd got my Black Belt by that time so I taught down there, through the *IFA*.

"I've done four semi-contact fights and one full contact, in 2009, in Birmingham, which I won against a Welsh girl. We fought three, two-minute rounds and I won that.

"The training and discipline of kickboxing was really tough at first. For those first four months I worked really hard. I'd be really crying; had black eyes. I began with Semi-Contact fighting. I didn't wear makeup, my hair was a mess. I'd be running, skipping and training, but it was worth it. I'd be at the club for hours, but that's how dedicated you've got to be.

"I run around Edgbaston Reservoir as part of my training although I don't do as much training as I used to, at the moment, because I've got one or two injuries, back trouble, so I can't. As a Foot Health Practitioner, my profession is related to having a healthy body too. It's hard work, but it's good. I did a Drama-Media-Arts degree at London," concludes Emma.

Shirley interviewed Emma at one of my Gym Open Days. The ladies classes are becoming more popular; she teaches every Wednesday here at my gym.

Like Emma, Jay Sokhi, pronounced Sewki, has been a student of mine for many years. She first met me when she was twenty-four and I was teaching at the *Handsworth Leisure Centre*. She has trained with me for the past eleven years.

"I was quite scared when I first went to the Gym," Jay remembers, "with Kash being so tall and disciplined. But as you get to know him, as the other person as well, outside of the Gym, then you realise that he's just as normal as anyone else. But in the Gym he kept us all very much under control.

"There were different levels, although I started at the basic level first, so there were three or four classes. Initially there were around twenty-five of us altogether. There *are* a lot of new faces, but also a few of us who started out together.

"I still keep fit, and try to maintain a training schedule on a daily basis, before I go to work, but not *every* morning. After work I go to my local gym, *Fitness First*, in Stirchley. I also combine it with fighting classes with Kash and technique classes, at Kash's gym.

"At the moment I do Tuesday evening fighters classes with Kash; Sunday with Kash, doing a two-hour fighting class; I do a Wednesday Technical Fighting Class and sometimes on a Monday I'll do a Cardio-Workout Class.

"I won the *Midland Area* title five or six years ago," Jay continues. "I was one of the first ladies to get a title for Kash. I had about seven fights, including one loss, over the space of about two years. That's when I had the chance to go for a title fight, which was my last fight.

"I love sparring. Kash has always said that he'd like to see me teach. I'd love to one day but at the moment I have a full-time job. I don't want to give Kash my word and then not be able to keep it – I don't want to let him down.

"For my first fight I was very nervous," Jay recalls. "The girl that I was supposed to fight couldn't fight, so I had to have a replacement. My opponent's name was Brodie. She was all got up like a bloke and she looked really fiery! She was a lot taller than me.

"When Kash was preparing me he said, 'Stop looking at her – look at me'... really making me focus. Obviously you don't know what to expect, never having been in the ring before and then you come out to all this audience. But when you're in the ring, you forget everyone around you.

"You're only aware of the audience when you're walking in," Jay continues. "When you start fighting you're in your own world; even with Kash, obviously coaching you by your ringside, sometimes you don't even listen to the instructions. It's not because you're not listening, it's that you're not *hearing* it.

"I'd always go by what Kash tells you, but because your nerves are everywhere, you don't hear the instructions: you're oblivious to it. But then something kicks in: hang on, your trainer's trying to tell you something here! And when you start listening that's when you start doing well. Everything you've learnt comes into play too – everything you've put into it," concludes Jay.

UB40's Brian Travers comments: "Kash stood out like a flame – this is why I supported him. He stood out like a rose in the thorns. He was the first Asian guy to become famous in a full contact sport. The young Asian boys could look at him and go: 'That's one of our own.'

"He encourages young people to channel their energies into sport and about keeping fit and eating properly; instead of stuffing themselves full of McDonalds and smoking 'weed'. I've never heard a bad story about Kash – going on a door, or bullying anybody; beating anybody into a coma or using his skills in a bad way," Brian continues.

"I saw, as an outsider, the effect that he was having as a performer; the same with Howard Brown as well. Black sportsmen have been celebrated for a lot longer – in America and in England – you know, Jesse Owens in the 1930 Olympics."

The second half of the 20th Century was an incredible period of change and creativity, a huge melting pot of all these cultures.

"After the war, yes," continues Brian, "with the invention of Youth Culture. Youth came alive, when young men and women didn't want to dress like their moms and dads anymore. Youth Culture saved Art, especially in England, because before that it was the domain of the Cambridge or Oxford Dons: that's when you became a' writer, if you mixed with the right publishers. It was 'who you know', not 'what you know'."

Wayne Elcock, another role model, has a mobile gym, called *Box Clever*: a boxing fitness and training programme, which he designed himself.

Wayne explains: "It was something that I put together, as I came to the twilight of my career. I decided to help some of the more disadvantaged kids. As you go further up the ladder you probably only box in matches about three or four times a year, so you've got a lot more time in between.

"People were asking me to train young kids that many times it was unreal, but I didn't have the time, because of my training schedules. I was going out to train in Portugal and other training camps abroad, so I wasn't here.

"To cut a long story short, in November 2009 I had to pull out of a major fight. So I took somebody up on the offer over in Solihull, some young kids over there. It's part of a government initiative. I've got a lot of experience in the game, but I wasn't sure how I'd take to the coaching side of it, but it seems to be going well. I use boxing as a tool, to change their mindset.

"I've got such good results from that; the key workers couldn't believe it! The kids were now getting to school; not back-chatting their parents. Because I'm a local lad they can relate to me. They can't turn round and say to me: 'You don't know what it's like. You didn't grow up around here,' because I did! And I took the right direction. So I've had some great results. I thought: 'Hang on – this is something I can do on a more permanent basis.'

"The use of school buildings after 6pm can be a problem. So I got the freestanding truck and equipment. Now all the schools have to do is provide me with the kids and the space – and you've got a training session. That's how *Box Clever* was born.

"When I give talks to the kids, I'll say: 'I know many of you in this room think that you're going to be a great professional footballer, a gymnast or whatever, but get an education.' When you work with people like those that I worked with in the boxing world, and they hand a big contract to you, I would have had to pay someone to go through that contract if I hadn't had an education.

"I suppose you could say that champions are born, not made; it's probably in the genes," Wayne continues. "Kash's father was a champion wrestler back in the Punjab and my dad was very sports-orientated... he put that drive into me. It's also the area you grew up in; it all adds to the picture.

"The kids can't believe how much technique is involved in boxing; it's not just about two blokes getting in there and knocking hell out of each other. The best boxers in the sport today are the ones with brains, because you have to outsmart your opponent.

"After only twenty-two professional fights and collecting five titles to date I believe the best is yet to come – and there's still plenty of life left in the old dog yet!"

According to Tom Ross it's intelligence that had made the real difference to my success: assessing how my own strengths can be used to combat a particular opponent's weak points, even if that opponent is bigger and stronger. Cyrille Regis points out that whatever the sport, all players or fighters have to do that, but it's just that some individuals are much more *expert* at doing that.

Wayne has a similar ability. "From early in my career I could predict what was going to happen in a fight. After the first round I'd go back to my corner and say to my trainer: 'I'm going to give you an early night tonight!' Then I'd go back out there – bang! The fight's over."

Peter Wilson, BBC *Midlands Today* Home Affairs Correspondent, comments: "I've done lots of stories in inner city areas of Birmingham, about different people who are mentoring people: keeping them out of gangs. Kash is doing that as well; helping kids to follow a different path, in areas where the only people to look up to are drug dealers, because they're driving around in fancy cars and making lots of money. Sport is a real force for good, in places like Birmingham and Kash is one of those people who are a force for good."

Peter spoke to students from across Birmingham, at my Holte School Gym.

"Some of them had built up relationships with people from different communities. That was important to them," he recalls, "but things were sometimes difficult out on the streets. The fact that Kash was a former champion, who was working within their community, meant a lot to them."

If someone wants to join my gym, the first stage is to try it out. If he or she wants to go ahead we'll enrol them in the club, and explain about how we work: about uniform; how we grade; how you can get a Black Belt – how long it takes. The idea is to inspire people to do well: how they can become a champion and fight in competitions.

Firstly, we'd just give them a 'taster': teach them how to make a fist; how to stand, how to move – it's all exciting! But it's up to the individual. The ones that *want* to do it really get into it. There's actually no full contact, for the first four months; they're learning all the basics.

There are so many different styles, with martial arts. Some of them are quite traditional, but are written in Japanese; others are modern and written in English, which many people prefer. We use more realistic styles for the street: Thai Kickboxing is more realistic, whereas Traditional Karate is not. It just gives them that confidence within themselves that they can hold their own. It's good for all people: after five or six lessons they feel confident, from five years up to sixty-five.

Tom Ross comments: "That energy or aggression has to go somewhere, so channel it into sport; it's a fabulous way to do it. Kash has provided a better community service than anybody, because he's taken kids off the street and given them a purpose, a direction; self discipline, self respect – all those things that they wouldn't have got."

According to footballer Kenny Cunningham, "I think Kash, as a coach, may be getting even more satisfaction, despite what he's achieved himself. It's a similar thing in football. I've finished all my coaching qualifications, so I understand the satisfaction that it can give, when you get hold of a young player and give him some direction, to develop his skills, helping him to mature both professionally and personally."

Joe Egan and myself have become good friends over the last three or four years. He came to the opening of my gym.

"A guy called Larry took me there and introduced me," explains Joe. "We'd met before, over the years. I knew who Kash was because I'd been a fan of his; because of his achievements he stands out from other fighters. I wish him all the success in the world. He's putting so much effort back into the sport that he loves."

Joe does loads of charity work too, including Third World Children's charities. He works with the Caldwell Children's Charity and attends events all around the UK.

Phil Upton has interviewed me within the last couple of years or so, primarily about my coaching.

"But also about going into the community and meeting those kids... getting them into kickboxing or the other martial arts," explains Phil. "About getting them off the streets and how he was very much a mentor for kids like that, who might otherwise come under very negative influences, rather than Kash's positive influence; helping to keep them on the 'straight-and-narrow'. So obviously he's been fulfilling different roles, in the different interviews that we've done. I did a radio interview with a *Mentor* theme, where he actually came into the *Mail Box*."

At the end of Kash's Holyhead School talk, in 2010, Leslie Edlington, who was then Head of Corwen College, remarked: "One of my earlier memories of Kash was at *The Handsworth Fun Run,* in the early 1990s. As soon as Kash appeared a whole crowd of kids went down from Holyhead School and swamped him. I think he signed over two hundred autographs that day. Better than that, word spread on the Handsworth grapevine; their mates came down and Kash signed *their* autograph books too. You don't get many chances like that guys, to chat to a World Champion."

Ross Trafford, who now holds Leslie's former position as Head of Corwen College, explained: "The reason that we contacted Kash was that when we look at extra-curricular clubs they are all basically for traditional games: football, cricket, rounders and things like that. I wanted to do something that had a bit of a fitness, discipline and confidence-building angle as well. Students don't traditionally attend after school activities in the community, so this gives them an option that they might follow.

"With a lot more martial arts being featured on the TV and with boxing at the school too," Ross continued, "we're trying to give them just that little bit of extra interest, as an option that they might pursue, outside of those traditional games. After we've gathered a bit of momentum, we're thinking of perhaps subsidising some places down at the club, so that some of the kids can go there at a reduced rate and get involved in it."

Since 6 June 2011 I've been going to schools five times a week, working with a cluster of seven schools within Ladywood, which is the catchment area for my Gym. I focus on Health and Fitness and Coordination at these presentations. It's important to keep a relaxed atmosphere and have a little conversation with them. To your students you're a social worker, teacher and parental figure too.

NEWS FLASH

Kash was single-minded… he had a 'dream'. He knew that he wanted to be Number One, at a very early age. Now some of us would have been poorer in our aspirations, but Kash was very ambitious. He knew what he wanted to achieve and by setting his goal that high, all of his training and preparation has been geared up to that world level. He put phenomenal energy into his training and he went that extra mile. He was always running, sparring.

Resham Gill

In this final Round, various contributors describe those qualities in Kash that have made him a Four times World Champion, juxtaposed with his faults, to present a balanced picture. This particular Round, the first part of Round 4 and all of Round 18 are the only sections where I'm taking the role of Principal Narrator, so Kash's comments are within speech marks, but mine aren't.

We conclude with some of the most recent and significant events that Kash has been involved with.

On Sunday 24 July 2011 Kash held an Open Day at his Icknield Port Road Gym in Birmingham. As his co-writer, I did six additional interviews at the event, with Norman Nelson and Craig Saunders, who has helped Kash with many events. I also met photographer, Gurmej Badesha, Anthony Whitehouse, Jay Sokhi, featured in Round 19, and Emma Fitch.

Norman Nelson and Tony Whitehouse both teach at Kash's gym. I asked Norman to define those qualities in Kash that have made him a Four Times World Champion.

"His determination…. Sometimes he'll call me and I know that something's wrong, so we just have a talk. I'd originally decided that if I was going to be taught by someone then it should be a four times world champion.

"He can be quite bluntly-spoken, but if that happens I just tell him that I need to chat things over with him and we get it sorted," observes Norman. "Kash has such a lot to think about, like with this event today. There's so much going on in his mind. But I'm just Norman – what you see is what you get!"

Professional photographer Gurmej Badesha has known Kash for over twenty years. Many of the photos on the Gym walls were taken by him, at Kash's various championship fights and events. True-to-form he took photos throughout the Open Day. Gurmej is a good friend of Gurdip's family, which is how he originally met Kash. A significant number of photos in this book were taken by him.

Emma Fitch attributes Kash's success to "…his determination for himself. He has a great passion for kickboxing. I've known Kash both as an instructor and a friend, since I was twelve. He trains so hard, even when he's on holiday; he's obsessed with the sport – that's his life. I've got great respect for that. I've only done one Full Contact fight, against a Welsh girl. The training for that was very hard. He's done *loads* of fights.

"Kash made me cry a few times when I was younger, he'd pick on me," Emma continues. "But in kickboxing classes he *had* to be strict and he'd help me all through. Occasionally, we go out for a drink together. In here he's my instructor, but out there he's my friend. It's good that we have that balance as well."

"There's a former American Ice Hockey Coach called Don Cherry," explains Tom Ross. "He managed the *Boston Bruins*. They were an unfashionable team, but he took them to win the *Stanley Cup*, which is the be-all-and-end-all in Ice Hockey. He wrote in his book, 'Never underestimate the power of desire over ability'. And Kash had that in bucket loads. If you have ability without desire, it's a waste of time. Kash had epitomised that 100%, as I said in one commentary 'he had a heart the size of a bucket.' If you've got top class ability and desire then you have a world champion."

Tom continues "There's so much nonsense talked about motivation, it's impossible for one human being to motivate another. What you have to do is create an environment whereby people are motivated from within, to do whatever the aim is.

"This is where Kash comes into his own, because he creates that kind of atmosphere. I speak to his fighters and it's perfectly clear that they want to do it for Kash," observes Tom… "and that is motivation!

"It's Kash's nature: he's what we call in Birmingham a 'proper bloke'. That means that he's an upfront nice guy, but you wouldn't take advantage of him. In the ring I've seen him angry, but outside the ring, he just doesn't get irate. He looks at a situation, analyses it and deals with it. That's a big strength," says Tom, with genuine admiration.

"Everywhere I go, people say what a nice guy Kash is. There's a theory on sport: nice guys don't win – but he's disproved that theory. There's no room for prima donnas in regular boxing and kickboxing," Tom explains. "In team sport it's easy for that to happen, because they have a lot of people looking after them if they are having a bad day; in the ring, Kash could not afford a bad day.

"I've done regular boxing in a charity situation and once the bell went I've gone: 'Oh my God!' It made me realise what warriors Kash and all those other guys are, who go into the ring for real.

"Kickboxing needs TV exposure; it needs money invested, from A List sponsors. That is the sport's biggest problem. Kickboxing had its chance and I think they blew it. People became distrustful of it, in certain cases, because they were let down. Kash has worked tirelessly to change that attitude and should be recognised for bringing credibility back to the sport. However, he still has to get the sporting world to take it seriously, because it was so badly run, at one time.

"Firstly as a man, Kash is warm-hearted, astute and intelligent... but he's nobody's fool, that's for certain! Inside the ring, he's got it all; as a boxer he had it all; he had an innate ability that he was born with it. But he added to that natural ability, with dedication, training, focusing and deciding that he was going to be World Champion," Tom says, with more than a hint of envy.

"So that talent for sport is definitely in the genes, because ability will not get you anywhere," Tom continues. "In football lots of players with ability never make it and lots of players with less ability do, because of the *desire*. We saw in the World Cup, in 1966, lesser players, like Jack Charlton and Nobby Styles, were an important part of the team, because of their desire to win – and all the other things that we just talked about. Kash has got all of those things – in abundance!

"Very often sporting people are great, but they don't know how to get other people to be great. Kash has this great ability to inspire other people and impart his skills to them. You can inspire people with words, but you've got to be able to back it up. He has this ability to show people how to do that.

"But he has a set of rules. I don't mean rules for the gym, I mean Life Rules. He probably doesn't realise it, but I'm sure if you sat him down and discussed it with him, he'd acknowledge it – and he wants everyone to realise that. So he has this ability to put that over, because they've been successful for him.

"When they did this fabulous book about the Bullring, I put Kash's name forward to be included in it," Tom explains. "He's an integral part of Birmingham. He's made a success of what he does. In my view he hasn't always got the recognition for what he's done.

"Kash should be recognised, not only for his sporting achievements, but what he does now for the community. I realise that he's got his gym – and that's a business. But those kids, when they get to that crossroads, they go to Kash's gym and become proper human beings, or they can turn rotten and become just another criminal on the wrong side of the tracks. Kash gives them an alternative to that – and I think that should be applauded.

"We all moan about the state of the country and how the kids are on the streets with their gangs – and about the youth knife culture," Tom says honestly. "I don't do anything about it, although I try to, by example, on the radio and how I live my life. But I don't actually *do* anything. Kash gets off his backside and does something positive.

"It's no surprise to me that he's gone on to work with the community, because he's got that warmth about him and a pride for the area he grew up in. I can't tell you what it is, but whenever you meet Kash, you're glad to be in his company. It's a kind of charisma. You think to yourself: 'I'm glad he's my pal, because he's a nice bloke.'"

Tom's description of Kash reminds me of my friend and co-writer Pat Roach... he made everyone he came into contact with feel as though they were his friend.

Kash recalls a conversation between Resham, and top amateur boxing trainer Frank O'Sullivan, during a trip to Yorkshire. "Frank said: '*Kash the Flash* is a big inspiration for the young Asian fighters,' not realising that Resham was my brother! So Frank respects me for what I've done for the fighting game too."

"When Kash brings his boxers in here, for interviews, he walks in and lights up the place 'cause he's a nice guy," Tom observes. "If somebody said they'd fallen out with Kash, I'd say: 'Well it must be your fault!' Me – I can be obnoxious... I'm easy to fall out with, but Kash is an all-round great guy and I'll always be chuffed to know him. I've seen the pride in his family when they watched him fight.

"I meet a lot of footballers and managers in my job, I know them well; they become good friends of mine, but there have been times when some of them would walk past you in the street. Kash would never do that, whether he was a World Champion *five* times over, he'd come up to you after every fight, put his arm around you and say: 'Come on Tom. How do you think I did?' He would also ask me how Blues had done, especially if he knew they'd lost! He never forgets his mates. I respect him for that as well and that's why I do what I can to help him now," concludes Tom.

Kash's sister, Binda, attributes Kash's success to "...his determination and the encouragement from my dad as well. He's very focused; that's all he did. It surprised me: I never thought he'd make a career out of it. It was a very unusual career."

According to Gamma, "Kash has a lot of discipline; he's slightly arrogant. He believes in himself and he is obviously gifted. When people went to his fights they got value for money. I personally think he's done alright out of kickboxing – and he's earned a living out of it. He's well known and he's got a lot of respect from the community... and all the kickboxing fraternity, so you can't do any better than that, can you?"

Cougar comments: "If he was fighting now and was receiving the advice that he's giving all his fighters, he'd have gone even further as a fighter. He'd have been there a lot longer and a lot less stressed. He wouldn't have had to worry about the attendance. Kickboxing is much more popular than what it was then.

"He's kept himself to himself. I don't know whether that's because of the upbringing, or because he lost his mom at a young age. He's always been like that. He's never been able to show his emotions as much as me, for example, but that's why I've always kept an eye on him."

According to Cougar's wife, Daljit, "Sometimes Kash thinks that he's right and he doesn't like being challenged. His brothers and sisters will leave it, because they don't want to upset him, but I'll say: 'Hang on a minute – you're wrong! You need to look at it from this point of view,' or 'Have you thought about this?'

"Kash and I have always got on. I'll help him to put things in perspective, but without an agenda. Kash is very level-headed," continues Daljit. "He's very business-minded, just like his dad, and he always thinks things out, so if he takes a risk with anything it will usually work out. Our son, Kietan, is good with computers, so initially he helped to put Kash's website together for him."

Cougar comments: "Kash has done so much to put Handsworth on the map. There are a lot of people who've grown up there, who'll see Kash working around there and say 'Hi Kash, how are you doing?'"

Daljit interjects: "Actually, we get stopped sometimes, because people go: 'Are you Kash Gill?'... to Cougar!" "Sometimes Cougar will say that he *is* me, just to get a free drink!" quips Kash.

Kash's younger brother, Gurdip, married just before his twenty-first birthday, to an Asian girl, whom everyone knows as 'Jan'.

"I've always used Kash as an example for our oldest son, Raajan," Gurdip explains. "People see Kash as a World Champion, but they don't realise the effort he had to put in, not just getting there, but *staying* there. He deserves every bit of success that he got, because he sacrificed a helluva lot.

"I'm really pleased that whatever Kash has set out to do, he's achieved. I remember how proud he was when he was up-and-coming; he'd bring his trophies home and wait for our dad to come home. It's sheer determination to succeed that has made him a champion. He's fantastic at what he does!

"Kash was a perfectionist in the gym, but if he was told to relax and rest, he didn't know how to, because he was so driven to wanting to succeed. I worry for Kash, with what he's going through at the moment, family-wise. I've rung him up a few times, to give him my support.

"I feel for Kash because kickboxing isn't regarded as a mainstream sport in this country; if it was, he'd be living on multi-millionaire's row," continues Gurdip. "But on the plus side it was something that he did as a hobby, but he made a career out of it. He's got a very good reputation. During a holiday in Egypt I met someone who said: 'You look like somebody that I know.' He was talking about Kash – I told him he was my brother.

"When I was a Special Constable, stationed at Sutton Coldfield, Kash used to run *two* gyms at John Wilmott School. A lot of police officers knew him; either they had children who attended the gym or they knew somebody, so they looked at him with admiration."

Gurdip has worked for Birmingham City Council for twenty-two years. He's a Security Supervisor, which is mainly day-to-day management of security officers, responding to emergency situations, the management of public buildings and city centre car parks and the recruitment and selection of staff.

"Growing up in Handsworth gives you nerves of steel. The situations I've been into it's sometimes 'fight or flight'. You have to hold your ground; but life teaches you to cope with situations like that," he explains.

"As an overview for this book, I would say yes, there were sad times as kids, but looking back, we had some *fantastic* times and as a family, I think we're strong. But I wonder, had Kash and I not gone through those experiences, would we have had such a strong determination to achieve? Our dad always used to say: 'Don't look at a person's wealth to measure their success... it's about being at peace with yourself.'

"He also said: 'Have a good work ethic. Look at what you're going to achieve next. Set yourself small, but achievable goals'. But I couldn't do the sixty or seventy hours of *physical* work that he and his generation used to do," Gurdip concludes.

Resham, the most highly-educated member of Kash's family, has worked for the Civil Service, throughout his career. His impressive list of qualifications include an HNC, a Masters Degree in Education; a Diploma in Management and an MBA.

"I've now moved to Wolverhampton Council, as 16-19 Education Manager. My wife, Mandy, teaches Hearing Impaired children at Secondary School," explains Resham.

"As regards personality, Binda and myself were quite even-tempered people, whereas Kash says of himself that he was a bit more stubborn over things. My father could be stubborn as well, but Kash used to bottle things up.

"The tragedy is that Kash wouldn't have known the love he had off his mother, because he lost her at such a young age... and what a wonderful woman she was: she put her kids before everything," explains Resham. "He probably doesn't remember the cuddles she gave him; the amount of love and pride she had for him, like every parent.

"If only she'd seen just *half* of what he's accomplished, she'd have been so proud; we're all very proud of him. Most people just know him for his kickboxing, but that's just a very small part of him," concludes Resham. "He was a well behaved, well-adjusted, nice child... a good little brother."

Apache observes: "Kash is ambitious; he's very focused – he's almost got it ingrained – from his father. He seems to have a good network around him, with members of his family. But he's stubborn, like me! I want to achieve what I've got to achieve: nothing can come in the way of that."

Dave Barnett's lifestyle and Kash's are similar in many ways in terms of dedication to their sport. They can phone each other up if either needs help.

Dave confirms: "We can talk about all that comes with football and boxing, being a world champion kickboxer in Kash's case, but the friendships that you have are more important than anything else.

"Kash is a very independent-minded person, but maybe he could benefit by listening more to advice, from people who know what they're talking about? However, to be fair, we got together recently – and he was taking on board what I was saying.

"But it's a subject in itself," Dave continues, "no matter who you're talking about: getting the balance right between your professional life and your private life; giving the right amount of attention to your chosen career, but also trying to manage a fully-fledged relationship and giving it all that you can. You could write a whole book on that, although not everyone's got the right answers!"

John Holcroft confirms: "Kash is not preoccupied with Race; that's what made him so popular. When he fought, he was flying the British flag. He genuinely likes people and he gets on well with them."

According to Hudson Richards, "Kash is a good example of the teleological tendency, because he is focused, has a lot of energy and the ability to make that energy contagious, so he can sell the dream. Due to his forthrightness, he can be very pragmatic and sees things in a particular way. Whereas I might see them in shades of grey, Kash might see them in black and white. So I sometimes take him with a little pinch of salt. I care for him deeply, but I'm not immune to the Kash tongue, so I usually time my response: 'Kash we need to talk about this!'"

Like several of our contributors Howard Brown ranks dedication as Kash's number one asset.

"Even later on in his career, when he was World Amateur Champion, European Amateur Champion, or a professional champion. He'd go abroad and have some really hard fights. A lot of his English fans have never seen his really hard fights. They were horrendous, but he came out on top… he won them!

"We've come home and it's been time for him to rest really," Howard recalls. "But the following morning he'd be in the gym! That made me feel quite proud, as well as his achievements. The other fighters in the gym would see the level of dedication that was required to achieve what Kash was achieving."

So does Kash have any particular faults?

"His aggression," replies Howard. "He doesn't walk around looking for fights and he's very placid in his day-to-day life, but he *can* be aggressive and if you rub him up the wrong way, he'll let you know very quickly. He can be a bit moody, but generally-speaking he's the most 'fun' person that you can be with. If you're going to have a night out with Kash, you know it! It's going to be fun and he gets all the attention. And that's the way he is to this day. That rubs off on everything that he does.

"We all get more placid with age. But that fire is part of youth – it's the same fire that *makes* you. You have to take the rough with the smooth. I've got many faults as well, personality traits that are unpleasant, but you live with it," observes Howard. "There are people who are still my friends, because we take each other's rough side; but the fun side outweighs that rougher side by a lot."

Kenny Cunningham recalls: "When I met Kash I found that he really enjoyed the physical aspect of his sport: the actual training and conditioning. He's very dedicated. It wasn't a chore like it is with some people. It was something that he embraced and that he actually enjoyed!

"He's got a very affable way with him, but we were interested in where he was coming from too – the kickboxing. Sportsmen of any sort always have a genuine interest in other sportsmen, so that was the initial topic of conversation.

"Obviously his particular field isn't as well paid as premiership football, which may be the motivation for *some* players. Clearly with someone like Kash, in his profession, there's no huge financial incentive.

"I've met him quite a few times, outside of the gym too. You can pick Kash out! Doing karate kicks down the street; he has got that 'beanpole' look about him! I see him around the area. I've bumped into him a couple of times when I've been jogging – I'm usually overtaking him at the time!

"On a couple of occasions when I've arrived at the *Virgin Gym* I'd see Kash coming up the stairs, obviously having jogged from his house, basically in a black bin-liner and a pair of trainers. This black puddle of water would be following him up the stairs. And I'd be looking at him thinking: 'Oh Kash, I don't particularly want to say hello to you at this minute! Just dry yourself down and then we'll have a conversation!'

"But inevitably he'd spot me. The whole gym would part like the Red Sea and he'd come over and shake my hand, quite oblivious to the situation –

and start a conversation. Kash isn't much of a drinker, so we don't go to the pub together. But in the number of conversations that I've had with him, over the years, I like him as a person. He's got a very human side to him and is quite directly-spoken: I'd rather have people like that than trying to read between the lines," concludes Kenny.

Paul Clifton comments: "Kash wasn't simply fighting for the UK. He was fighting for anyone and everyone who had experienced the kind of setbacks that he had in his childhood... he was fighting from the heart. When he fell into the world of martial arts he found Discipline, Etiquette, Courtesy, Manners and Respect and tempered those with the ability to fight. I've got a great deal of time for Kash."

Paul poses the question: "If Kash could go back, would he have done Kickboxing? Thai Boxing has more appeal and the commercial element. Would he have gone into the Mixed Martial Arts, if he was coming into the fight industry today? Or would he go for Thai Boxing or still kickboxing? The *MMA* would give him more financial success, so whether he would go for that, with hindsight, is an interesting question."

Kash replies: "Yes, it's a bit like Bruce Lee. He had an era for Kung Fu and he was a legend: I was a big fan of his and everyone watched his films. But I set a goal, similar to Howard's, to create a new era for Kickboxing, so that my name became a legend in the 1990s. Even though nowadays you can get all these vitamin supplements you couldn't compare with *Kash the Flash*. But it's a bit like the 100 metre sprinters – they're getting quicker and quicker aren't they?"

"If you threw Kash into a prison, with no weapons and no allowable group gang killing, just on a one-to-one basis," continues Paul, "I think Kash would do very well and become, if you pardon the expression, the 'Cock of the Prison'. He would always try to get to the top because he has got that determination. Combined with over thirty years experience in the fight game, he would definitely come out on top!"

"Regarding kickboxing nowadays," Kash interjects, "I feel rather sad when I go to some of the shows around the country. Paul holds Ronnie Green in high esteem. If he came to one of my shows I'd get him in the ring and say: 'This is Ronnie Green, World Class Thai Boxer.' If Mike Tyson walked in, that would happen straight away. Why are we not getting this in our sport? We're not recognising our own heroes. That's why we've got a lot of jealousy and we're not moving on. No one's working together because of the jealousy and the rivalry. Until that day comes there's no moving forward. There are too many egos," Kash concludes.

Andy Walker assesses Kash's success from the perspective of a friend and colleague.

"I have to confess that before I started working on the *Solihull News/Times* the name *Kash the Flash* Gill didn't ring any bells. So I've seen not the competitive side of Kash, but the Entrepreneur, or the big-hearted charity person. He's the text book 'Gentle Giant'.

"Kash goes out of his way to welcome and greet people," continues Andy. "I've always been a bit of a stranger to kickboxing, but at any events that Kash has invited me to, he's always made me feel welcome, asked me to present awards and so on.

"When Kash contacts me he can be very single-minded. I had a colleague come across and say: 'That Kash Gill – he doesn't give up, does he?!' I was dealing mainly with sports stories, so if there was a community story I'd pass it on to the relevant person. If I hadn't followed it up straight away I'd have Kash back on to me and obviously the chain continued. But it's a side of Kash that shows why he's done so well: he never gives in!

"If you're a professional footballer you know that you're going to become a multi-millionaire," continues Andy. "You'll never get that with kickboxing, so in some ways you need *more* dedication. He's always got so much on, yet he's still got to juggle his gym in the background and his classes. Kash always wants to be the biggest and the best; that's why he describes his events as 'Flash' – in e-mails! And he's true to his word."

According to Phil Upton, "I found Kash to be an honest man; very straightforward; very 'dry'. In that respect he's a 'Proper Brummie'... he tells it how it is. He's very laid-back: I don't see him get very animated or excited; he's very chilled, very calm. I would have thought that that inner calmness was what you need in the martial arts. But he certainly comes across that way.

"Kash could have quite easily walked away from the sport and found another aspect of his life and dealt with that," Phil continues. "What's to his credit is that he's kept kickboxing to the fore and tried to find another generation of kickboxers, to achieve in that sport. He's raised the profile of the sport. A lot of people wouldn't know about the sport, had it not been for him, so the Birmingham kickboxing community must be grateful for him having done that.

"He became very much a role model for his community. It's become quite a cult thing nowadays: Indian entrepreneurs; the guy who recently won the Gordon Ramsey cookery contest is an Indian guy – and all of that is really fashionable. Well Kash came onto the scene when it wasn't really fashionable."

Former Chief Superintendant David Webb sums up Kash's qualities as follows:

"First of all he's got the ability and the physique, but he's also got the mental qualities: he wants to win. If you've got the determination to go on trying no matter what, it can all happen. He's always had that."

Peter Wilson points out two contrasting aspects of Kash's personality.

"At the *Virgin* gym he was very relaxed and jokey; I should imagine that he's also something of a practical joker, but at his *own* gym I could see the focused, hard work and intensity that made him a world champion. Also, hearing him coach young people, especially the talented ones whom he felt could rise to the top. It was very different from his non-work persona: very sharp and focused and obviously an incredible expert... the best in the world."

UB40's Tony Mullings shares a good sense of humour with Kash: "Most definitely. I have to be, because I'm a professional musician!"

According to champion bodybuilder Dorian Yates, "There are people who are born with certain gifts, which make it easier for them to become successful, but without the mental aspects it's like trying to build a house with no glue. You've got all the pieces there, but the 'glue' is the mental approach: I think it's crucial to have the motivation and drive.

"With Kash, it was mental focus and the fact that he was the first Asian guy to be in a contact sport. I'm sure that there are a lot of other Asian kids who got into the sport because of Kash. He made them realise that anything was possible.

"It's the same as me, coming from Birmingham, from a little backstreet gym, being in a sport that no one in the UK really understands, so no one gives you any real encouragement. With me it was 'Oh you can't go to America and beat those guys!' I'm sure Kash had the same thing: an Asian guy coming in to do kickboxing. You've got to put all of that negativity behind you and just focus on being a success. That's what he's done and that's what makes him different to everybody else. He was a 'one-off' – a trailblazer.

"He doesn't look physically very strong," acknowledges Dorian, "but it's not all about physical strength. He surprised them before they could gain the advantage. But the main thing is that he could push on and overcome mental prejudices, negativity. Any situation can be positive or negative, but you can use it to drive you on... you've just got to believe in yourself. That's what sets Kash apart."

Boxer Frankie Gavin comments: "Skills pay the bills but you still need to train really hard too. But when I'm not in training I *do* go and have a drink – I think most boxers do. To not have a drink is *unbelievable*, but Kash might unwind in his own way, maybe go and have a walk or something. If I was having trouble I know that he'd be there for me."

Bob Sykes observes: "Being a kickboxer requires a very special person. Kash has been brilliant at channelling the energy inside him into sport, in a very positive way. Everybody has a certain drive, but I think the fact that both Kash and I lost our mothers when we were young, has something to do with our drive for success: I was eleven years old and Kash was nine, when that happened to us. It provides us with an emotional relief, because we didn't have that approval and support that our mothers would have provided us with.

"Unfortunately, in some cases, it can be channelled into drugs alcohol and crime, so it's very important to spend time encouraging young people to channel that energy in a positive way, as Kash, myself, Apache Indian and others are doing nowadays, in our various ways. Kash can sometimes be stubborn, but then a lot of martial arts guys are."

On page 63 of *The Journeyman*, Bob Sykes wrote:

"Nowadays Kash and myself are good friends, furthermore I feel honoured to have shared the ring with him. His past is partly my past and my past is partly his. It was a golden age of kickboxing, a special era in which the events were full of character, the spectators were numerous and the fighters had magic in their eyes."

According to Brian Travers, "The most important thing that Kash did was he became a beacon for all of those young Asian kids. He demonstrated, internationally, that they were *not* second class citizens, that they shouldn't be cowed by institutional racism. Apache Indian Steve is in some way, half of a result of Kash Gill.

"These were very formative days for the Asian community and for Birmingham in general. I don't really like to talk about Asians or West Indians, as being separate; we're all in this together. Kash is a good man, and we all come from this city. That's what we should be talking about, but we're referring back to a very uncomfortable time in Birmingham's history. It was incredibly racist, but despite that, against the odds, Kash Gill came through and evened out the playing field.

"There's a challenge for a young Asian kid, who loves that sport... try and beat Kash Gill. But that's inspirational," continues Brian, "that's a challenge that he's set. It's like our *UB40* achievements. I wonder who the next band out of Birmingham will be who will sell a hundred million albums and have fifty Top Twenty hits – more than the *Bee Gees*, more than the *Beatles*?

Brian advises: "Take what you *do* incredibly seriously, but not *yourself*: once you do that, people can chop you down. And they will do that, because for every fan, there's somebody who resents what you're doing... who wants to be you. So good luck to Kash... good luck with the book!"

Kash's former kickboxing student Stuart Nicholls comments: "Kash is totally down-to-earth and has genuine concern for people. It took me ten years to get my Black Belt, because I had a fulltime job. At times when I was getting a bit fed up he'd say: 'Just take it easy – you'll get there.' I've got nothing but praise for Kash and I'll be interested to read your book. I'd like to find out more about him."

Gringo observes: "For Kash to have achieved what he's achieved is unbelievable, because Handsworth at that time was one of those places that could have held him down. He's maintained his enthusiasm for life, not just for kickboxing and I feel privileged to know him.

"He got into a little scrape once, so he phoned me up to ask for advice. I gave him what I thought was common sense. That led to him and somebody he's had a bit of Road Rage with settling it between them, without anybody being arrested. Also, he regularly invited me to watch him fight, with front row tickets. I didn't turn up because people would think I was 'on-the-take' – but I would *love* to have seen him fight live.

"I've enjoyed being in the police force, it's like a big family," continues Gringo. "But the lovely thing for me, over those thirty-nine years of service, is that I've met people like Kash, who have made it all worthwhile."

EVENTS:

Kash has participated in many special events over the years. The following is a brief selection of the more recent ones:

At the 2009 *Vaisakhi* Festival in Handsworth Park, thousands of people crowded round watching *Kash the Flash!* "They called me up onto the stage and presented me with a *Lifetime Achievement* award for all the years of fighting – and being a pillar of the community. Even on YouTube, under 'Recognised Sikhs', *Kash the Flash* comes up. I didn't realise that until a few weeks ago. I felt really proud receiving the award, because at the time I began in kickboxing the sport wasn't recognised," Kash explains.

"But I always felt predominantly main stream: I never said that I was Asian or Sikh. It's only years later that I thought: 'Well yes, I am actually Asian and I *did* become World Champion'. I hadn't thought of it like that previously.

"The *Handsworth and Soho Community Awards* was a black tie affair, on Thursday 18 November 2010, held at West Bromwich Albion Football Ground. Councillors from Handsworth were there. People within the Soho Ward won the awards: schools, clusters of schools and business people. I was invited by Midlands Promoter Jon Pegg to share Top Table at a meal with boxing legends Nigel Benn, Steve Collins and Richie Woodhall."

Kash did a phone-in for Phil Upton's breakfast programme at the end of Feb 2011 regarding Motivation. It was in relation to Birmingham City's success in winning the *Carling Cup* that month. Because Kash has been at the top of the tree for so long, Phil asked him about motivation in sport.

A range of Kash's interviews can be found on YouTube. These include a March 2011 interview for the Brit-Asia TV Channel for the series *Outstanding British Asians*. James and Amir Khan were amongst others interviewed for the series.

Kash had the great honour of being invited to Downing Street, on Wednesday 13 April 2011, together with the BBC's Tommy Nagra, whom we introduced in Round 6.

Tommy was tremendously proud when Kash won his World Championships, but feels that Kash hasn't received the recognition or credit that he deserves, at a national level. Tommy featured Kash two or three times in the *Network East* programmes. For the *Desi DNA* programme, around 2004-5, they did a profile of Kash as a promoter. At that time Tommy was Head of Asian Programmes for the BBC, based in Birmingham.

Satnam Rana of BBC *Midlands Today* was also invited to Downing Street. She interviewed Kash prior to the event, on the BBC WM radio programme, *Midlands Masala*, on Friday 8 April. Kash quipped: "I did say to one of the newspapers that I was thinking of asking the Prime Minister if I could swap roles with him for one day!"

Satnam elaborated: "In the West Midlands we now have the largest Sikh community in the UK, in terms of numbers; it used to be London but we've just outnumbered them at the end of last year, according to figures just released by the Office of National Statistics. Happy Vaisakhi Kash and I'll see you on Wednesday – at Downing Street!"

Kash later described the occasion:

"Downing Street was inviting high-profile people in the Sikh community and considered me to be one of them. I've done a lot for the event, in the past. George Osborne was hosting it. Unfortunately David Cameron had to be called away at short notice, because of the Gaddafi situation in Libya. They apologised for the fact that he couldn't be present. It began at 5.30pm and lasted for about three hours. I managed to have a few photos taken outside Number 10 and outside the gates.

"On Sunday, 24 April 2011, I took a Demonstration Team of younger fighters to Handsworth Park for the Vaisakhi Mela Festival, as I do every year. Hopefully it may also encourage other youngsters present to come to the gym."

A highlight of Kash's career was being admitted to the illustrious *Hall of Fame* at a ceremony on Saturday evening, 26 November 2011. He allowed himself a rare stiff drink, to celebrate: "After thirty years in martial arts with so many great names under one roof, it was good to see no politics and no fights – Ha ha!"

Shortly afterwards, at a day's notice, Kash flew to Kazakhstan, for the weekend of 3rd-4th December 2011, to take part in a USA 3-round Exhibition Bout with world-renowned movie star Don 'The Dragon' Wilson:

"I finally made it back home after an amazing long weekend. What can I say? It was arranged by matchmaker and friend Cynthia Rothrock. Muay Thai rules in the end. It was a great experience getting back in the ring and enjoying the move around with legend and actor Don Wilson.

"I had VIP treatment in a 5-Star hotel with 5-Star treatment, with fellow guests Michael Madson, Armand Assante and 'Tiny' Lester. It was for a children's charity in Kazakhstan, so I thought I would help the Dragon Don out, in Flash style!" Both fighters went the distance, with Kash losing on a narrow points decision. But it was amazing that he could summon kickboxing skills of such high quality, at very short notice!

On Wednesday 25 April 2012 Kash and I attended the official launch of *InBusiness with South Birmingham College*. It was held at South Birmingham College, Digbeth Campus, in Birmingham. This is a unique networking strategy, designed to expand organisations and create opportunities for students. Kash was appointed as one of a select team of ambassadors, from a range of professions, who will be working to improve students' skills and broaden their experience, in Kash's case through sport. Wayne Elcock, also featured in our book, was appointed as an ambassador too.

A photograph shows Kash with guest speaker at the event, Sir Doug Ellis OBE and South Birmingham College Principal Mike Hopkins. The *Harp* subsequently covered the launch.

Kash the Flash continues his charity fundraising. On 21 October 2012, the day after our Birmingham Launch for this book, Kash took part in the BUPA Birmingham Half Marathon.

On May 12-13th 2012, Ronnie Green and Kash featured prominently in the *Martial Arts Show Live* at the NEC, Birmingham, where they hosted seminars for the fans and signed autograph photos. They also had radio and television interviews.

As our book draws to a close, here are some final thoughts, from Joe Egan:

"Every fighter that climbs through the ropes dreams about being a World Champion. I wasn't good enough, but I shared the ring with a lot of world champions. Well Kash not only got to live the dream once – but four times! Four times Champion of the World, you know? It's a fantastic... massive achievement!

"All sports don't just need good athletes they need good ambassadors for the sport. I don't think they come any finer than Kash, in kickboxing, because he's such a lovely man. I'm not just saying that because I'm here with you Shirley, he really is a gentleman. So he's a great ambassador for the sport *outside* of the ring and he's also a great fighter *inside* the ring."